P9-CRZ-636

Farewell, Israel!

Farewell,

Israel!

Ephraim Sevela
(*Efraim*)

Translated from Russian by

Edmund Browne

HOLY LAND STATE
COMMITTEE
2025 EYE STR. #505
WASH., D.C. 20006
(202) 775-0277

GATEWAY EDITIONS, LTD.

South Bend, Indiana

Copyright © 1977 by Ephraim Sevela
All rights reserved. Except for use in a
review, the reproduction or utilization of
this work in any form is forbidden without
the written permission of the publisher.
Manufactured in the United States of America
Library of Congress Catalog Card Number: 77-81437
International Standard Book Number: 0-89526-699-7

325.247
S 497 f

234141

This book is dedicated to the memory of those who died for Israel. May it not be considered an act of blasphemy. The longer the silence, the greater the sin.

Contents

Farewell, Israel!

At eleven A.M. Moscow time on the twenty-fourth day of February, 1971, in a country where the tongues of men were chained by fear, in the very center of Moscow, by the Kremlin Wall, an event took place which at first no one noticed. Here, beside the entrance to the president's reception hall, where behind walls of stone he is hidden away from the eyes of the people, they gathered one after another, twenty-four men and women, twenty-four Soviet Jews, defenseless, armed only with their desperate resolve to issue a challenge to Goliath.

chapter one

THE DUMB SPEAK

Under the shadow of the massive red star perched atop the barb of the Spassky Tower the chimes call sweetly to one another, like the antiphonal ringing of all the bells of Moscow, until the great hand of the clock pauses on the XII.

Bon–n–n–g...

The dull, thunderous blow rolls over Red Square; for a long moment the tremors linger in its wake, until another blow crashes through the frosty February air of blizzard-blown Moscow.

Bon–n–n–g...

Eleven measured blows rain down on Red Square; the sound descends heavily, as though pressing the deserted Square into the earth.

Three figures in grey overcoats, in time with the thundering blows—three and yet one, three fused into one—march across the Square. They stride out with precision, lifting black boots high in time with the sweep of their right hands. Like three mindless robots, rifles pressed to shoulders,

3

bayonets gleeming coldly, the three soldiers move toward the granite pyramid of the mausoleum.

Bon–n–n–g. . .

Their boots strike the frozen stone.

Bon–n–n–g. . .

The toes of their boots fly right up to their chests.

Bon–n–n–g. . .

Clenched, gloved fists slash through the icy air.

Bon–n–n–g. . .

Above their heads the points of the bayonets move jerkily along the short name in the granite, piercing it letter by letter.

L E N I N

Bon–n–n–g. . . bon–n–n–g. . . bon–n–n–g. . . The cold metallic ring floats across Red Square.

The solemn changing of the guard is taking place.

One pace forward. Feet together.

One pace to the right. Feet together.

About face. Feet together.

A sweep of the arms. A rifle is torn down from the shoulder and thrust forward. The bayonet is still by the face of stone. A further sweep. The rifle freezes by the foot.

Hear, O Israel! The Lord, our God. The Lord is one. These are the words of a prayer, as old as the world, with which a Jew begins his day. O Israel, we call upon You. We believe neither in God nor in the devil, for so we were taught by Soviet power. But now we no longer believe even in Soviet power.

Hear, O Israel!

Our forefathers invoked your name on the walls of Jerusalem as they fought to repel the attacks of the Roman legions.

With these words, in the ruins of the besieged fortress of Masada, our ancestors slew their wives and children lest the enemy should defile them. They then took their own lives.

On the bonfires of the Inquisition the scorched lips of our kinsmen breathed these words.

With these same words, they entered the gas chambers and, by the gaping holes of mass graves, ranged themselves before the barrels of German machine guns.

Hear, O Israel!

We took up this cry, this summons, like runners in a relay, and became Jews, sensing in ourselves a strength unsuspected in our former existence. Looking back on it all later, my wife, a Moscow actress, possessed of no exceptional heroic qualities, said: "Destiny gives every man his finest hour. If this had not happened to us, I would have felt that my life had been robbed of something."

The twenty-four of us staked our lives. We plunged irrationally and without thinking into the abyss, to set an example for others, to breach with our bones the wall separating Soviet Jews from the rest of the world. And however it might end (my illusions have long since disappeared), to the end of my days I shall recall that finest hour, that flight of the human spirit, and thank fate for joining me to the company of those who were unafraid.

Hence the uncharacteristic pathos and exaltation of style when I write about these things. I shall not conceal my pride in having taken part in the *first* public, political sit-in to take place in Russia in the entire history of Soviet power. It happened when a handful of sane and sensible men and women leapt voluntarily into the gullet of Leviathan in the name of an idea and for the good of many.

Yet in reality it seemed prosaic and ordinary. The atmosphere was tense and inauspicious. Some friends got cold feet and boycotted the idea; our relatives felt dread and despair; and there was the strain of enforced inactivity, since the desire to emigrate to Israel led automatically to dismissal from work. You have already reached the stage where, without thinking, you sign collective letters, any one of which would provide more than enough evidence to pack you off to prison. By clandestine routes these letters reach foreign journalists accredited in Moscow, and from them, via mysterious channels, the letters seep through to the West. They return to you through the ether of voices of foreign radio announcers. Not only do *you* hear them, so does everyone who listens to his radio—and, first and foremost, those who listen professionally, the officers of the State Security Service. So as not to make their job too difficult, the announcer enunciates clearly not only your full name but your home address, too, as if to say, "There, go and catch him while he's still warm in bed. After all, he wrote it himself, so he's consciously drawing your fire." And you wait for the fatal knock on the door. You've even got everything ready, including a change of underclothes and a travel case, so that you can be off quickly when they come to get you.

For us, the past was gone and looking to the future was like gazing into impenetrable darkness. All that was left was the present, *this* particular day, *this* hour, while one was still free. We lived in a kind of ghostly, unreal world, as if we were waiting for an inescapable cataclysm.

Not all my friends turned their backs on me after such revelations on the radio. Those who remained loyal, a few Russians and some Jews, too, demonstratively began to visit us almost every evening. This called for courage, for the sharp eyes of the KGB watched everyone who came to my home and the microphones hidden in the walls relayed not only words but even whispers to the sensitive ears of the police. All that was left for my guests to do was drink— drink more in order to talk less—brightening our loneliness with their presence and keeping us from despair. It was like a feast during the plague.

And only quite recently our house had been full of joy, and many had envied our prosperity and the carefree way in which my wife and I seemed to stride through life. We had everything that a man and a woman can dream of in the Soviet Union: a fine apartment in the center of Moscow; a very high and steady income, which gave us enough spare money in the bank to last for the next five years; work I loved in the film industry, which brought me success. The first sweet taste of fame was already beginning to turn my head. My wife and I were among the small, select number of Soviet citizens who frequently traveled abroad. The resorts of the Black and Baltic Seas were at our disposal, as were special creative-work centers for those engaged in the arts, where, amid wonderful countryside, in peace and quiet, looked after by deferential servants, we, the elite, could grow fat at government expense and serenely enjoy life.

Anti-Semitism, which had sprung up in the USSR from the moment that the state of Israel was created, hardly affected people like ourselves. The Soviet government needed us and our talents, and it solicitously set us apart from the crowd and protected us from day-to-day disorder and the squalidity of Russian life. So what was it that prompted my wife and me to give up this life, to make the excruciating wrench from all that tied us to it, and to plunge headfirst into the depths of the unknown?

At the time we ourselves couldn't have given a clear answer, and we didn't seek one. We leapt into the embryo Jewish movement, which was like a fast-flowing river, and were swept through the rapids by its powerful currents, bleeding where we had been hurled against the rocks and choking with happiness and our first taste of total, overwhelming freedom. No looking over our shoulders, no trifling cares, no past, and no ... no future.

Yet this was not merely the caprice of people spoiled by an easy life, nor was it a thirst for excitement. All that my wife and I had achieved in Moscow had been hard won, after our first blush of youth and at the cost of going without

a great deal when we were young. There were, unquestion-
ably, profound and serious reasons behind our decision to
renounce the success we had grasped with such difficulty
and self-denial. Much later, after we had already left the
USSR and were experiencing a series of crushing disillusionments, I delved agonizingly into the motives that had
prompted me to break up my previous, well-regulated life
for the sake of a vague and obscure future. I realized then
that it was nothing irrational that had impelled me to do
this but a host of contributory causes: at the root of each was
a lifelong, unquenchable yearning to be an honest man.

The pampered gilded cage in which the Soviet government had placed us, the hothouse life of the privileged elite,
could not prevent us seeing what went on around us. Un-
blinkered, we saw the evil and the violence, the lies and the
hypocrisy, that permeated the whole of Soviet life. We had
long lost our faith in the ideas of communism, ideas which
had been dinned into our heads since we were children, but
along with so many others we hypocritically pretended
that we still believed. Consequently, one of the chief
motives for our actions was the desire to have done with
hypocrisy and to begin a fresh, morally purer life. To do this
we needed to make a conclusive break with Soviet power
and with the Russian nation, which was being crushed beneath the ruthless heel of this regime.

I can state today with complete confidence that the
movement among Soviet Jews for emigration to Israel was
born as a form of protest against, and rejection of, Soviet
life, first and foremost on the social level and only then on
the national level. National feeling, however, was quite a
significant factor. Official anti-Semitism, which after 1948
descended like coals of fire on the heads of an almost-
assimilated Jewish population, contrived to halt this process of assimilation and to precipitate an unhealthy form of
national consciousness. The Soviet propaganda machine's
onslaught of attacks on Israel, monstrous in its falsity and
spite, provoked a feeling of injury and indignation in every
Soviet Jew, however hard he endeavored to conceal it be-

neath a mask of loyalty to the USSR. A barrier ran between us and the country we lived in. For example, when I observed the ever-growing flood of threats made by the Soviet government against Israel, I clearly envisaged the possibility of direct military intervention by the USSR in the Middle East conflict and my own unenviable role in such a situation. I was a reserve officer and would, against my will, be sent into battle and obliged to annihilate my fellow Jews, that sorry remnant which had survived the Nazi extermination camps. For me, this prospect was totally unacceptable and was precisely what prompted me to cast off my former life and to fall suddenly and morbidly in love with an Israel I did not know. I plunged into an arduous struggle almost without any hope of success in order that I might go there, to the ancient land of my forebears, to fuse with my nation and become one of its defenders rather than the involuntary accomplice of its executioners.

Thus, late one evening in that cold and snowy February of 1971, as my guests were sitting about in my apartment, drinking, eating, talking of anything save politics, even laughing and joking (for if you lose your sense of humor in a situation like that, the only way out is to put a noose around your neck), the moment came.

At the height of all this feigned and wistful cheer, there was a ring at the front door. I opened the door, quite indifferent as to whether they had come to arrest me or whether it was just some passing friend drawn in by the light. It was Yasha, one of my new friends, the ones I had become close to after getting involved in Jewish matters. He was a biologist who had been dismissed from the university for having expressed the wish to emigrate to Israel and had earned his keep thereafter by driving a Moscow taxi.

He spoke no words of greeting but simply nodded his head and glanced enquiringly toward the living room where the sounds of guests could be heard. He passed quickly in front of me along the hallway, glanced into the bedroom, and, having ascertained that there was no one in there, motioned me with his eyes to follow him and closed the door behind us. I too was silent, realizing that he did not wish the sound of his voice to betray his presence to the eavesdropping authorities. He took a sheet of paper from his pocket, placed it on the bedside table, and, without sitting down, quickly wrote in pencil:

"I'm in my cab and not being tailed. It's urgent and very important. Tomorrow, we're going to occupy the reception hall of the Presidium of the Supreme Soviet."

I was dumbstruck.

"We shall enter the building near the Red Square unobtrusively, one by one," he wrote, "and when we are inside we shall declare a hunger strike. We shan't leave until we are received by President Podgorny. We shall issue an ultimatum: Free emigration to Israel."

I smiled sardonically. In answer he went on writing:

"I can understand your skepticism. This kind of step is unheard of in the history of the USSR. It will be the first strike of its kind—and, possibly, not the last. In all probability we shall be arrested and given long prison sentences. No less than ten years. We must be prepared for such an outcome. But it's better than sitting here doing nothing. Our arrest will create a storm throughout the whole world. Are you coming with us?"

He lifted his eyes from the paper. My throat tightened, and I heard my blood pumping wildly in my temples. If I agreed, I would lose my freedom for ten interminable years, perhaps even longer. My wife, chatting animatedly with our guests in the next room, would become a widow; my little daughter, sleeping in her bed, an orphan. Our family and our world would collapse. And just because a late-night guest called on me and not on some other Jew. After all, thousands dream of escaping to Israel.

I took his pencil and with a hand over which I had little control wrote on the paper beneath his uneven lines:

"Who else is going?"

He smiled and wrote down a few names. They were my new comrades—forthright and honest people whom I had grown to love.

"Agreed," I wrote. "When?"

"At eleven A.M. Go to the Lenin Library Metro station. From there, singly on foot."

I nodded. Yasha patted me encouragingly on the shoulder, lit a match, and put the flame to the corner of the sheet of paper covered with our writing. He placed the blazing paper in an ashtray, allowed it to burn out, and then ground the ash into powder with his fingers. He then left quietly, endeavoring not to be noticed by the guests.

When I had closed the door behind him, I encountered my wife's enquiring glance and used sign language to make her understand that she should ask no questions. Only when the guests had dispersed, the dishes were washed, and we were alone in the quiet, deserted apartment did I explain to her on a sheet of paper, trying to write clearly, what I had agreed to do and that she should expect my arrest on the following day. I expected tears, to be reproached for egotism, anything but what my wife wrote in answer on the paper: three words; "I'm coming too."

The next morning we sent our daughter off to school. Suspecting nothing, she dashed off into the frosty morning, her satchel on her back—a tiny thing in her white fur coat. I caught myself thinking that the next time I saw her, after I returned from prison, she would be quite grown up. My wife locked the front door and, jingling the keys, said:

"We can throw them away. We shan't be coming back here anymore."

"Who knows?" I said, shrugging my shoulders. "Give me the keys. They might come in handy."

We emerged from the entrance, and cold wintry Moscow swallowed us up.

*   *   *

The huge entrance to the reception hall of the Presidium of the Supreme Soviet of the USSR, decorated with dense stucco moldings. Doors of oak with panes of thick and heavy glass. Ponderous brass handles.

People are coming in and going out past the bored and listless militiaman in black. At this point a young fellow in a warm short overcoat goes up to the door. He tries to look casual. He is one of the twenty-four. Here's a woman wearing an old-fashioned overcoat and wrapped up in a shawl. A grandmother, she has the face of a kind old lady, and a gentle, frightened look. She is one of the twenty-four.

A man with a small black moustache, his face almost hidden right up to the eyes behind the fur collar of his winter overcoat, pauses at the entrance when he notices my wife and me. It is one of our new friends, Ephraim Bluvstein. We both nod to him perfunctorily and move toward the door, when Ephraim takes hold of my wife's hand and whispers quietly:

"Why have you come?"

"She didn't want to stay at home," I said.

"I won't let him go alone," my wife interrupted.

"Now let's just get this clear. We shall all land in jail. That's by far the most likely thing that will happen. Only one member of each family can come. You've got a daughter at home. Who's going to look after her?"

My wife became thoughtful and bowed her head.

"Go back home," I said, smiling tensely. "Get supper ready. I'm sure to be hungry when I get home." And I followed Ephraim through the doors.

The marble walls of a vast hall. Stretching along the walls like hedgerows are benches with black leather upholstery. There is a glass door reaching halfway up one wall. Opposite, one can see the heads of officials of the Presidium reception hall through two small openings in a huge sheet of glass. On the left, looking bored, sit typical petitioners: invalids on crutches, poorly dressed women with hordes of unwashed children, men and women with patiently anxious, downcast faces. All the woes of Russia flow down into this pool in a never-ending stream of everyday complaints about the shortages of apartments, pensions not being paid, or unlawful dismissals from work.

The Jews settle themselves along the wall on the right. There are twenty-two men and two women. The expressions on their faces are totally different from those on the faces by the left-hand wall: not a single ingratiating glance; not a trace of the typical languor of defeat—quite the reverse. One can sense an excited alertness, a kind of spiritual illumination. At first they don't even talk to one another. They just exchange quick glances of encouragement.

Ephraim Bluvstein nods to two other men, and together they make their way to one of the windows in the wall of glass. They thrust a piece of paper to the official and stand waiting silently while he reads it. The eyes of the rest, who have remained on the bench, fix on the aperture in the glass.

Finally, the official looks up from the paper and, staring hard into the faces of the three Jews, remarks through the aperture, "What's this supposed to mean?"

"Just what is says," Ephraim said, even managing a fleeting smile.

"The person whom you wish to meet will not see you."

"Why not?" said Ephraim with naïve surprise. "We are ordinary Soviet citizens trying to arrange a meeting with the president of our country. Surely there's nothing illegal in that?"

"No, of course not." The official did not think of the answer at once. "But he's busy and won't be able to."

"But we don't want you to answer for him. First ask the man himself."

"I know whom to ask," said the official angrily as he snatched up a telephone and began poking his fingers into the dial. "You'll have reason to regret this provocation of yours. Nobody is going to see you."

"Then we shall stay here," said Ephraim firmly.

"Until President Podgorny sees us," said the second man.

"You tell him," added the third man, "we're going on a

hunger strike in the building of the Supreme Soviet of the USSR.''

"Wh-a-t?'' said the official, half rising from his chair and freezing with the telephone receiver in his hand.

My wife didn't go home. She stood close by the entrance to the reception hall. As always there was a stream of pedestrians passing along the pavement; cars, buses, and trolleybuses swept by. As usual the bricks of the Kremlin Wall emitted their menacing red glow, and the five-pointed stars on the tops of the towers gleamed with the same ruby light. And yet she felt that something new and intangibly alarming was beginning to happen.

Aware of someone staring at her, she turned around. A man in a civilian overcoat but with a military bearing was peering at her intently from beneath the fur of his deerskin cap. When he met her glance, he looked aside with feigned indifference. A mere two paces from her on the other side, another man, also in civilian clothes, clicked a camera with practiced dexterity and, when my wife looked his way, calmly fastened the case and began to whistle. He was wearing the same kind of deerskin cap. She glimpsed a third such hat in front of her. That man too was watching her.

A grey Volga drove up to the entrance to the reception hall. Four officers in the black overcoats of the militia and with a worried look about them got out and quickly entered the building. The grey Volga drove off immediately and a second one drove up in its place; the doors flew open and more black militia overcoats emerged. Two green army buses stopped at the pavement's edge and a large group of KGB officers emerged from them. In a car with a two-way radio aerial, parked behind the buses, an officer barked sharply into a microphone. An ever-increasing number of deerskin caps flitted in and our among the people on the pavement. The beady eyes beneath them scrutinized anyone approaching the entrance.

By this time, the entire lobby was filled with officers; but not one of them entered the reception hall. The people sitting inside saw them clearly through the glass door. All twenty-four Jews were seated on a long black bench against the marble wall. Each one of them had taken up a comfortable position: some had crossed their legs and were leaning back against the wall; others leaned forward with their elbows on their knees. Above them on the wall were three portraits—the triumvirate of the Soviet Union—Brezhnev, Podgorny, Kosygin.

The people on the bench had already got used to their situation. The nervous look had disappeared from their faces, although, despite the relaxed appearance of the comfortable postures each had taken up, tension could be sensed in their every movement. One took off his overcoat and restively placed it beside him; another quietly exchanged a few words with his neighbor.

Who are they, these friends who share the risk I take? Well, for a start let's take that old woman, Hannah Gold. What has brought her here?

*   *   *

Mikhail Gold is standing on the stage, a pale, thin young man in evening dress. He is just finishing a Neapolitan song accompanied by a rather rubbishy orchestra. Loud applause follows. A Jewish girl with a bouquet of flowers runs up to him and whispers loudly:

"'Beltz.' Please sing 'Beltz.'"

He quickly shook his head.

"'Beltz!' 'Beltz!'" The loud shouts came from the tables.

The singer looked in desperation at the accompanist, a Jew with a long mournful nose, who also shook his head no.

"'Beltz!' 'Beltz!'" The shouts in the restaurant grew louder and more emphatic.

A fat, bald, hook-nosed man jumped up on the platform and, motioning for silence, announced authoritatively: "Citizens! Stop behaving like hooligans! Or else I shall call the militia."

"'Beltz!'" The customers in the restaurant, both Jews and Russians, were in a frenzy. The singer motioned the manager aside with one hand and held up his other for silence in the hall. The restaurant became quiet. The manager went off into the wings and watched the singer distractedly.

"Beltz," unaccompanied, almost in a whisper, Gold sang, "Beltz, mein shtetele Beltz." The violin sobbed, the accordian sighed. The timid pianist kept his eye on the manager, but his fingers found their own way to the notes.

"Beltz, mein shtetele Beltz," the singer began again and the words of the song poured into the stuffy depths of the hall like a bitter lamentation.

"Mein haymele dort, vu ikh hob
Meine kindershe yorn forbrakht."
[My home over there, where I spent
my childhood years.]

The manager was speechless and stared at the singer, but he didn't dare to stop him. He seemed both spellbound and dispirited by the sadness of the melody.

"Beltz, mein shtetele Beltz
Mein haymele dort, vu ikh hob
Meine kinder khaloymes getrakht."
[...where I dreamed my childhood dreams.]

Together with the singer the whole hall took up the chorus. Tears glistened in their eyes.

An icy blizzard sweeps along the street, which is little more than a maze of trenches, hemmed in by the somber hulks of unfinished houses with empty windows like pits of darkness. As it shakes in the wind, the occasional street light snatches briefly from the darkness the silhouettes of the cranes and the excavator standing silently by a foundation pit. A lone bus with frozen windows has just left the stop after picking up the last few passengers. Mikhail Gold has missed it and arrives only to see its red lights disappear. He stands alone in the deserted street in the pool of light cast by a street lamp. Clutching his suitcase and drawing his head into his upturned collar, he stamps his feet against the cold. Four figures in identical overcoats and fur hats pass across the boardwalk over a trench and stop beside him. One of them looks around, winks at his comrades, and reels over toward Gold.

"You don't happen to have a smoke?"

"I don't smoke," Gold answered, looking into his face and sensing at once from his look that something was amiss. Gold quickly turned his head to look at the others. They were moving silently toward him. One had slipped behind his back.

"What do you want?" stammered Gold, turning pale.

There was no one else to be seen anywhere. The wind moaned sadly, tugging at the fabric of a banner stretched across the wall of an unfinished house. The large white letters of its slogan stood out from the red material: *"Let us greet the 24th Congress of the Communist Party of the Soviet Union in the proper manner."*

The four figures closed in on Mikhail Gold.

"If it's my watch you want, take it," he said, taking off his wrist watch. "I have no money. Please leave me in peace."

"Jewish tricks," snarled one of the four, his face twisted in a contemptuous grin. He knocked the watch from Gold's fingers. It smacked against the ground; with deliberation the man placed his foot on it and ground the crystal into the pavement.

"Are you Mikhail Gold?" the second man asked sharply, as though it were an interrogation.

"I am, and what of it?" Gold trembled.

"So, you're hoping to go to Israel?"

"That's no business of yours," he answered quietly, though no longer fearfully.

Surrounded by the four identical overcoats, his slim, narrow-shouldered figure seemed overshadowed by doom.

"We'll give you Israel, you dirty kike."

Mikhail Gold reeled from the first blow to his face. He raised his suitcase in an attempt to protect his head, but the blows showered on him from all sides—clinical blows of trained fists. His suitcase fell to the ground, spilling open. Out tumbled a black frock coat, a corner of white handkerchief protruding from the pocket, and a fan of sheet music. He couldn't even fall down as the unceasing hail of blows descended on him from every side. With each blow came the hoarse indictments:

"That's Israel for you."

"Here's a bit of Israel for you."

Gold collapsed at their feet. They gave his head a few last kicks with their boots, scuttled across the boardwalk, and disappeared into the depths of an unfinished house. Silence descended. The blizzard howled, and the red banner, its white letters greying with frost, flapped on the wall: *"Let us greet the 24th Congress of the Communist Party of the Soviet Union in the proper manner."*

A bus with frozen windows pulled up to the curb.

A large room with a black grand piano. On the walls there are colored posters, some of which bear the smiling portrait of Mikhail Gold; others simply display his name in large letters. The bearer of the name is lying on the sofa wrapped in a rug with his head swathed in bandages. The taxi driver Yasha is seated on a chair in front of him with a notebook on his knees. Hannah Gold, Mikhail's mother, keeps peering in at the door like a disturbed brooding hen.

Yasha wrote. "It's a pity you're sick. Tomorrow we're staging a sit-in at the reception hall of the Supreme Soviet."

Hannah brought her eyeglasses from the other room; looking over Yasha's shoulder, she began to read what had been written on the paper.

"No!" shouted Hannah. "My son's not going."

Mikhail covered her mouth with his hand. Hannah started, frightened; regaining her self control, she seized the pencil from Yasha.

"In the first place," the pencil began to twitch nervously on the paper, "my son is ill. He has to stay in bed. In the second place, he mustn't be put in prison. He'll lose his voice there. I may be his mother, but I don't exaggerate. He's a singer of genius."

Both Yasha and Mikhail couldn't help smiling.

"I'll go in his place," Hannah said out loud abruptly and, with another start, began to write quickly on the paper: "My son is a famous singer. I'm his mother. The mother of a famous singer also has a name."

She looked at them both, ashamed of her lack of modesty. Both were silent and looked at the old woman who, as though depleted of her strength, went on slowly writing on the paper: "At my age, in prison or out of it, you're getting nearer death all the same."

Yasha took the sheet, already covered with writing, and tore it up into little pieces. He embraced Hannah and kissed her shyly.

*   *   *

Bon-n-n-g...

The dull, thunderous blow rolls over Red Square; for a long moment the tremors linger in its wake, until another blow crashes through the frosty February air of blizzard-blown Moscow.

Three figures in grey overcoats, in time with the thundering blows—three and yet one, three fused into one—march across the Square.

Their boots strike the frozen stone.
The toes of their boots fly right up to their chests.
Clenched, gloved fists slash through the icy air.
Above their heads the points of the bayonets move jerkily along the short name in the granite, piercing it letter by letter.

L E N I N

Bon–n–n–g... The cold metallic ring floats across Red Square.

The twenty-four Jews are still sitting on the black bench by the marble wall, but by now they have changed their postures. High above their heads Brezhnev, Podgorny, and Kosygin stare from their portraits into the emptiness of the hall.

And who is this boy whose face not only isn't Jewish but is so strikingly Slavic? His name is Sasha Ivanov.

*   *   *

There are four inhabitants of this typical Moscow apartment—two rooms, a small kitchen, a toilet. Sasha Ivanov, his brother Yuri, and Yuri's wife, Vera, with little Vovochka in her arms, are standing, looking at the door that has just closed, exchanging perplexed glances.

Sasha is well built, athletic, and fair haired; his brother Yuri, although two years older, is smaller, more delicate, and dark. The table in the room is still covered with dishes that have not been cleared away after dinner.

"We should have seen her on her way," said Sasha breaking the silence. "When all's said and done, she's an old lady and from out of town."

"It's like some sort of bad dream," said Vera, nervously rubbing her temple with her hand. "Life's going along smoothly. And suddenly, 'How do you do, I'm your aunt.'"

"And not just any old aunt!" Sasha said, rolling his eyes in great amusement. "But Aunt Rakhil Abramovna. I've lived for thirty years thinking I was a Russian, and it turns out that my mother was Jewish. I, Sasha Ivanov, am the son of Sarah Abramovna. And you, Yuri Ivanov . . . are her son too. Ha, ha!"

"I don't think it's funny," Yuri muttered through his teeth.

"Wait a minute boys," Vera butted in. "This whole thing needs sorting out. I think the old girl is in her second childhood and has got everything mixed up."

They all went through into the living room and back to the dinner table, Vera continuing excitedly, as though she had hit upon a way out of the situation:

"You both grew up in an orphanage and didn't know your parents. It's only from your papers that you know that your father, Vassily Dmitrievich Ivanov, an officer in the Soviet army, was killed in action when you were tiny babies, and your mother died of hunger in the Leningrad blockade. That's true, isn't it? You know neither your mother's name nor her face. All her papers were lost. Why do we have to believe that old woman when she says that your mother was a Jew and that she is her sister? Where's the logic?"

"And these photographs she brought," said Sasha, ignoring Vera and taking a yellow photograph from the packet on the table. "This is my father; he's like me, or, more accurately, I'm like him, like his twin brother. Yura, old chap, that's you sitting on his knee as large as life. You've not changed much—one can tell it's you. And this little angel in mother's arms is me. You know, I even find it almost flattering that I was such a pretty baby. By the way Yura, you're very like mother."

"You stupid fool!" Vera burst out. "Do you realize what this means? Why can't you be serious? Good God, Yura," she said wearily after a pause, looking at her husband sadly, "you really do look like a typical Jew."

"And you're a complete idiot," Yura barked back testily.

"Keep calm, keep calm," Sasha stopped them, smiling. "We don't want a row in a cultivated household. Both Yura and I were Russians, and Russians we'll remain. And we'll forget Auntie Rakhil Abramovna just as if she never existed. Anyway, after the reception you gave her, Vera dear, she won't show her face in our house again. She didn't even leave her address."

"Thank God for that."

"Now, why look at it that way," said Sasha, pouting his lips reproachfully. "She's a lonely old woman who was really overjoyed to have found her nephews. And her little nephews are scum. Surely she's not to blame for that? All right, I'm joking. Well, at least that's got the smiles back on your faces. Peace has returned to our family. Soon things'll be really fine." He put his arms round Yura's and Vera's shoulders. "I'm getting a one-room flat, and then this'll all be yours. In six months' time I shall be going abroad as our newspaper's own correspondent if, of course, I don't fail my examinations in English. I shall be able to send you all kinds of foreign schmattahs: cardigans, blouses, minis, and midis. So, chin up."

Vera gave a sidelong glance at the photograph in Sasha's hand. "That needs removing," she said. "If anyone drops in and starts asking questions, we shall have to explain to everybody."

"There's no need for any explaining," said Yura. "Remove it without a trace."

He tried to tug the photograph from Sasha's fingers, but Sasha wouldn't let go of it.

"But why, Yura old chap," Sasha said mockingly. "Let me keep it. I'm not a sentimental person, but after all it is the only picture we have of our mother. I'll keep it to remember her by."

"It's a time bomb," said Vera, nodding her head

vigorously, "which will go off one day. Oh, you'll be sorry, Sasha."

"But you're both out of your minds," said Sasha, growing angry. "What difference does it make? A Russian, a Jew, or, for that matter, a Turk. We're all Soviet people. You talk as though we lived in Germany under Hitler."

Vera looked him up and down sardonically. "You're a big fellow Sasha, but your brains don't take up much of that space. Take your position with the paper. That career of yours is like a soap bubble. You've had no experience of that sort of thing yet. There's a girl called Sofa Zisman who works with me. This is the third year her daughter's been trying to get fixed up in an institute. Her examination results are excellent, but they won't accept her. And why, do you think? Because of Section 5, my dear—her na-tion-al-i-ty! What's going to happen to our Vovochka? Have you thought of that?"

The muscles of Yura's cheeks began to twitch. "You know I've never cared for Jews; now I think I'm beginning to hate them."

"Whom?" said Sasha, narrowing his brows. "Me?"

"What have you got to do with it?"

"I happen to be Jewish. Like yourself."

"It's a lie!" shouted Yura. "I'm a Russian! Russian! I was born a Russian, and I'll die a Russian."

Sasha fixed him with a scornful glance: "You won't die a Russian. You'll die a worm."

The editor's office. It is large and spacious, with official furniture—a desk and, at right angles to it, a second one for conferences. The occupant of the office is a grey-haired man getting on in years. Eyes, intelligent but lazy, look out from beneath swollen lids.

"Alexander Vassilyevich," said the editor wearily to Sasha, "you're not a kid. You should be able to see what's going on."

"Where?"

"Well, on the foreign scene let's say . . . our relations with Israel. . . . You yourself will soon be working abroad. . . . Do I have to spell it out for you? I like you, and don't wish you any harm. Don't chatter about this thing too much."

"What thing?"

"You know as well as I do. The whole editorial office is talking about nothing else. If it goes any farther I shall have to alter your clearance form."

"I don't understand."

"If you don't watch your tongue, you'll understand soon enough. That's all I have to say. You may go, Comrade Ivanov."

When Sasha had left the office, the editor pressed a bell and said to the secretary who pushed her head languidly through the doorway, "Bring me Ivanov's personal file."

Sasha is in his room, settled deeply into an armchair, tuning a transistor radio, which he is holding on his knee. At first he hears snatches of sentences in various languages, then the beat of a jazz band bursts through, then the doleful crackle of Soviet jamming fills the air for a time before disappearing, only to come through again, covering, drowning the voices of the announcers. Nevertheless, through the bristling radio interference, at first faintly but then more clearly, comes the Israeli radio's theme song. Sasha tunes in to the wave more exactly, and when he gets clear of the jamming, the announcer's voice, speaking in Russian, can be heard in the room:

"This is Radio Israel speaking. In Israel the time is. . . ."

Sasha squints at the door and into the next room, and turns down the volume so that the broadcast can only just be heard. He looks up at Vera, who is standing in the doorway.

"What an odd language. Don't you think so?" he asked, smiling and nodding toward the transistor. "I can't get used to the idea that it's just as much my native tongue as Russian is."

"It'll never be your native language," said Vera dully.

"I wonder," said Sasha thoughtfully.

"Make your peace with Yura," Vera urged him after a pause.

"No. He has insulted our mother's memory. He and I are both half Russian and half Jewish. At the moment in Russia it's more advantageous, more convenient, to be Russian than it is to be Jewish. But you can't turn your back on your own mother. Her blood is in our veins. And if in our country it's a disgrace to be her son, then I'm on her side, and I want things to be as hard for me as they would have been for her if she had survived the Leningrad blockade. I am a Jew. Today and always. So long as there's a single anti-Semite left in the world."

The editor's office.

"Well, Ivanov," said the editor to Sasha, "you've signed your own sentence. You won't be allowed to go to Israel. You can take that as final. Nobody's allowed to leave the Soviet Union for a foreign country."

"Why? What are we then? Slaves? Serfs who are bound to their masters?"

"You know that as well as I do. There's no point in discussing it. And you can't go on working in the editorial offices. With views like yours . . . well, you must realize. . . . Let me have a letter of resignation."

"And if I don't?"

"We'll bounce you."

"And the reason?"

"We'll find a reason."

"I'll tell you. Maybe up till now I wasn't quite certain of the rightness of my decision, but from now on I'm going to fight to the very end."

"And I can tell you where your end's going to be," said the editor sadly. "In Siberia."

Sasha, who has grown thin and has deep hollows under his eyes, is standing in the center of the room with his arms behind his back and is looking provocatively at the people who are sitting at a table covered with green cloth. It is the employment commission of the district (municipal) executive committee. The chairman of the commission, a bloated bureaucrat with a shaved head, leafs through the papers in a file, muttering in annoyance.

"Ivanov, Alexandr Vassilyevich ... mmm ... Jewish. It's absurd, young man. You should have changed your surname."

"Why?" Sasha demonstratively straightened the brass Star of David on his chest. "I'm proud of my father's name—just as I'm proud of my mother's nationality."

"Where do you work?"

"Nowhere."

"What are you living on?"

"I'm selling my remaining things. I got rid of my typewriter yesterday."

"So you want to go to Israel, then?" the chairman of the commission looked at him and at the Star of David on his chest with undisguised disdain. "A fine one you are, eating Russian bread for thirty years."

"You might say," said Sasha, grinning wryly, "that it's a long time since anybody ate Russian bread. We all eat American bread. There isn't enough of ours to go around. We have to make it up with other peoples'. And the main thing, which you'd do well to put in your pipe and smoke, is that I want to go to Israel because there nobody will reproach me for eating bread, whatever its origin."

The chairman began to cough and splutter, looking helplessly at the other members of the commission. A woman sitting on the chairman's left came to his aid: "There's a war on in the Middle East." When you get there, they'll take you into the army."

"If they do, it'll be a great honor," smiled Sasha.

Her eyes widened. "What do you mean by that?"

"Aren't you the people who've been teaching me since I was a child not to know fear in the face of an enemy, not to be afraid of difficulties, and to do my duty to my motherland honorably? Israel will be my motherland."

"Do you know what you're saying?" said the chairman, turning a little crimson and banging on the cloth with his pudgy fist. "A time will come when you have to shoot across the Suez Canal at my son."

"Your son has no business to be anywhere near the Suez Canal!" Sasha raised his voice. "He'd do better to stay at home."

"Now you listen to me, my lad," the chairman rose to his feet, looking bad tempered and red faced. "You've got as much chance of ever seeing Israel as you have of seeing your own ears. We'll see you rot here! On Russian soil!"

*   *   *

Two more busloads unload their burden of militiamen by the entrance of the president's reception hall. Men in civilian clothes, wearing identical overcoats and deerskin caps, have stationed themselves by the windows, endeavoring to use their backs to prevent the passersby from looking inside.

Inside the marble hall, the Jews are the only people left. They sit on the bench as before. By now they are pretty tired and are listening attentively to the blows of the Kremlin chimes.

An official walks through the hall and, without looking at anybody, says as though to himself: "The working day is over. Please leave the building."

No one stirred. But this was what he was hoping for because at once he issued a loud instruction: "Begin cleaning."

As if a signal had been given, five cleaning women dressed in dark blue overalls and headscarves, with mops and buckets in their hands, came through the line of officers, who stepped aside to let them pass. Five middle-aged women worn down by life and indifferent to all that was happening there put their buckets down on the stone floor, splashed some water down, and set to work apathetically with their mops, without raising their eyes. Like a line of attacking soldiers, they advanced upon the people who were sitting by the wall. When the lathered tongues of water began to flow near the benches, the people started to lift their feet, but they did not stir from the spot.

An official waited silently by, tugging the strings one by one, lowering the plastic venetian blinds. Large chandeliers lit up the whole hall brightly. A light was burning in the corridor, where behind the glass the grey overcoats were tightly packed together, the glare reflecting on their buckles and hat badges.

A stern-faced man in a black suit and tie entered the hall, followed respectfully by two others. Everybody sensed that this man represented the authorities and got up from the benches in tense expectation, but not one moved toward him. He and his escort stopped in the center of the hall. For a long time he examined each individual in turn, as though testing their powers of restraint, and only when the examination was concluded did he give a dull, authoritative cough.

"I am the deputy head of the reception hall sent here by Nikolai Viktorovich Podgorny, president of the Presidium of the Supreme Soviet of the USSR. My name is Dumin. I demand that you leave the building at once."

"We won't go! Go ahead and arrest us! We won't go! Not until we're allowed to go to Israel!" everybody chimed in at once.

Dumin raised his hand to call for silence.

"Do you realize what you've done?" he said, raising his voice. "Do you understand the meaning of your actions? You've seized Soviet power! Is that clear? And our laws punish that sort of thing severely. They show no mercy."

With a slight movement of his head he indicated the rows of grey overcoats on the other side of the glass.

"I'll give you one last chance to clear out of here, and no harm done. If you don't, then you've only yourselves to blame. If you don't leave the hall, things will end very badly for you. Soviet power knows how to deal with its enemies."

"We are not enemies! We demand what is our legal right!"

"The tribunal that tries you will decide what you are. That's all I have to say!"

And he and his escort left the hall. No sooner had the door closed behind them than the chandeliers flickered and blinked off, and the hall sank into darkness. Looking into the lighted corridor, they saw the wall of grey overcoats, and, in the darkness of the hall, they whispered to one another nervously:

"Now they will take us."

"But we shouldn't go voluntarily. Only by force!"

"We'll not get less than a year."

"You'll thank God for only a year. Ten you don't want?"

"They can't execute us..."

"Well, you know, times have changed. They'll give us each ten years of hard labor. Mind you, that's no joke either."

"Shut up, you Jews. Have you lost your grip? Anybody want to listen to the radio? I've got a transistor."

"Let's have the radio. If we're going to die, let's do it to music."

All twenty-four of them crowded like apparitions around the tiny transistor with its faintly gleaming antenna. The set began to squeak till at last there burst through fragments of music and voices speaking various languages. Eventually, their attention focused on a far-off voice speaking Russian:

"This is the BBC. According to the reports from corre-spondents of foreign press agencies in Moscow, a group of Jews who had been refused permission to emigrate to Israel today occupied the building of the Soviet parliament and went on hunger strike there. The building is now cordoned off by police and soldiers. The attention of the whole world is riveted on the course of this desperate struggle.

"These twenty-four men and women are the representatives of tens and hundreds of thousands of Soviet Jews, who have for years, with no success, been trying to achieve their legal right to live in their historical homeland. According to un-confirmed information. . ." But the snarling rumble of the jammer drowned the announcer's words. An impassioned whisper filled the darkness of the hall.

"They know about us."

"Friends, we're not alone!"

"They'll be afraid to do anything to us."

"You think they'll be afraid? There's nothing that will stop them."

"But we aren't afraid either. We've been afraid for long enough! Let's put an end to our fears!" Ephraim spoke, drawing himself up to his full height above the people crouching over the gurgling transistor. One after another people straightened up and stood beside Ephraim. Pressed closely against one another, indistinct in the darkness, they stood facing the illuminated glass behind which, hat badges and buckles gleaming, stood the wall of grey overcoats.

*   *   *

The high bays of a large machine shop in a modern en-gineering works. The whine and roar of hundreds of machine tools, bursts of blinding light from electric wel-ders, lift trucks scurrying about with loads of iron castings. Above the heads of the workmen, grasped in chains, soar bundles of metal pipes.

At the end of the bay is a plywood stand, to which are attached a large number of notices. A man whose clean suit and tie mark him out from the greasy overalls pins a large sheet of drawing paper on to the stand. The words stand out boldly in black india ink:

TODAY
at 6 P.M. there will be
a closed Party meeting.

AGENDA
1. The case of Communist Party member
Comrade Bluvstein
2. Other Business

Works Party Committee.

Beside this stand is a second one bigger than the first and with an ornamental frame. It is dominated by a hammer and sickle, surrounded by banners. In embossed wooden letters are the words, *Our Best Workers.*

There are neat rows of photographs of men and women— the pride of the factory. The man in the clean suit and tie goes over to this stand, runs his eyes over the photographs and examines the first one. Large, dark eyes look down from the photograph; the face is handsome with cheeks sunken through illness, and a small, black moustache. Underneath is written: *E. L. Bluvstein, shop manager.*

Thumb tacks secure the photograph at each corner. The man in the clean suit digs out one of them with his finger nail. The edge of the photograph curls up; he turns his attention to the second tack.

"Aren't you burying me rather early?" a voice from behind his back spoke reproachfully. Behind him, wrinkling his eyes sadly, stood the shop manager, Ephraim Bluvstein. In the photograph he was wearing a white shirt and tie. At work he wore dark blue overalls, his neck hidden by the turned-up collar of his sweater.

The man in the new suit blinked in confusion. He was clearly one of Bluvstein's subordinates and continued to regard him as a boss.

"It's not me. We got orders from above."

A sad smile touched Bluvstein's handsome face. "The Party meeting will decide my fate ... in two hours time. Why all the hurry?"

"Well," the man in the suit giggled brazenly, "we know already what the decision will be. We're small fry ... orders from above. ... But if you're against it, I can leave the photograph up for another two hours."

"Give it to me."

Bluvstein tore the photograph from the stand without even removing the thumb tacks, leaving its torn corners behind. He rolled it up and shoved it into the breast pocket of his overalls. As he was opening the door of his small, glass-partitioned office, he was stopped by an old man, a foreman in a greasy jacket and an equally greasy cap, pulled down on his head like a pancake.

"Comrade manager, it's him again—Syomin. He's been up to his tricks again. He pointed to a middle-aged, burly giant of a man in dirty overalls who was standing nearby. He had a puffy, flabby face. One eye was half closed guiltily; the other, the glass one, gleamed straight ahead, its gaze fixed in perpetuity.

"Well Syomin, what have you been up to now?" Bluvstein asked wearily.

Syomin spread his hands in a gesture of resignation and bowed his curly, already balding head.

"He fouled up two parts, one after the other," the foreman explained. "And why? He's come to work half drunk again. You can smell it a mile off. He got a warning last week. And here he is again."

"Come into my office, both of you." Bluvstein held open the door, first for the foreman and then for the clumsy, lumbering Syomin.

In the little office everything was in perfect order. On the walls were engineering drawings; on the table, a pile of files; shiny measuring instruments were nearly laid out. The whole shop was visible through the glass and, within, the rumble and scraping of metal was only slightly deadened.

Syomin crumpled up his dirty cap in his hands and stared at the floor with his single eye. The foreman turned toward the window. Bluvstein laid his chin on his hands, which were folded on the table, and, though his sad black eyes were fixed on Syomin, his thoughts seemed far away.

"I only had a couple of shots," mumbled Syomin. "With a friend—this morning. It's the last time. You have my word."

"Foreman, put him down as absent without good reason, and send him home from the shop to sleep it off. If it happens again, you'll be sacked."

"What are you going to write 'absent without good reason' for, boss?" Syomin flared up.

"That's it. There's nothing more to say." Bluvstein got up from the table.

"You're a very hard man, boss. Your last day in charge, too."

"I don't change my rules, even on the last day."

He looked into Syomin's face, and his look expressed not resentment but pity for this seedy drunk. Syomin grinned.

"You're wasting your time, boss. They won't think any better of you. You'll get bounced, and I'll stay on. Seeing as I'm a Russian and you're a Jew. D'you get it?"

The foreman became agitated and tried to manhandle the huge Syomin toward the door.

"Go on, go on . . . for that sort of thing, I'd bash your face in . . . if it were up to me."

Syomin staggered out of the office, walking unsteadily; as he passed the board of honor, he noticed that the photograph had been torn down from its place above the shop manager's name. He blinked his one good eye in amazement, took his glass eye out of its socket with his dirty fingers, rubbed it on the sleeve of his overall, and popped it back under his eyelid.

"What did I tell him?" Syomin laughed triumphantly. "The Jews are finished."

A closed Party meeting is in progress in the spacious room of the Party bureau. On the walls are portraits of Brezhnev and Kosygin. In the corner on a little table stands a plaster of paris bust of Lenin. Behind it is displayed the velvet cloth of a Red Challenge Banner.

About thirty Communists sit on the chairs closest to the platform; the back rows are empty. In the middle of the room, dividing the rows of chairs, is an aisle, along which runs a strip of carpet, which reaches as far as the raised portion of the room. Here the leadership sits at a long table—a number of factory personnel and a representative of the district committee, who conducts the meeting. Bluvstein is in the front row. There are a number of empty chairs on each side of him.

"Your shop manager, Ephraim Lazarevich Bluvstein, has been dismissed from his post, and today we have to decide the question of whether or not he is to be allowed to remain a member of the Communist Party."

"And why has he been dismissed?" someone's voice rang out.

The speaker was displeased and looked round to find the person who had asked the question.

"The order will be hung up in the shop. It explains the whole thing."

"Excuse me." The old foreman, who had brought the drunken Syomin to Bluvstein, rose from his seat. "Ephraim Lazarevich has been in charge of the shop for three years and has turned it from one of the worst in the plant into one of the best. Until he came along, however hard we tried, we had no success. It's true that he's a stern man; he maintains a high standard of discipline and as an engineer he knows what he's doing. As you know, the working man has no love for the bosses, but in our shop we look upon him as a father."

"What's your name?" the district committee representative cut him short.

"People have been calling me Samokhin for fifty-eight years, and for thirty of them I've been in the Party."

"Well then, Comrade Samokhin, your 'father', as you put it, is an anti-Soviet element. And today you're going to expel him from the Party—as an alien element who is hostile to us."

"For what?" once again the voice was heard.

"For slandering Soviet power and the Party. He wrote a letter to the general secretary of the Central Committee of our Party, Comrade Brezhnev, in which he clearly expounded his views."

"What sort of letter? Read it. We want to know," the voices rang out.

"I've no intention of reading the letter to you. It is anti-Soviet propaganda."

"Well, what next!" said the old foreman, leaping from his seat and throwing up his hands. "We've got to expel him for the letter, but we aren't allowed to know what was written in the letter. It's like a blind man trying to walk a tightrope."

"Comrade Samokhin," the representative of the district committee said threateningly. "Judging by your remarks, you seem to share Bluvstein's views."

"What views? We'd at least like to know what we're supposed to be talking about."

"Comrade Samokhin." The old man got a rebuff from the platform. "Will you please come to order. Nobody gave you permission to speak."

"And they needn't bother," Samokhin growled out and sat down, lowering his head.

"Very well," said the representative of the district committee. "I can give you a brief summary of the letter's contents." He coughed very significantly. "Former shop manager, Communist Bluvstein, slanders the Party's Middle East policy, accuses the Party of conducting a campaign of anti-Semitism, and demands that Jewish traitors be allowed to emigrate freely to Israel.

"Well, isn't that enough?" The district committee representative looked round the silent hall like a prosecutor.

Bluvstein nervously got to his feet.

"Sit down!" shouted the district committee representative. "Nobody gave you permission to speak."

"I would like you to read my letter. You have distorted its meaning entirely."

"You want a platform here for your anti-Soviet views? We won't allow that."

"I want to explain my behavior to my brother Communists before they make a decision, even though you have already made yours. I'm a Communist, and I will always be a Communist. It is my faith as long as I live. And as an honest Communist I wanted in this letter to save the Party from taking steps which would be wrong and compromising. The duty of a Communist is to uphold the honor of his Party—not to stand by indifferently when the good name, which it won in 1917, is trampled into the dirt."

"Slander! Silence! Remove him from the hall!" the shouts came from the platform.

"Let him speak! We want to know!" came the shouts from the hall.

"I know that I am speaking to you for the last time," Bluvstein said quietly, "and I want to have my say. My letter is in keeping with the Party statutes, where it says clearly that a Communist may put his criticisms in writing and send them to the highest levels of the Party, who are obliged to give him a hearing. They may agree with me, or they may disagree. If they disagree, they must then explain where I have made my mistake. Why was I trampled on and shouted at in all the Party commissions? But they couldn't answer a single question I put to them—because they don't want to know the truth. And the truth isn't very pleasant.

"There is anti-Semitism in the USSR—crude, undisguised anti-Semitism. Even if all a man's relatives live in another country, he's forbidden to leave ours, just as if he were in a concentration camp. We are losing billions of rubles in the Middle East. They are being taken away from the people. And why? To help the Arabs? It's not true. We need military bases on the Mediterranean Sea, but Israel is a stumbling block. So, why not destroy Israel and the few remaining Jews—those whom Hitler didn't have time for—for the sake of our imperialistic goals? And this is being done by the same Communist Party which declared that its main aim was the happiness of men on earth.

"No honest Communist can agree with such a policy, and that is why I wrote my letter to Comrade Brezhnev. But he hadn't the courage to answer me. And that is why I am on trial now. It would appear that I, a Communist, have no right to vote and must ask no questions. I am only allowed to do one thing—to applaud my leaders.

"Which of us has infringed Party statutes, if those statutes are nothing more than a piece of paper? I put the question to you, to you Communists, with whom I have worked for three years in the same shop. I know that you are honest men. You are my comrades."

"A wolf is no comrade for a lamb," the man who had taken Bluvstein's photograph down from the board of honor blurted out from the platform.

"Hey, that's enough," someone snarled back from the hall. "We won't have anybody insulted."

"Well, there you are, comrades," said the representative of the district committee, rubbing his hands in satisfaction. "It turns out that the whole Party is wrong, and Bluvstein is the only one in the right."

"Why the only one?" objected Bluvstein calmly. "Today only I had the courage, but tomorrow others will ask even more ticklish questions. You can't shut everybody's mouths. Times have changed."

"Well, I think everything's clear," said the representative, spreading out his arms. "There is a motion to put to the vote Bluvstein's expulsion from the Party."

"Why expel him here and now?" asked someone uncertainly. "Perhaps our comrade made a mistake, went a bit too far. He needs putting right."

"He's beyond putting right," said the man who had taken Bluvstein's photograph down from the board of honor.

"May I ask one question," said the old foreman, getting to his feet. "We're told we have Party democracy, but how does this work out in practice? You refused to read Bluvstein's letter to us, but we're supposed to expel him on the basis of his letter. That's one thing. In the second place, everything he did he did in accordance with the Party statutes. That means the statutes are invalid. In the third place . . ."

"In the third place," the steely tones of the district committee representative interrupted him, "the question of your behavior will be reviewed separately."

The incipient murmur of discussion in the hall immediately stopped. The old foreman spat angrily at his feet and sat down.

"We'll put this matter to the vote. That Ephraim Lazarevich Bluvstein, formerly a shop manager, should be expelled from the Party for slandering its policy and for anti-Soviet propaganda. Those in favor, please raise your hands."

All those on the platform raised their hands instantly, but those in the hall vacillated. Slowly, hesitatingly, arms of lead were raised. A few remained undecided. The gaze of the district committee representative rested on each of the wavering faces in turn. Mutely, one by one, hands were raised. His eyes fell on the old foreman. The latter squirmed on his chair under the look. His face took on a tortured expression. He seemed about to burst into tears. His hand, which was lying on the back of the chair in front of him, twitched but did not move from the chair. The whole platform was looking at the foreman. He did not raise his hand.

"Carried unanimously," sighed the representative of the district committee. "Will Bluvstein please leave the meeting."

The cheeks of his pale, sickly face had sunk even more deeply, his eyes were like black coals. With his head held high, he walked up the aisle in the center of the hall. As he approached each row, people frowned and lowered their eyes in shame; they drew their heads into their shoulders, huddled up uncomfortably. No one dared to look him in the face.

"We will now move to the second item on the agenda," the voice of the district committee representative grated out triumphantly behind him.

The bowed figure of Ephraim Bluvstein, huddling down into the upturned fur collar of his overcoat, shuffles along the street. He walks past shops with empty windows, past a long line of women with purses in their hands, stretching along the pavement to a salesman doing a lively trade in canned goods. On the corner is another line, of men, arranged before a beer stall. A woman, her face nearly obscured by her fluffy scarf and her many layers of clothing covered by a greasy smock, is pumping foaming beer from a barrel into glass mugs. She tops up each with warmed-up beer from a large kettle, which she keeps taking from an electric stove. Those fellows lucky enough to get some beer drink it then and there, standing out in the cold. They blow the foam off the beer with gusto and help it down with a piece of sun-dried fish, which they have divided in comradely fashion.

"Ephraim Lazarevich," a familiar voice called to Bluvstein from the crowd. It was Syomin, fighting his way from the beer stall toward Bluvstein with a mug of beer in each hand, one full, the other half empty. He had no overcoat over his oily overalls and was bareheaded.

"My friend. Don't bear a grudge. Have one on me."

He was already quite merry and his one eye looked benevolently on Bluvstein. The frost was making his glass eye watery.

"I don't drink, Syomin."

"You don't want to join me?" asked Syomin, ready to take offense.

"No, Syomin," smiled Bluvstein. "I'm not allowed to drink."

"And why's that?" said Syomin, mystified.

"I'm a war invalid, too. As are you. My stomach was cut to bits by shell splinters. I've got to keep off most things. I can't have beer or vodka. Nothing spicy, nothing salty. Just diet foods and medicines."

"Not much of a life," said Syomin with genuine sympathy. "Enough to drive a man to drink. Well, your good health, Ephraim Lazarevich. Forgive me if I said something I shouldn't have. I respect people like you. D'you get me? Stuck to your guns. You did right, Lazarevich. You're one of the best!"

He drained the half-empty mug and handed it to Bluvstein. Then he dealt with the second in the same way and handed that to Bluvstein, too. He wiped his lips on his sleeves, clumsily put his paws round Bluvstein, and kissed him on the lips.

"Fellers!" he shouted tearfully addressing himself to the crowd by the stall. "You're all shit! And I am too! Have you got that? We save our own skins and to tell the truth we've got no guts. Here's a man for you! He showed them all where to get off!"

He poked his finger toward Bluvstein, who was clutching the two empty mugs to his chest.

"And I offended him!" Syomin continued his drunken confession to the crowd. "I didn't respect him! At the side of this man I'm nobody. How can I look people in the face now?"

In front of the whole crowd Syomin pulled his glass eye out of its socket and, in a fit of temper, dashed it against the pavement, smashing it into little pieces, and began to trample on them with his foot.

The crowd began to hoot with laughter. There was the sound of a whistle, and a militiaman in a sheepskin coat trussed up in squeaking shoulder straps placed his hand, which was incased in a heavy sheepskin mitten, on the shoulder of the weeping Syomin.

"Citizen, will you come with me to the station."

Two men in civilian clothes, who seemed to appear out of the earth, converged on Bluvstein from each side and took him by the arms. He was still clutching the two empty beer mugs to his chest. One of the men took the mugs from him and carried them back to the stall; the second twisted his arms behind his back.

"What are you taking him for?" Syomin snarled drunkenly.

"Shut up!" shouted the militiaman. "You'll be told what for at the station."

The hall of the People's Court is narrow and cramped, like a pencil box. The walls are scratched, and it's been a long time since the panes of the one and only window have been cleaned. The seats set aside for the public are empty. Flanked by two militiamen, Syomin and Bluvstein stand before the table of the people's judge.

"For hooliganism and rowdyism in a public place," the judge droned on, peering shortsightedly at his papers, "Citizen Vassily Ignatyevich Syomin, a worker of No. 12 Works, is sentenced to fifteen days imprisonment. No appeal."

"What did I tell you!" Syomin grunted submissively, scratching the back of his neck as he did so. "We will rest awhile from our righteous labors."

The judge looked at him with displeasure, and then once more buried himself in his papers.

"For hooliganism and rowdy behavior in a public place, Citizen Ephraim Lazarevich Bluvstein, unemployed, is sentenced to fifteen days imprisonment."

"What have you sentenced him for?" gasped Syomin. "He was sober. As sober as a judge. He's not even allowed to drink."

"No appeal," said the judge in a dull, creaking voice, looking somewhere over their heads.

Bluvstein smirked and simply shook his head.

Syomin and Bluvstein are sitting opposite each other on their plank beds in a prison cell, which is lit by a dim bulb behind a grill on the ceiling.

"Ephraim Lazarevich, you must forgive me," said Syomin looking at the wall in embarassment. "It's all on account of me. They took you because you were with me. How many times have I said I'd stop drinking. And now I've got a decent fellow into trouble."

"You've got it all wrong, Syomin. It isn't the first time you've been drinking, but you've never been here before."

"That's right," Syomin nodded.

"And you wouldn't have got here this time if you hadn't stopped me. They're on my heels all the time—always looking for an excuse to arrest me. Well, there I am standing with a drunk and clutching two beer mugs into the bargain. What else could they want? Hooliganism. Served up on a plate. The truth is you're here because you were with me."

The keys grated in the iron door. A guard came in with a tray. On it stood two iron bowls of steaming liquid and two hunks of black bread. A second guard remained by the door.

Syomin immediately placed his bowl on his knee and began to gulp the food down noisily, biting off large pieces of the black bread.

"I shan't eat that," Bluvstein remarked calmly.

"Don't you like it?" the guard smirked. "This is not a restaurant."

"He's a sick man. He's supposed to be on a diet," said Syomin, going on chewing as he spoke. "And medicines. You got that?"

"This is a prison, not a hospital."

"I've been sentenced unjustly. As a protest, I'm going on hunger strike."

"You refuse to take any food," the guard stated, indifferently putting on the tray the untouched bowl of soup and the bread.

The door banged closed, and the key grated in the lock.

"There's pigs for you," said Syomin looking at the door with his single eye. "They've taken it away. I'd have downed that. There wasn't enough there to keep a bird alive," he nodded at his own empty bowl.

Ephraim Bluvstein is lying on his plank bed with his arms folded under the back of his head. His face has become even more sunken, and a thick crop of black bristles has appeared on his cheeks. Across from him, Syomin is hastily guzzling down a bowl of thin soup. A guard with a tray on which there is an untouched bowl of soup gives a sidelong glance at the officer standing in the doorway.

"Leave the food in the cell," the officer orders. "He might feel a bit weak after five days."

A tiny spiral of steam rises from the bowl of cloudy liquid, which has been placed on a stool by Bluvstein's head. He runs his tongue round his parched lips and gazes uninterestedly at the damp ceiling and the iron grill in the top corner, which admits a tiny ray of faint light into the cell.

"Lazarevich," Syomin cautiously touches him on the shoulder. "To hell with all that, have something to eat. You'll finish yourself off altogether."

Bluvstein shook his head—once.

"What do you think you'll prove to them?" asked Syomin. "Surely you don't think you'll find any justice here?"

"I'm not going to eat." Bluvstein pulled his dry lips apart. "You can eat it."

Syomin began to fidget on his plank bed, groaned a little, his eye all the time on the bowl. He sighed uncomfortably. "As you wish." Putting the bowl on his knees, he began to spoon the soup down at high speed. There was a click from the peephole shutter on the door and the grating of the lock; in ran a guard. Syomin threw his spoon aside and, almost choking himself, began to drink the soup out of the bowl, having first shoved half the piece of bread into his mouth. The guard snatched the bowl from him, dumping its contents over Syomin's knees, picked up the remainder of the bread, and stalked out of the cell.

Bluvstein's face is deathly pale and overgrown with a beard. His cheeks are great hollows, and his eyes are sunk deeply into his head. He has become so weak that he cannot even raise his hand. Two men in civilian clothes, supporting his back, sit him upright on the plank bed, lift his limply hanging hands and dress him in a straitjacket, then they lay him down again and tie the long ends of the sleeves across his stomach as if he were a parcel. A man in a white coat, beneath which are visible officer's boots, takes his instruments out of a case and puts them on a stool. Syomin is sitting on his plank bed with his back pressed against the wall, his single eye round in horror. The two men sit on Bluvstein's legs. He winces but makes no sound. The doctor takes a long rubber tube and sits down on the edge of the bed.

"Well, my dear fellow. You've been without food for thirteen days; we shall have to feed you forcibly. In two days time you're to be set free and you can't even stand up. We are humane men. We even spare our enemies. I can tell you quite frankly this whole scheme of yours is pointless. All right, you went without food, and what of it? Not a single person in the world knows about it. Not a single person can either pity you or praise you. It's all in vain and to no purpose. Please don't offer any resistance. It's pointless."

He brought the end of the tube up to Bluvstein's nose. A tortured grimace twisted Bluvstein's face and he shook his head with the remainder of his strength.

"Listen," he wheezed in a scarcely audible voice, "you mustn't ... I'm very ill ... Don't do it ... I could die."

"That's quite possible," said the doctor without a shadow of doubt in his voice. And the two men sitting on Bluvstein's legs smiled.

"We have already foreseen that eventuality."

He fumbled in his breast pocket, brought out a paper, unfolded it and put it in front of Bluvstein's eyes.

"There you are, read it, if you're still capable of reading: your death certificate. It's all been filled in. And the reason's given: a thrombosis of the myocardium. All we need is the date. What date is it today?" he asked Bluvstein politely.

"Doctor." Syomin's voice called out suddenly. The doctor turned to him. "Are you a Communist."

"Yes," he drawled in surprise. "I've been in the Party for twenty years."

"You're lying, doctor. You're no Communist. He's a Communist. But you're just a lot of pigs. And you'll never be forgiven for what you've done!"

"Take him away!" ordered the doctor, throwing down the rubber tube. He leapt up from the plank bed; the authoritarian note could be clearly heard in his voice. "Put him in the cells!"

The two men in civilian clothes, who had been sitting on Bluvstein's legs, rushed over to Syomin.

*   *   *

Bon–n–n–g. . .
The dull, thunderous blow rolls over Red Square; for a long

moment the tremors linger in its wake, until another blow crashes through the frosty February air of blizzard-blown Moscow.

Three figures in grey overcoats, in time with the thundering blows—three and yet one, three fused into one—march across the Square.

Their boots strike the frozen stone.

The toes of their boots fly right up to their chests.

Clenched, gloved fists slash through the icy air.

Above their heads the points of the bayonets move jerkily along the short name in the granite, piercing it letter by letter.

L E N I N

Bon–n–n–g. . . The cold metallic ring floats across Red Square.

My wife emerged from the Metro tunnel. A deerskin cap bobbed along in the crowd that ascended the steps to the street. It was the man in civilian clothes who had been trailing her since the morning. By the very edge of the pavement in front of the reception hall of the Presidium of the Supreme Soviet of the USSR stood what seemed to be a barricade of closely parked buses; their idling engines grumbled impatiently and threateningly, belching out grey clouds of exhaust fumes into the frosty air.

The people on the pavement were hurrying about their business, not suspecting why so many identical buses were cordoned off. Anonymous in the crowd, my wife went over toward the windows. They were impenetrably black. She pressed closely to the glass in her anxiety. She discerned the vague outlines of people and knocked on the glass with her fist. She saw someone's face emerge in front of her on the other side of the glass; it nodded to her, but in the

darkness she could not make out who it was. She felt someone's hand on her shoulder and she heard a dry, commanding voice in her ear:

"Move on, citizen. You can't stop here." And she went
away; she dared not look back.

At that moment the lights in the ground floor windows
blazed on simultaneously. The sudden light revealed the
strikers in all parts of the hall. Some were hunched up on
the black benches; others were standing about in twos and
threes.

As if he had risen out of the parquet floor, Dumin stood in
the center of the hall with his same two-man escort. This
time no one approached him. With weary indifference to
everything, they remained motionless, rooted in the positions that they had taken up before the lights came on.

"Listen carefully to what I have to say," Dumin announced solemnly. "I have been instructed to give you the
following message: Your request has been granted."

Expressions of disbelief, confusion, and astonishment
flickered across the faces of the men and women. They
moved toward the center of the hall, surrounding the man
in the black suit and his escort.

"Are we allowed to go to Israel?" exclaimed someone, not
believing his ears.

"Wait a minute, wait a minute," Dumin waved his hands.
"The authorities have decided to form a state commission to
study the question of emigration to Israel. All of you are
invited to its first session."

"And will they let us go to Israel?" Hannah asked.

Dumin was at a loss, but finally he made up his mind to
speak: "I think they will. You may go to your homes and
come to the session of the commission on the first of
March."

"Have we all got to come?" someone questioned him.
"And what about the rest? Thousands of Jews are wanting
to go to Israel."

"They'll all be summoned to appear before the commission. There's no need to worry. Everything will be taken care of."

"But what guarantee do we have that this isn't a trick?"

Dumin hesitated but nevertheless found an answer: "Well, what about the fact that you haven't been arrested." He gave a sidelong glance at the line of officers of the State Security Service on the other side of the glass. "And finally, you have the word of the chairman of the Presidium of the Supreme Soviet of the USSR."

Everybody was silent; motionless. A sort of numbness had descended on them: they could not take in what had happened.

"Go to your homes," Dumin requested. "That's it. It's all over."

"And can we be sure of getting to our homes?" asked someone behind me. "Where's the guarantee for our personal safety?"

"The word of the chairman of the Presidium of the Supreme Soviet of the USSR."

"Well, Jews," grinned Yasha. "Shall we take him at his word? Perhaps he'll actually keep it? What do you think?"

Both sides of the door in the entrance were thrown open. Through the ranks of grey overcoats the Jews walked out into the frosty evening air of Moscow. Yasha, Hannah, Yosif, Sasha...

Dozens of deerskin caps, massed on the pavement, held back passersby, clearing the way for the Jews. They walked past the identical buses, whose idling engines emitted an impotent yet sinister rumbling, and through the evening lights of Moscow. Above the Kremlin towers the ruby-colored stars were shining, the traffic signals flashed their red-and-green lights, people were eating and drinking at the restaurant windows—as if nothing had happened.

The Jews moved along the pavement in a group. They were stunned and as yet were not fully aware of their victory. One of them, smiling broadly, suddenly said loudly so that everybody heard him: "Jews! Remember this day. Israel's children, her poor schoolchildren will curse you. Just think how many bad marks they'll get in their history lessons because they couldn't learn all your names by heart."

*   *   *

The sun, already up in the eastern sky, has turned the glass cube of Moscow's Sheremetievo Airport to silver. The airlines, like great aluminum cigar holders, glisten with frost.

People are going up the steps into a plane. And behind the metal barrier hundreds more are waving, shouting, weeping. Hundreds of Jews, impatiently awaiting their own hour, are seeing off the first lucky ones. An old lady, who is apparently paralyzed, is carried into the plane on a mattress. Raising her grey head from the pillow, a head which seems as old as the Jewish people itself, she triumphantly calls out a prayer to the cold sky: "This is how we came out of Egypt thousands of years ago. We are coming to you, our country. Hear, O Israel!"

Up the stairs go those whose faces we remember from the Supreme Soviet, and others—people whom we do not know. But they are also Jews. More and more Jews mount the stairs. And it seems there is no end to them.

And behind the metal barrier, those who are left wave, weep, and shout.

After the twenty-fourth of February, 1971, a mass exodus of Jews from the USSR began. Thousands of people poured into Israel; now the number of Soviet immigrants there is more than a hundred thousand. Twenty of the participants of that memorable sit-in were allowed to travel to Israel, but four are still languishing in the USSR for "reasons of state," to use the official Soviet phrase. In telling this epic story I have simply changed the names of the characters so as not to endanger their relations living in the USSR.

I have been an Israeli citizen for more than five years now. Not long ago, I met a former Russian film producer, a man who had had an excellent reputation in the Soviet film industry. It turned out that no one had any need of him in Israel and he was glad to be offered work in a warehouse; his boss, an ignorant local man, had no compunction about sending him to the shops like a young lad to get cigarettes for him. These terrible words this Moscow acquaintance addressed to me can serve as an epilogue to the story I have told:

"If it were in my power, I would put up twenty-four gibbets and stretch the necks of every last one of you. You and your sit-in caused unhappiness to thousands of people who rushed after you through the opening you made. I was one of them."

I tried to joke my way out of the situation, saying that twenty gibbets would do, as four of the original group were still in the USSR and imprisoned there most of the time.

"Make it twenty then," he agreed with a wave of his hand. "Anyway, why bother to hang you. The fact that you're in Israel is punishment enough."

chapter two

I, A JEW?

The whole world is now scratching its head over this riddle: How could it happen that Russian Jews—completely assimilated for two generations and not knowing their own language, culture, or history; not only speaking Russian, but even thinking in Russian; Jews whose parents were among the main protagonists of the Russian Revolution and creators of a mighty world power—that precisely they suddenly felt that they were a separate national group and began to wage an unequal struggle with an all-powerful state in pursuit of their right to leave the country, a right which in the Soviet Union is denied to every man.

What are the reasons for this? There are many of them. It is possible that in time we shall be able to systematize them and sort them out one from another. All we know at present is that it happened. Tens of thousands of people who, if you had suggested to them a year or two earlier that they would dare to do such things, would have told you that you were mad; who a year or two earlier would have come to terms with all kinds of havoc and humiliation and tried to live like everyone else, closing their eyes to what was going on around them, have now, like sleepwalkers, shaken themselves free from the burden of day-to-day cares and with maniacal persistence are hurling themselves against a brick wall, breaking it down brick by brick. And what is most improbable of all—they are getting through it.

Not all of them, it is true. And it is also true that the price they are paying is a frightful one. They must part from their friends and relations. They are reduced to extreme nervous exhaustion. They are deprived of their property and all their life savings.

How did this happen? Where did it all begin? I am myself at a loss to explain. Perhaps the story of what happened to me will explain something. The story of how it was brought home to me for the first time in my life that I was a Jew. How I, an equal citizen of the "freest and most progressive" state in the world, collided head on with a wall of flagrant, official anti-Semitism.

There is nothing fictitious in this story. I have retained the original names of the places where events took place and the real names of the people who took part in them. It happened in Brest, the most westerly point in the Soviet Union, a small town whose tree-lined, tidy streets stretch lazily along the banks of the river Bug, which is also the border of the Soviet frontier with Poland. This town was soon to become famous, albeit belatedly, for its fortress, whose garrison did not surrender in 1941 but fought on for several months when it was already far behind the German lines. At that time, however, this was not mentioned because Stalin was still alive and he, as is well known, regarded every man who was taken prisoner as a traitor.

Where the memorial stands today and where tourist groups and visitors are now led reverently, goats then grazed among the crumbling ruins of the brick bastions. Small boys collected the tarnished, spent cartridge cases and found the occasional hand grenade, which they exploded to stun the fish in a muddy little river called the Mukhavets, a tributary of the Bug.

Brest is the town where I took my first independent steps in life. I was sent there after I graduated from the university and arrived at the editorial offices of the regional newspaper *Zarya* ("The Dawn"), complete with my journalist's diploma. The newspaper, the only one in the town, was published by the regional Party committee.

Formally speaking I was not a Communist, i.e., a Party member, but like all the rest of my generation, I had been nurtured in the spirit of communism literally since the time I wore diapers. I fully shared the Party's ideals, believed in its infallibility, and regarded the Party's adversary as my own personal enemy. We, my entire generation, believed the Party's every utterance, deified Stalin, and would readily have given up our lives for him in an ecstasy of patriotism.

The events of 1937–38 took place while we were still children. We were, however, already Young Pioneers, organized into disciplined units, and the words *The Party* and *Stalin* had for us a sacred significance and were spoken with a sincere thrill of emotion.

Consequently, the trials of the so-called enemies of the people, the mass executions, the searches that took place at night, and the arrests in neighboring apartments were regarded simply as the intensification of the class struggle and the natural victory of the Party over its most deadly enemies. This although only a few days before the same individuals had been respectfully referred to as the dads of Mischa, Tolya, and Vova, my young pals in the neighborhood, and I had even been in the habit of sitting on their knees, without suspecting in whose awful embrace I was held.

We, and also those who were a little older, believed everything that the radio and the newspapers said.

At that time, the news of Pavlik Morozov's epic deed

spread throughout the country. In a remote hamlet in the Ural forests, a Young Pioneer called Pavlik Morozov had denounced his own father to the NKVD. His relatives took revenge on the boy, however, and killed him in the forest. For this both his father and all the relatives were executed.

Pavlik Morozov became our idol. We cut his photograph out of the newspapers and stuck it on the walls of our rooms. We sang songs honoring our youthful hero and, at solemn gatherings of Pioneers, swore, to the sound of bugle and drum, to continue the work of Pavlik Morozov and to be like him.

I feel very sad now when I recall my childhood. How foul the venom that poisoned our immature consciousness. With ardent looks and feelings of ecstasy, we swore to betray our parents and to denounce them to the authorities. With the instinct of the hunter and with unchildlike suspiciousness, we eavesdropped on the conversations of our elders in an attempt to scrape together any shreds of evidence against them in order, then, to run with all speed to the NKVD and tell all so that afterwards the whole country would applaud us as heroes.

Yes, this was the formative atmosphere in which my generation was brought up. This picture needs neither touching up nor toning down. This is the sort of people we were. And at twenty years of age, with my university diploma in my pocket, this is the sort of person that I was still. I banished the doubts that crept unawares into my heart. I believed, and I had no wish to doubt anything.

And I was young and bursting with health. My blood did not flow—it pounded through my veins. My muscles rippled at every movement. I thought I was handsome, and actually the girls often did stop and look at me.

Twenty years old and already a journalist. I had no trouble finding work. Not a cloud was to be seen on my horizon. I loved my country, its rivers, its forests, and fields, with the same love that I felt for each board of the wooden floor on which my mother had taught me to walk. I loved its people, my fellow citizens, like my own brothers and sisters, with a love that brought tears to my eyes and pierced my heart with a sweet pain. I was ready to raze mountains to the ground, to move the banks of rivers, to make my country the most beautiful in the world.

Initially everything appeared to be working out perfectly. The editorial office was short of staff. I was greeted warmly. I was fixed up with a room in the only hotel in town. I didn't have a room of my own but slept in a room containing three beds. The other two seemed to have a new inhabitant each time I returned there. I didn't even have time to get to know them all.

For the most part they were army officers—young fellows, noisy and cheerful, who had so much money that they didn't know what to do with it and were ready to squander it on drink with everybody they met. They whiled away the period of waiting in Brest until immigration or emigration formalities were completed and they could continue on their way either to Germany or back home to Russia.

There was drinking in every room, and I was invited to join in. Since they had nothing to do and I was working, I could always find a pretext not to get drunk. The atmosphere in the hotel was like a carnival—loud, loutish, and raucous. One officer actually drowned when he passed out in his full bathtub.

Every day I would go off to work. Even then there was no escape from the drunks. The editorial office was staffed for the most part with veterans of the front line, demobilized officers, who, having nothing else to wear, were still wearing out their military tunics, complete with the stripes for their various decorations and the yellow-and-red stripes showing that they had been wounded in action.

Practically everybody in the editorial office drank. They drank a lot, without any restraint, to the point of total insensibility. The corridors and offices reeked of stale, vodka-laden breath. But the newspaper came out daily. And the articles were handed to the compositors on time. Vodka did not interfere with work. Moreover, there were five or six Jews on the staff, also veterans, but happily nondrinkers who steered clear of those who were in search of fellow tipplers.

As a callow, inexperienced member of the staff, I was not at first allowed to engage in any actual journalistic activities but was used as a proofreader. Thank heaven, I was more literate than the others, always sober, and could be relied upon not to let a mistake get into print.

This suited me well enough. I wanted to get my bearings and learn a thing or two from other people before tackling my first article. But things in fact took such a turn that I never got started on it at all.

It was 1949. Far away in the Middle East, Israel, the Jewish state, had undergone the agonies of its birth. There were three million Jews in the USSR. By linking these two facts, we discover the cause of an outburst of official anti-Semitism. A campaign against "Cosmopolitanism" and worshiping the West was being unleashed on the whole country. Individuals with Jewish names to whom absurd antipatriotic sins were attributed began to crop up all over the columns of the newspapers. They were singled out and vicious reprisals were called for.

I read all this and believed every single line of it. I didn't even see anything suspicious in the fact that every one of the culprits was a Jew. I assumed this was indeed the case. And may they get the punishment they deserve. Soviet power is stern but just. Of that I had no doubt.

There was only one thing which troubled me. This was the unimaginable fuss made over everything Russian—immodest, absurd attempts to prove the superiority of Russian science in literally everything. Caustic jokes came to my ears in which this ubiquitous madness was maliciously mocked, and it pained me to see my country's prestige and reputation being undermined. I consoled myself by assuming that this phase of boastfulness would soon pass, like sickness in a child, and everything would be as before.

Cosmopolitans were everywhere sought and found. Each town left no stone unturned so as not to lag behind the others. They found their cosmopolitans in all sorts of places, and they were always Jews. Finally the waves reached the frontier itself and eventually the town of Brest. Here the trail led to the editorial office of the newspaper *Zarya*. There were five or six Jews there, all working on ideological matters, and it was at them that the accusing finger pointed.

Events developed with bewildering speed. The whole staff was assembled in the dingy hall of the editorial office club. Not only the journalists were there but the printers too, the make-up men, the proofreaders, and even the messengers, caretakers, and cleaners. It was to be an open Party meeting, that is, a meeting called at a place of employment for all the people who worked there; this one was concerned with the fight against cosmopolitanism.

At first I wasn't in the least alarmed by this. I had been to various meetings and took a condescending view of the usual empty chatter one heard there. These were the feelings of most other people too. You have to sit there and be bored for a while before you can go home. Every day we were printing stuff about Cosmopolitans, and everybody felt sick merely at the thought of such monotonous fare. No one expected anything new.

But in fact there was something new. Some Cosmopolitans had been found in the editorial office itself. And who should there be among these enemies who had been so deftly unmasked? The senior secretary of the editorial office, Zaretsky, stern, pedantic, formerly a captain in the army. When he came to the editorial office to attend a Victory Day celebration, he had two rows of military decorations and medals on his new civilian jacket; Kagan, quiet, unobtrusive, perpetually hunched over galley proofs, the secretariat's literary specialist; old Zolotaryov, a wit and a joker from Odessa, who was in charge of the newspaper's literature and art section. During the war he had been a correspondent at the front line. There was the head of the propaganda section, too, puny, sickly, Rafik Bukhartsev, a man with a cartoon-type Jewish appearance, a favorite Aunt Sally for the anti-Semites. Rafik published in almost every issue his huge, pompous articles about Stalin and the Party, in which he dubbed Stalin "father," "bright sun," "fount of knowledge," "wisest of the wise," and the Party he referred to as "mother." Only a madman could have doubted his devotion to the cause of communism.

Without exception the Jews on the staff were Communists. They were all told to sit on a long wooden bench on the right-hand side of the platform in front of the whole assembly of non-Party members. They submitted without objection and sat down; their faces, in advance, gave evidence of guilt; crushed, they waited submissively for their fate to be decided.

On the left-hand side of the platform, at a table covered with red cloth, huddled together in a tight cluster were the editorial office's remaining Communists—the Russians. They were almost all drunk and had red shiny faces. Their eyes, bleary from vodka, had a predatory gleam as they savored the reprisals they were about to take on these defenseless people. Only one, who sat separately from the others at the end of the table, was completely unfamiliar and alien. Small, puny, with the little round head of a monkey and a puffy, unhealthy face like a baked apple, he remained indifferent, as though what was going on around had nothing to do with him, but his quick eyes, which were never still, darted about the hall from one face to another. This was the provincial Party committee secretary for propaganda, Comrade Lutskin. His presence alone, without any word, served to direct the whole drama.

I sat at the back of the hall and looked at the stage, unable to believe my eyes. Something improbable was happening. I knew all these men. Everyone knew them. Previously no one had doubted that they were honest and respectable people. No one had a personal score to settle with any of them. Moreover, all they had written in the newspaper was in no way different from what the others had written. And here were their colleagues, who only the previous day had been slapping them familiarly on the back and in flushes of drunken frankness assuring them of their lasting friendship, who had served with them in the army, suffered with them in the trenches, and moaned in pain beside them on hospital beds—these men with fiendish spite cursed them as their sworn enemies, heaping upon them one absurdity after another, each of which was inflated to the extent of becoming a crime against the state.

No one mentioned the word *Jew*. Other fashionable expressions did duty for it: "Cosmopolitans without kith or kin," "passportless vagrants," "men without family and name."

Zolotaryov was charged with having published a critical review of a film called *The Ballerina*, although the film was actually trivial and worthless. But this, it was said, was part of his general plan as an enemy saboteur who had infiltrated into our ranks to discredit the whole of Soviet art and poison the minds of our readers.

This same sort of thing was said about everybody who was sitting on the right-hand bench. Zaretsky, it transpired, had been seen in one particular article to have used the epithet "of genius" five times in connection with Stalin's name and to have replaced it on one occasion by the word "great." This was now seen as a hostile deed, a base, crafty design. The drunken prosecutors, who could hardly remain steady when they spoke, cursed unashamedly, and sadistically gloated over the Jews, who cowered beneath the torrent of abuse in a pitiable bundle on the bench opposite.

This was a pogrom. It was the first time in my life I had seen anything like it, and I sat stunned, unable to realize what was happening. The entire hall listened in silence. The stillness crushed and squeezed one's very heart. It was like being present at a public execution, where innocent heads were rolling in full public view.

But the worst was yet to come. The Jews to a man admitted their guilt, accepted all the accusations and repented, beat their breasts, and in pitiful, whining voices asked for forgiveness, assuring their judges like little children that they would never do anything like that again, that they would worthily repay confidence if they should be spared.

I could hardly breathe. The incredibly tense atmosphere reached breaking point when they launched into Rafik Bukhartsev, the last person on the right-hand bench. This puny, bespectacled little gnome, with his perpetually dripping, pendulous nose and moist lips, suddenly leapt from the bench, began to dig feverishly in his pockets and, finally, finding what he was looking for, pulled his passport out and held it high above his head.

"Comrades!" he yelled in a heartrending voice, and, hurrying and choking over his words—because he feared that he might not be allowed to have his say—he blurted out, "I am an Armenian!"

The prosecutor stopped short and stared dully at him.

"Yes! Yes!" Bukhartsev half-danced to the middle of the platform and reiterated, his steamed-up eyeglasses gleaming in triumphant ecstasy, "I am an Armenian. Look at my passport."

Yegorov, the secretary of the editorial office Party bureau, ill-temperedly barked at him from the far side of the table, "Come on then, over here. Let's have a look!"

Bukhartsev readily hurried over to the table and obligingly held out with trembling hands the precious document. Yegorov screwed up his eyes, leafed through the passport, and returned it to Bukhartsev in disgruntlement.

"Yes-s-s, quite right. You may go and sit down in the hall." And off Bukhartsev scuttled, tripping over his feet and without a backward glance.

The show bubble had burst. The case of Bukhartsev had with merciless frankness revealed all the cards. Only the Jews were on trial. And they were on trial only because they were Jews.

But no one in the hall grasped the whole tragicomedy of the situation. Only one man burst into loud peals of laughter. It was I—twenty years old and far too healthy to be afraid of anything at all. Even here my sense of humor had not entirely deserted me.

I must say, by the way, that I was the only Jew who hadn't been dragged out on to the platform and submitted to a trial. And really the greatest determination in the world could not have found anything to accuse me of. I was a new boy in the editorial office, the youngest member of the staff, and, what was most important, I hadn't had a single line printed in the paper. I even believe that not everybody had even guessed that I was a Jew.

But I burst out laughing, and that was sufficient pretext for the accusers, who were embarrassed by the gaffe they had made with Bukhartsev, to remember that I too was Jewish.

Yegorov, the secretary of the Party bureau, came from behind the table on to the front part of the platform. His box-calf boots squeaked, and as he walked he straightened his army-style field shirt beneath his broad officer's belt.

"We'll have you instead of Bukhartsev!" he said, poking his finger at me.

It was stuffy in the hall. I had taken my jacket off and was wearing only a white tee shirt. This tee shirt had the same effect on Yegorov as a red cape has on a bull, for this tee shirt was an American one. I had received it when I was still a student, in the form of aid from the stores of UNRA, the international relief organization for war victims. All my pals had received either a shirt or a pair of shoes, and my portion had been this tee shirt. It was a cheap cotton thing, but emblazoned right across the chest was a cowboy galloping on a horse and the word *OKLAHOMA* in bold letters. At the time the state of my wardrobe was such that I valued it very highly and wore it proudly, much to the envy of the other lads.

Now this wretched tee shirt became the shred of evidence

that Yegorov seized upon and used to construct a charge against me.

"You rootless Cosmopolitan!" he cried with pathos, his finger directed threateningly toward me. "You passportless tramp! Look at what he's wearing! His ideal is not Moscow, but Oklahoma, U.S.A. A man without kith or kin. He grovels before a cheap American rag. For a miserable pittance he's ready to sell Russia to the imperialists."

"Now that's going a bit too far," said someone in the hall, no longer able to contain himself. Even his drunken cronies sitting round the red table on the platform looked at him askance. But to stop Yegorov wasn't all that easy.

"Comrades!" he tried to attract the attention of the hall by using a normal oratorical tone. "I had good reason to say that his place was among the accused. This is no ordinary Cosmopolitan. He is their ringleader. The guiding spirit in a wasp's nest of saboteurs. Oh yes. And now I will give you the facts."

He paused to savor the impression that these words had made. The hall waited tensely for what he would say. I waited too. Admittedly, I had a sardonic and disdainful grin on my face and was ready to burst out laughing over his next ineptitude, but I began to feel a chill of alarm creep over me.

"Well then." Yegorov stuck his thumbs in his belt. "Quite recently this Cosmopolitan expressed his doubt about the fact that Antarctica was discovered by the Russian voyagers Billinshausen and Lazarev. He brazenly mocked the pride of the Russian nation."

I must admit that sitting in the office in the evenings we often made ironic remarks about the flood of nonsense concerning the preeminence of Russian science that was being printed in the paper. Yegorov, perpetually drunk, agreed with what we said, as he too was amazed by the absurdity of what we were printing. I honestly cannot remember whether I had ever said anything about the discoverer of

Antarctica, or whether I had doubted that the Russians had been first to reach that continent.

Yegorov, however, hurled this in my face like a dreadful accusation and elevated me to the rank of guiding spirit in this conspiratorial cell of Cosmopolitans, thereby deftly turning all the fire on my person. In this way, he infused fresh blood into the veins of the dying meeting. The orators, hardly capable of keeping their feet, rose from the red table and deluged me with their righteous anger. Soon I had been depicted as a most sinister figure, a major criminal against the state, who for some incomprehensible reason had not yet been put behind bars.

Things were beginning to get hot. The people sitting next to me in the hall automatically began to move away from me, eyeing askance and with suspicion the cowboy and the OKLAHOMA inscription on my tee shirt. They forgot completely about the benchful of Jews on the platform, who sat awaiting their fate.

I demanded an opportunity to speak. This was denied. Words of unequivocal abuse were already being hurled at me from the platform. With the ardor of youth I insisted, and was finally given permission to speak for no more than two minutes.

I had not yet realized that the anti-Semitic spirit of the meeting was not just the loutish act of this band of alcoholics with Party cards in their pockets but had been inspired from above and was becoming an accepted part of Soviet life. In the naïve belief that truth was on my side, I began to speak with fervor.

"I am young, and my life is only just beginning. I am preparing myself to become a Communist. But I could never belong to the same Party as you do. These Jews here call themselves Communists." I pointed to the wretched figures sitting on the right of the platform. "Knowing that they have done nothing wrong, they repent and ask for mercy. How can such people be called Communists? I would sweep them out of the Party like the garbage that they are—as I would you at the same time." I pointed to the left-hand side of the platform where the awe-inspiring Russian "judges" were sitting. "You're even worse than they are. They have families who need to be fed. Because they're afraid of losing their jobs and being left to starve they humiliate themselves and cover themselves with filth. But what about you? You're the people who've pushed them into this degradation. You walk all over your Party comrades. What kind of Communists are you? You're just anti-Semites and that's only a step away from fascism. There's no place in the Party for people like you."

How naïve I was then! I was trying to shame people who had not the slightest notion of what shame was. I spoke to them of the ideal of a Communist as I understood it and of the Party as the embodiment of such people. My childish speech simply added fuel to the fire. Chernykh, the head of the agricultural section, made a speech. He had a puffy, hollow-cheeked face and horn-rimmed glasses with thick lenses. His heavy-set figure was suggestive of peasant gawkiness. His incipient paunch was tightly pinched in a field shirt of black cloth and belted with a broad officer's belt that had a bronze star on the buckle. Wide black riding breeches gripped his bowed legs at the knee from which his box-calf boots went accordion-like down toward his ankles.

He was so drunk that he rocked back and forth on his heels, seeming on the point of tumbling down from the platform. In order to keep his balance, he kept thrashing his hands about as a bird flaps its wings, as though he were trying to get a grip on the air. He was incapable of coherent speech; he stumbled over every word, but he was bursting with anger and he sobbed and wept drunken tears, as he spoke of me and the insult that I had dealt the Russian nation.

"He has spat on what we hold most dear," he sobbed. "He has wounded our national pride ... the memory of the immortal Russian voyager ... that ... what's his name? Matvei

Matveevich Bil–lins–hau–sen," said Chernykh, scarcely able to pronounce this difficult, un-Russian surname.

"Listen, Chernykh," I interrupted him. "This Billinshausen that you're so fond of wasn't called Matvei Matveevich at all. He was called Fadei Fadeevich."

A slight ripple of laughter ran through the hall. Chernykh lapsed into stunned silence and then barked out for everybody to hear such a foul oath that a murmur of displeasure rose from the women. He was led back to the red table, and, in the general hubbub that ensued, the chairman adjourned the meeting for lunch.

From feelings of shame and discomfiture, people avoided looking at one another. Everyone felt that he had witnessed something very unseemly. The editorial office staff disappeared to their rooms.

I was left alone in the long, narrow, deserted corridor into which the doors of all the offices opened. My whole being boiled with indignation. I didn't even notice that the black figure of Chernykh had appeared in front of me. He stared dully, yet provocatively, into my face through the thick lenses of his eyeglasses. He wanted to take revenge for the defeat he had sustained during the meeting.

"Listen, Cosmopolitan," he said, "who do you think you are?"

"And who do you think you are?" I said, deliberately answering his question with another one.

"I am a Russian!"

There could be no doubt. He wanted to dot all the i's and cross all the t's.

"You're not a Russian," I answered calmly. "You are Chernykh, a lump of shit. If you'd been alive in the time of the czar, you'd have been one of those people from the Union of Michael the Archangel who took part in pogroms, and in 1917 the Bolsheviks would have stood you against the wall."

I spoke clearly and loudly, not for the ears of Chernykh alone. The doors of all the offices had opened slightly into the corridor, and, drawn by the whiff of scandal, both Jewish and Russian noses were poking out. The whole editorial office fell silent, listening closely to our conversation. What had been left unsaid at the meeting had to be made clear now.

"Are you saying that the Bolsheviks would have shot a Communist like myself?" Chernykh answered in a threatening tone of voice.

"Who else but you and your ilk. You're no Communist. You just happen to have a Bolshevik Party card in your pocket. It should really be a Nazi Party card."

"Ah, you lousy kike!" said Chernykh, choking with anger.

This was just what I'd been waiting for, the logical conclusion of our conversation. Chernykh had said what all the accusers at the meeting had had on the tips of their tongues. Under Soviet law he should have been severely punished for that statement. I had witnesses (the noses that were poking out of the doorways) and I decided that it would be quite just and legal if I were to give him the punishment he deserved.

I struck him with full force on the jaw. The thick lenses of his glasses splintered all over the floor. Chernykh, arms flailing, flew backwards along the corridor. He was falling, but his bowed legs managed to find a foothold, and he tottered backwards at high speed. With a crack like machine-gun fire, the doors of the offices slammed shut as he approached them, clearing a passage, so to speak, for his further progress. The noses went into hiding. Nobody wanted to be a witness.

Waving his arms, weaving this way and that, but managing to keep his feet, Chernykh staggered almost to the very end of the long corridor and there he slumped down. Slowly and attentively, as though all this was happening to somebody else, I rubbed my bruised fist with the palm of my hand.

After the lunch break there was no more meeting worthy of

mention. The loutish behavior of Chernykh, which had completely exposed all the ugliness of what was happening, had disconcerted even the most thoroughgoing anti-Semites. A resolution was hurriedly passed in which most of the attention was devoted to my person. All my sins were enumerated, and it was decided to purge the editorial office of its nest of Cosmopolitans by firing me and handing the case over to the investigating authorities, i.e., the NKVD. And since most of the blame fell on me, the rest of the Jews, whose exposure had been the original reason for calling the meeting, were hastily given a stern Party reprimand and demoted. For them, it was miraculous salvation, and they did not hide their triumph. Only when they walked past me did they avert their eyes in shame.

Oh, and to make things look quite fair, Chernykh was simply reproved for "behaving in a manner unworthy of the Party." So for a few days he spent his time sobbing in the Brest beer houses, complaining to his drinking companions about the injustice that had been done to him, the low price that had been put on his patriotism, and that the kikes were out to ruin him.

That evening I was sitting in my hotel room with my current roommate, a lieutenant-colonel, a military engineer, and an intellectually minded young man, with whom I had become fairly close during the week we had shared the same room. He heard out my story in sad silence.

"Things are going to be very bad for you, my friend," he sighed. "You're too young, and you've no idea what it's all about. A black period in the life of Russia is setting in. Another time of troubles. Things won't only be bad for the Jews. Everybody will feel the draft. But you fellows, as usual, will feel it most of all. Prepare for the worst."

Out of tact he didn't use the word *arrest*. But what he meant was clear enough even so.

The next morning the floor clerk summoned me to the telephone, and an unfamiliar voice dryly suggested that I appear at the regional Party committee building in an hour's time. The grey concrete structure that housed the regional committee stood in the main street next to the NKVD building. I was no longer in any doubt—the regional Party committee had been mentioned to serve as a shock absorber so that I shouldn't get wind of the truth: I was expected at the NKVD. My roommate was of the same opinion. Incapable of helping in any way, he said goodbye to me, but at the last moment he decided not to go to work and to remain in the hotel until I returned. He wished in this way to leave me some small ray of hope that things would end well.

I could not have cared less. A mood of complete mental and physical exhaustion had descended upon me. That was the day in which my youth came to an end, and I did not even want to speculate about what lay ahead.

When I got to the regional committee building, I was taken into a vast, almost empty office, the floor of which was covered with brightly colored lengths of carpet. For what seemed to be a long time, I walked along these carpets toward a massive desk at the far end of the room. Poking up above the desk was the familiar monkey-like head with the puffy, sickly little face that reminded one of a yellow baked apple. It was the Party regional committee's secretary for propaganda, Comrade Lutskin, who had sat all day yesterday through our meeting in the editorial office without saying a single word.

Now, head withdrawn into the padded shoulders of his jacket, his eyes bored inquisitively into me. Above him, like a slab of plaster of paris, soared a bust of Stalin wearing the epaulets of a generalissimo.

Our conversation was short and surprising.

"You know what will happen to you?"

"I do."

"How do you propose to live your life from now on?"

"I don't know."

"I like you."

Had I misunderstood? Did he really say...?

"And that's why I want to save you." He had a thin, piping voice like that of a Lilliputian. He half lowered his eyelids. "We were all young once. Youth is a splendid time, but a dangerous one too—the easiest time of all to get your head chopped off."

"So I was right then?" I said, unable to believe my ears. "You think so too."

"That isn't what I said," he opened his eyes, and I could read unconcealed sympathy. "I wish you well."

"Just a minute, what about what they said about me? You don't agree with that," I began to press him further in a hope nourished by returning faith.

"You are interested in my opinion?" a cunning, twisted smile flittered across his thin wrinkled lips. "The Party is always right. And you are just a young pup who seems bent on jumping into the soup."

In some way I had managed to impress this hard-boiled, cynical Party bureaucrat, in whom all feelings were long since dead, and it is possible that with my fervor and naïve faith I had stirred up in his mind memories of his own revolutionary youth, when he had been just as fervid and believed just as naïvely as I did now. I don't know. These are just my conjectures. But surely the age of miracles is past.

He got up, appearing to become only slightly taller, skirted the huge table, and stopped in front of me, looking down into my face.

"Off you go. Pack your things. And be out of the town by this evening. You'll get a clean set of papers."

He shook my hand limply.

"I hope that in the future you'll be more discreet."

And off I went along the huge length of carpet, across the hollow emptiness of the vast office; when I reached the door, I turned round and set off back again with rapid steps.

"But tell me. Who, after all, did discover Antarctica?"

He seemed taken aback.

"Young man," he said sadly, looking at me as one might look at an incurable invalid, "if you're told tomorrow that white is black, then say it is black. And don't have so many doubts, young man."

It was precisely then that the first doubts crept into my mind. They have never left me in peace since.

Don't have so many doubts, young man. So many doubts.

And who discovered the Antarctic I do not know even now. I do not believe any sources, neither Russian nor foreign. At the mention of this frozen land, a spasm of nausea rises in my throat. I do not want to know who discovered it! The hell with it! The hell with this cold and empty Antarctic. Confound it!

chapter three

LESSONS IN DEMOCRACY

We who have come from a totalitarian world, where we were born and brought up in an atmosphere of stern dictatorship and arbitrary rule—I am thinking of emigrants from present-day Soviet Russia—respond to any manifestation of democracy and absorb its every nuance like a dried-up sponge, insatiably.

Israel, the most democratic state not only in the Middle East but, if one is to believe the local press, perhaps in the whole Western world, taught us our first lessons in democracy.

The first lesson was both amusing and sad.

My friend and I were traveling from Jerusalem to Tel Aviv along the modern multilane highway that gently weaves its way across the low ridges of the hills of Judea, through gorges carved out by the hand of man. All around the bright green foliage of young pine woods, also lovingly planted my man's hand, caresses the eye.

Where before there had been bare stones and crags, the

71

trees now murmured; where the caravan routes had wound their way, the black ribbon of the highway now runs.

"And all this has been created by Jewish hands!" my friend said with the exuberance of a child. He had arrived in Israel not long before and, like all of us at one time, was in a semideranged state of total, irrational infatuation with all that met his eye. "We are a great nation! We created from nothing a state that is an example and a source of wonderment to the whole world. I am proud that I am Jewish!"

I did not interrupt his ecstasies. I had no inclination to deprive the man of brief delight, and I had no doubt that life would soon turn this delight into ashes. But then again, five years earlier I myself had gasped and blathered ecstatically about anything and everything while driving along just such a highway—not here but closer to Haifa. I cooled off and was brought to my senses, as if I had had a bucket of cold water poured over me, by the sober voice of my neighbor in the bus, an Israeli citizen of long standing. Gazing at my enraptured face with irony and sadness and being evidently somewhat nauseated by my immoderately joyful exclamations at every bend in the highway, he said:

"Don't make so much noise. You look ridiculous. Of course, there's nothing wrong with this road. But it wasn't Jews who built it. It was Arab workers. Paid with American money. This road has swallowed up so much money that if you were to dig up the surface you'd find pure gold a meter deep. In other countries seven roads would have been built for the same amount of money. That's the kind of great nation we are. Probably the only one capable of pouring so much money down the drain."

Then, seeing that I was beginning to look sour, he took pity on me: "But nevertheless there is a road. And thank God for it. And we two Jews traveling along it have a state of our own, even if it is a bloody useless one."

I could have said the self-same thing to my friend at that point and evoked in him just such hostility as my neighbor in the bus had in me. After all, quite recently this same stretch of road along which we were traveling had had some bends removed, and I had seen hundreds of Arabs attacking the rock-hard ground with picks and shovels. I had seen the orange bulldozers and graders that had been donated by American Jews. More than that, I already knew that these woods too had been planted not by Jews but by Arab workers, hired with the resources of Keren Kayemeth Leisrael, the international Jewish organization for making green the land of Israel. All this wasn't our own; it was a donation, built by someone else's hands, paid for out of somebody else's pocket.

I said nothing to my friend, who was taking his first steps in the new homeland he had begun to love long before he reached it, before he knew it, and which he had endowed from afar with every conceivable and inconceivable virtue. Just as I had five years earlier—just like any Jew setting his foot on that soil for the first time.

Meanwhile we were approaching what appeared to be the hulks of burnt-out, obsolete motor vehicles, apparently abandoned in the roadside ditch. They had been arranged along the edges of the road and painted bright red, as a memorial to those who had died there in 1948 during the War of Independence, in their attempt to break through in columns of vehicles to come to the assistance of beleaguered Jerusalem. My heart skips a beat whenever I pass these places where pure and honest Jewish boys gave up their lives. They escaped from the claws of the Nazis in Europe only to soak with their blood every meter of this dry, stony land—a land that the world had unwillingly yielded to them so that they could build themselves a refuge from the hatred that chokes the earth.

Hundreds of cars, from patched up old jalopies to the latest models, roared along the highway at high speed. The drivers' turbulent, southern temperament made the vehicles quiver impatiently as they thundered along in a mad gallop, striving at any price to pass other drivers, force them onto the hard shoulder, into the edge of the road, leave them behind. The cost is immaterial, be it even the cost of their own lives, not to mention the lives of those careless enough to travel in front of them or alongside.

We had only just passed the red-painted car hulks—the memorials of 1948—when we caught sight of a brand new Alfa Romeo abandoned in the roadside ditch, squashed like an accordion. The accident was apparently quite recent. Splinters of broken glass still glistened on the pavement, not yet swept away by the tires of other vehicles that incessantly and relentlessly roared by on the way to fresh accidents. We flashed by a tiny Fiat, whose upturned wheels protruded from the ditch, and at a turning in the road a huge green Leyland mobile concrete mixer lay like a collapsed elephant.

My friend's face, craning out of the car, expressed surprise and anxiety. He had never in his whole life seen such a large number of accidents, one after the other, nor had he ever while traveling in a car felt himself to be so likely a candidate for a journey into the next world.

The insanity that grips Israeli drivers as soon as they get onto a main highway makes experienced drivers from New York, Moscow, and Paris shake in their boots. No one observes the rules. Each one drives as fast as possible, and even the instinct of self-preservation, which every man possesses, vanishes like smoke on the roads of Israel.

One former Moscow cab driver with many years of accident-free driving behind him admitted to me that behind the wheel in Israel he is petrified with fright, like a novice driving a car for the first time. Two other motorists, friends of mine, who recently arrived in Israel, one a sailor from Odessa and the other an aeronautical engineer from Tashkent, already rest in their graves after quite a brief acquaintance with the mores of Israel's highways.

On this particular hairraising journey with my friend—who did at last become disgruntled—we too came near to experiencing the cold sweat of catastrophe, when a crazy

Mercedes started to overtake us on the inside, forcing us to lurch away from him and almost collide with another vehicle. The Mercedes broke every rule of the road with impunity and got out in front of us as if nothing had happened. Blazing with righteous indignation, we raced after him to catch up with him and halt this potential murderer. We caught him, stopped him, and pulled him out from behind the wheel of his car. He wasn't in the least afraid of us, nor was he the slightest bit ashamed. He parried our indignation with disarming frankness:

"This is a democratic country, and I drive as I like."

The word *democracy* is shamelessly exploited in Israel at every turn as a cover for the most primitive anarchy, which has become deeply rooted in the fabric of a shaky and insecure society. Israelis have latched onto democracy and play with it untiringly, as might unattended children with a box of matches, transforming democracy into its antithesis and giving base instincts free rein. Democracy, thus abused, is not the sacred right of every citizen to be protected from those who aspire to spit in his face but, on the contrary, license for anyone to encroach on another's inviolability. This kind of "democracy" engenders a barbaric lack of respect for the individual, tacitly proclaiming the superiority of the brazen and the strong over the weak and the defenseless, devaluing and setting at naught human life itself. Official statistics reflect like a mirror the twisted visage of this type of democracy. In a very short space of time, Israel has established a number of quite lamentable world records, capable of plunging into the deepest melancholy anyone who cares in the least for the fate of the hapless Jewish people.

In a country with a population of only 3 million, according to the figures for 1971, more than 80,000 were killed and injured on the roads. These road hogs, with their idiosyncratic understanding of democracy, mow down in a year the same number of children as attend the average-sized school.

The former chief of Israel intelligence, now Israel's ambassador to the United Nations, Reserve General Chaim Hertzog, quite recently made a shattering revelation based on a simple analysis of certain figures from military statistics. He had been studying the data for one of the "quiet" years when scarcely any armed hostilities had taken place on the frontiers. And what did he reveal? During that year, only five Israeli soldiers were killed during exchanges of firing or as a result of mines laid by enemy saboteurs, but a report on losses of army personnel listed more than 250 dead. The difference was made up by soldiers and officers who died not on the field of battle but as victims of ordinary road accidents or accidents during exercises. Still more alarming is a report on industrial accidents at plants and factories in Israel, where equipment, if one believes official propaganda, is the last word in science and technology. In 1971 alone, more than 100 people died as a result of injuries sustained at work through failure to observe safety requirements and tens of thousands escaped with injuries of varying severity. What monstrous indifference to human life lies behind these figures! What a low level of civilization! And all this is happening in the country of a most ancient people, which gave the world the Bible and the Ten Commandments, a principal foundation of the world's moral and social structure. Unbridled anarchy in the guise of democracy causes the people of Israel to sustain more palpable losses than all the wars of a quarter century.

In the Russian-language Israeli newspaper *Tribuna* [Podium] N. Gutin looks at the seamy side of life in Israel from a different angle in an article unequivocally entitled "Invitation to Violence":

Mordecai Moshiashvili went six times to the Kupat-kholim clinic in the town of Tirat Carmel seeking urgent medical aid for his wife, who suffered from a serious heart ailment.

Every time that Moshiashvili, breathless with haste (he was afraid that his wife's condition might deteriorate during his absence), came to the reception desk, the duty nurse gave him the same answer—the doctor could not come to his house as he was attending to patients.

In despair, Moshiashvili went to the police station and sought the help of the police to persuade the doctor to come and examine his wife. He was told, however, that in Israel police do not bring pressure to bear on doctors.

Moshiashvili attempted a seventh time to persuade a nurse to come to his house, but without success. Then, as a last resort, he produced a knife and compelled a doctor to come with him. . . .

Five months ago the entire Israeli press reported a case of a soldier, seriously ill with acute appendicitis, who went to a hospital, was sent to another hospital, from that hospital to a third, and from the third back to the first, where, in fact, he ultimately died on the operating table. This case was discussed in the Knesset, and the minister of health promised that there would be no more similar cases in future.

What conclusion do we draw from this? If the soldier had drawn his gun, let's say, and begun to threaten the doctors and nurses in the first or even the second hospital, would he still be alive? In all probability, he would, for according to the conclusion of the doctors' report he died because medical aid was not rendered in time. But he was a civilized man, incapable of threatening doctors with a knife or, let's say, a submachine gun, and so he died. . . .

For years Israeli doctors put up with the fact that their European colleagues earned five times more than they did, trying to get their salaries raised through reasonable methods. But they spoke too softly and no one paid any attention to them. Eventually the cup of their patience was brimming over and they decided to have recourse to violence. . . . Thus once again violence triumphed. . . .

And what about getting an apartment? Officials, dying of boredom, seemed simply to be waiting for you to bang your fist on the table before they would do anything to help you. This probably provided some kind of embellishment to the dull routine of their daily work. Consequently, those who shouted loudest and made the most fuss got their apartments more quickly than the soft spoken and well behaved.

One man shouts because no one hears him when he talks quietly; another because he finds himself in an impasse. A third shouts because he wants a bigger slice of the cake. But in each case, a shout is a more effective and convincing argument than a polite request.

Have you heard of a single substantial wage demand being granted without a strike?

Of course, one cannot equate every strike or demonstration with an act of violence. Strikes and demonstrations are an accepted means of defending one's rights in civilized, democratic society. But when nurses go on strike and operations have to be postponed, when the doors of clinics and hospitals are closed, when food destined for export rots and the state suffers huge losses, when airplanes don't take off—these things verge on violence and sometimes on blackmail. . . .

All the machinery of life, public, social, and political, functions extremely badly. The only lubricant which, for a time, makes it work normally, are acts of violence in a broad interpretation of that word. Our bureaucracy, arranged as it is, sometimes simply craves violence.

I have purposely quoted exhaustively from this extensive article to illustrate the fact that I am not the only one who sees the seamy side of life in Israel. As the saying goes, "You can't get away from the truth."

And so my dear reader, you have seen the nature of democracy in this country in ordinary everyday life, but perhaps in the state as a whole, in the country's legislative and executive bodies, in its socio-legal structure, we shall discover the principles of a genuine democracy, the praises of which Zionist propaganda is always trumpeting abroad. After all, there is in the country for all to see a multiparty system, free direct elections on the basis of universal suffrage, no evidence of a police state and its natural by-product, the ordinary citizen's dread of the powers that be. Isn't this democracy? We in particular—we who come from totalitarian Soviet Russia, with its single ruling party, its joke elections where one candidate produces one deputy, its repressive KGB network, persecuting not only for acts but for thoughts as well—what have we got to complain about? We ought to be glad. But, alas, however hard one tries there's nothing much to be glad about.

Before mentioning my own impressions and conclusions,

I want to quote the opinion of another brand new citizen of Israel, an immigrant from Russia like myself, whom I know only through an article of his I read in the only surviving Russian-language newspaper, *Nasha Strana* [Our Country]. (The other one *Tribuna* [Podium], which manifested a certain independence, was successfully put out of business.) *Nasha Strana* is published by the former ruling coalition, Maarakh, and not noted, therefore, for its objectivity, and is very redolent of Soviet newspapers in both its style and its whitewashing, ultraloyalist tone. Articles like the one I quote from below are a rare occurrence in its pages, thus only making its testimony more valuable.

This is what Dr. S. Lifshits writes under the title, "The Costs of Our Democracy":

Democracy of course is society's great prize and blessing. However, as one gradually becomes involved in the social and political life of the country, one comes across phenomena that are difficult to explain.

Who can explain the meaning, the purpose, and the function of Israel's multitudinous political parties? Who can find his bearings amid the chaos they create in the country's political life, where the objective intertwines with the subjective, progressive political thought with a medieval outlook, and common sense with fatal irresponsibility?

Why in fact does Israel, with a population of three million, have a good three dozen political parties?

The Western European and American democracies manage with two or three or at the most five parties, but the Israeli voter is offered twenty-one different lists at an election—individual lists, moreover, that include two or three parties. Nobody seems to have been left out. A simple run through the titles is quite illuminating: there is an "Independent Liberal party" and a "Liberal party" pure and simple. Apparently, unlike the first, the second is dependent—but on whom?

"Progress and Development." This party seems to emphasize by its very name that all the rest are against progress and against development.

"Cooperation and Brotherhood" and "The Brotherhood Movement." The second party has apparently dispensed with cooperation, or else what need is there for them both to exist side by side?

There are Communist parties of varying persuasions: a pro-Moscow party, a pro-Chinese party, and some "house-trained" Israeli Communists.

There are parties which can be distinguished by color: "Black Panthers" and "Blue and White Panthers."

"The List of Revolutionary Socialists" is a party nobody has heard of, which at the election polled 0.08% of the votes on the strength of its own members—and, apparently, not all of them.

And here is a party which masks its ferocity beneath the elegant title of "Mary," and there many others with incomprehensible names and the Lord knows what kind of political programs.

One should observe, moreover, that the smaller the party numerically, the more noisy and arrogant its leaders, eloquently confirming the popular saying about the broken wheel which creaks loudest.

It is quite understandable, therefore, that those parties which do not win a single seat in parliament not only fail to depart from the political scene but continue to kick up a din and to arrange rowdy demonstrations. . . .

All this is well enough for the indigenous Israeli population, which takes a great deal in its stride and no longer tries to look for the point of much that happens—being convinced in advance that there is no point—but what about us, vainly trying to discern the innermost meaning of all these new experiences!

Like Dr. S. Lifshits—and why make a secret of it?—for quite a long time, I also endeavored to discern the forest among the trees in the jungle of the Israeli multiparty system, which I was predisposed to admire for its seemingly democratic character. Yes, that wasn't a slip of the pen. *Seemingly* is the operative word. I needed time to grasp that, behind this camouflage façade of chaos, there is a complete blanket of purely totalitarian power exercised by one or, at the very best, a group of related socialist parties. And the more tiny parties and little groups representing nothing and no one that there are in the country, the greater the quantity of empty political harangues, and the more convenient it is for the real bosses to exercise their dictatorship and govern the country by methods painfully well known to us from our Soviet experience.

For many years Israel has been ruled, not by a government

made up of the members of one particular party but by a handful of people in Tel Aviv, hidden carefully away from prying eyes, the all-powerful syndicate "GUSH." The members of this group deal the cards from the political pack, appointing and dismissing ministers with an iron hand, manipulating the "democratic voting" in parliament.

Whenever one attempts to do anything in Israel, one feels the deathly chill of this dictatorship on the back of one's neck. There is no point in thinking about promotion or getting a good position if you do not belong to the ruling coalition or openly express sympathy to it. You cannot dream of getting a loan on advantageous terms or the license to open a business enterprise if you are not closely linked to those who rule.

And how much better off are you in Israel than in the USSR for being able to disagree with the government at the top of your voice or even to stage protest demonstrations? Make as much noise as you like, for it will change nothing, and no one will listen to your screams; instead, the respectable decorum of phoney democracy will be preserved. It cuts both ways. In the words of the Russian proverb: "The wolves are full, and the sheep are whole."

In fact not all the sheep manage to survive. Particularly troublesome ones are quietly separated from the flock. There is no need to fling them into jail or beat them up at night in some deserted street, as is the practice in the unashamedly totalitarian countries. There are more flexible and gentler methods of educating dissenters, and in Israel these methods are practiced with great skill.

One such technique is slander. The dissenter or recalcitrant is ensnared in a sticky web of rumors. He is discredited by having the extent of his sins and faults slightly magnified. It may be said that he is anti-Semitic or engaged in spying on behalf of a state whose policies are openly hostile to Israel. People begin to shun such a person. They stop inviting him into their homes; his employer uses a specious excuse to dismiss him from his job. In no time at all he has

gone from Israel, seeking deliverance for his family in some
other country where there are not many Jews; for in those
countries where there is a large Jewish community he will
continue to be persecuted at Tel Aviv's bidding.

I myself have firsthand experience of such treatment and
when I call to mind certain events they provoke a feeling of
nausea and disgust. When I first arrived in Israel and was
still only taking stock of the situation and trying to get my
bearings, I was favored with a certain amount of attention
by the Israeli press. In particular the press in France and the
U.S.A. lavished flattering comment on me, almost turning
me into a national hero for having taken part in the first
political sit-in in the history of the USSR. But as soon as my
perplexity led me to ask questions (and there was much to
be perplexed about), the attitude toward me quickly
changed. People who, in order to appear in the newspapers,
had previously striven to be photographed at my side van-
ished by magic. My name was no longer on people's lips.
Wherever I was, I had a physical sensation of being surrounded by a cold vacuum of alienation. My every attempt
to find something to do and to do something useful, ultimately even to find work to support my family, inevitably
resulted in failure.

With a great deal of difficulty I managed to obtain a commission from abroad to make a documentary film. I rustled
up a film crew from among my comrades in distress—
former Soviet film men who had emigrated to Israel, only to
find themselves out of work and with no work in prospect.
Even people such as these, delighted to grasp my invitation
to work, were not left alone by my persecutors. Yuri Spilny,
a cameraman, soon told me confidentially that in the home
of a certain important Israeli official where he had been a
guest, he had been informed unequivocally that working
with me could have a damaging effect on his career prospects in Israel. Apparently because he did not heed these
solicitous warnings, Yuri Spilny also ended up on the
blacklist. Before long, rumors were reaching me that this

cameraman Spilny was no less than a KGB agent sent to Israel for a specific purpose. The fellow began to be hounded openly, and he took his wife and child and fled from Israel to Canada without a backward glance, where, to the best of my knowledge, he is now flourishing in Toronto.

I stayed on and continued to disturb the authorities by my concern for my fellow filmmakers who, following my example, had left the USSR for Israel. Finding no support anywhere in Israel, I turned for help and advice to the American Jewish community, addressing them publicly from the pages of the *New York Times*. I asserted that if the cultural force which had poured from the USSR into Israel—a country which can hardly boast of a plethora of its own talent—was not soon given proper work, then undoubtedly it would be forced to go looking for work and a crust of bread wherever it could, i.e., back to the diaspora, which it had but recently left in the name of the national state. This would signify the bankruptcy of the idea of Zionism.

No one—not in America nor in Israel—responded to my desperate cry, to this distress signal from a sinking ship. In Moscow, however, the journal *Za Rubezhom* [a Soviet-published digest of foreign press reports], not without a certain gloating, reprinted my dramatic interview from the *New York Times Magazine* (April 1972), thereby placing on the horns of a difficult dilemma many Soviet Jews employed in the arts who secretly cherished the hope of emigrating to Israel.

My gesture led only to the intensification of the atmosphere of hostile mistrust and malicious, petty rumors that surrounded me. The doors of many houses were closed to my family, and the already acute sense of loneliness and alienation was reinforced. But it would not be altogether accurate for me to say that I was completely forgotten. By some strange coincidence, I began to be called up from the reserves for active service with increasing frequency. I was called up three times in one year. It was even contrived to have me court-martialed on a patently trumped-up and absurd charge of dereliction of duty. It was clearly thought that the drudgery of military life would cool me down, knock the folly out of my head, and transform me into an ideal Israeli, an indifferent and apathetic citizen of the most democratic country not only in the Middle East but in the whole world.

That is one method of stamping out dissent. Another is that of quiet threats made face to face. A friend of mine, an immigrant from the USSR, obtained a modest government position in the town of Hertzliya and, taking the democratic nature of the social order at face value, dared at an election meeting to put a ticklish question to the candidate of the ruling party. That and no more. The next day when he turned up at work his boss sent for him and warned him behind the tightly closed door of his office that if he did not learn to exercise reasonable control over his tongue his service contract would not be renewed. Since then my friend, who has a large family to support, has lost his tongue. He has reverted to the state he was in when he lived in the Soviet Union, whence he fled thirsting for democracy.

They do not stand on ceremony with dissidents and uncooperative elements in Israel, however great their distinction in the state's eyes. The story of Esther Mostkov and her son, Israel Shamir, is a perfect and persuasive illustration of this somewhat unsavory side of life in Israel.

I knew Esther Mostkov when I lived in Russia. The name of this frail, middle-aged woman from Novosibirsk was known to Jews in many towns in the USSR. She was one of the most desperate and boldest people involved in the Jewish movement for the right to emigrate to Israel. She would travel thousands of kilometers to Moscow in order to take part in a hazardous demonstration. More than once she was arrested and sent into exile, but she did not surrender; she continued the fight, sending protest letters out of the country, keeping dangerous appointments with foreign journalists, and nothing, not even the tragic fate of her husband, could stop this amazingly courageous and noble person.

Much earlier than most Soviet Jews, Esther Mostkov began to dream of going to live in her ancient homeland. In 1948, the year in which the Jewish state was created in Palestine, Esther Mostkov bore a son in Siberia, and in honor of the state's birth, she named her son Israel. While Stalin was still alive and out-and-out official anti-Semitism was at its height, this Jewish family from Siberia took a step that verged on the insane: they openly demanded permission to emigrate to Israel. Esther's husband paid a cruel price for this. He was thrown into a concentration camp and did not live to see the beginning of the Jewish mass movement. Esther continued her husband's work, joined by her son when he was old enough. Both of them risked sharing the fate of their husband and father.

The son was the first to reach Israel. The Soviet authorities allowed him to leave when he was a student of twenty in order to accompany his infirm eighty-year-old grandfather. In his new homeland, Israel Shamir did not take advantage of his right to continue his university education but, gripped by patriotism, voluntarily joined the army as a paratrooper. He saw active service and after his demobilization helped to build a kibbutz on the Golan heights, toiling unremittingly as a zealot should, with no thought of gain or personal advantage.

Finally, after a long and exhausting struggle, his mother, Esther Mostkov, was also allowed to leave. She plunged headlong into the political life of her new country, reacting to her surroundings with characteristic honesty and directness. This woman's frank views—patriotic to the point of fanaticism—and her unselfish and constant concern for the fate of her country were not to the taste of those in power. Official Israel does not care for the likes of her. Her two university degrees and good knowledge of English were not enough to help Esther Mostkov find work. While other immigrants with less merit and inferior qualifications gradually found jobs, she received polite refusals or vague, unbinding promises wherever she applied.

Esther Mostkov forgot about her degrees and got a job cleaning the apartments of well-to-do American Jews. In this sphere, official Israel could not stand in her way. She needed nobody's references and nobody's protection to become a domestic servant. There is a dreadful shortage of such people in Israel.

In this democratic country, her son was dealt with even more unceremoniously. After serving in the army and working in a kibbutz, Israel Shamir came home to his mother in Jerusalem. By this time he had learned to speak Hebrew as well as English and, as he had a lively journalistic talent (at one time in Moscow we used to read his enraptured, vividly poetic letters from Israel), was given a job as a reporter in the Russian-language broadcasts section of the radio station, Voice of Israel. The bosses, however, did not praise their gifted, hard-working boy for long. It reached their ears that in private conversations the young man made no secret of his critical attitude toward certain facets of life in Israel; and without delay, at the first pretext, the former paratropper and kibbutznik was dismissed. Fed up with being unemployed and having lost the remains of his patriotism in the meantime, he left the country. Now he lives in England, where his qualifications were found sufficient to gain him a radio-journalist position at the BBC.

So much for democracy. It might have been the USSR, with the one possible difference that he was not locked up in prison.

Tens of thousands of Russian immigrants awaited the elections to the Knesset, the Israeli parliament, with understandable excitement. Having escaped from behind the Iron Curtain, from beneath the heel of a totalitarian regime, they saw the first chance in their lives to take part in genuinely democratic elections as the triumph of their freedom-loving aspirations that had culminated in their arrival in Israel. They prepared for this day as they would for a personal celebration, arguing in delight with one another until they were hoarse as to which party they should support and whom they should entrust with representing their interests in the state's supreme body.

They ran headlong into the real face of Israeli democracy—unattractive and even repugnant. The ensuing disappointment was sad and painful: they were not permitted to participate freely in the elections.

The Israeli Socialist bloc, which until recently had ruled the country, had no illusions about the sympathies of those Jews who had fought their way out of the country where socialism had already been built. Only the opposition could count on the votes of the Soviet Jews, and so everything was done to stop them taking part in the election. Most of the country's new citizens did not get the invitations they needed to give them access to the ballot box. Despite their poor or nonexistent knowledge of Hebrew, they tried vainly to discover why this had happened and received belated, incomprehensible replies to the effect that their invitations had been sent by mistake to other towns, where they had been living in temporary reception centers for immigrants immediately after entering the country.

In Hertzliya, all the houses on Brenner Street are occupied by recent immigrants from the USSR. Only a handful of the denizens of this street, those who had immediately sensed where the power lay and, so as to grab their share of advantages, had rushed demonstratively into the camp of the ruling party, received the invitation to vote. The rest never even found out where the elections were held.

I questioned dozens of my acquaintances in Jerusalem and always received the same answer: We didn't take part in the election. Only one of them, a wildly obdurate man, traveled the length and breadth of the town in his own car, managed in the afternoon to find the polling place where his name was on the roll and so cast his vote. My wife also showed exceptional persistence and obtained the desired ballot paper. With trembling hands, she placed it in the ballot box as if she were placing it on scales that determined the country's future. But the next day she became very aggrieved when she learned she had been taken in like a child. Elections for the local council and for the parliament took place at the same time in the same building. She had cast her vote on the ground floor where the elections for the council were being held, but because she did not know much Hebrew she did not discover—nor was she told—that voting in the main parliamentary elections was taking place on the second floor.

The first "free" election of their lives dissipated the illusions of many Soviet immigrants about democracy in Israel. Those, however, who tried to keep intact the vestiges of their beliefs were dealt a *coup de grâce* by the events that unfolded in the town of Beersheba, the capital of the Negev desert region.

It was here in the summer of 1973, and not in Jerusalem or Tel Aviv, where most of the immigrants are concentrated, that a congress of immigrants from the USSR was held. The very choice of the place boded ill. It was not easy for new citizens to get to Beersheba even as guests or observers. The journey to the far south from other parts of the country is long and difficult and beyond the pocket of someone without work. And to get a delegate's identification card...

The Israeli political hacks, who knew all the tricks and were responsible for the congress preparations, taught the new arrivals a lesson in democracy. The results of the elections for delegates were quite openly falsified. Instead of representatives of the current *Aliyah* [immigration of Jews to Israel] of Russians, about one hundred old men, elected by nobody and representing nobody, were brought to the congress from various kibbutzim with delegate cards in their shaking hands. To be precise, they represented the ruling party but certainly not the people on whose behalf the congress had been convened. Forty identification cards turned out to be completely phoney.

I was at this congress in the capacity of a guest (I got a day's leave of absence from my military unit) and witnessed the whole farce. Someone called Mintsovsky came to the microphone and announced loudly that there were many delegates in the hall whose cards were false. The party functionaries on the platform were extremely indignant and demanded proof. Mintsovsky waved his card high above his head in front of the eyes of the platform party.

"Here's one of them—a forgery! Nobody elected me! This card was put in my hands, and I was brought here."

But even this did not dismay the organizers of the congress. Divesting themselves of any pretext of democratic procedure, they conducted the whole charade along tested Soviet lines: previously compiled lists of suitable people, voting but not counting votes, only calling puppets to the microphone and on no account anyone whose political reliability was suspect. A real fight took place over the microphone and stewards dragged some people off the platform and ejected them from the hall.

The sheep's clothing was discarded, and the wolf's fangs were bared before the bewildered eyes of the erstwhile Soviet citizens. This was a graphic lesson, an almost inconceivable final collapse of illusions. And to crown it all, right there in the hall, Alexander Druz, a famous artist from the USSR, died of heart failure while still waiting for his turn to speak.

I knew him, this extremely kind puppet-theatre enthusiast who had contrived by dint of inconceivable efforts to bring from the USSR to Israel the fruits of long years of creative work—dozens of puppets—so as to delight the Jewish children of his new homeland with his joyful art. He vainly went the rounds of official institutions, begging them to assist him to set up Israel's first puppet theatre. The cold indifference he encountered everywhere discouraged and depressed him, whose life had been full of suffering, and the congress in Beersheba was the final straw.

For me and for many Russian immigrants, Alexander Druz's funeral was the burial of our own hopes, passionately cherished as we fought our way through the Iron Curtain, of a life in a democratic and just society.

We had miscalculated. This is now clear to each of us, and consequently I am not surprised to learn that an ever-increasing number of people refuse to take advantage of the right, won in battle, to emigrate to Israel and that there is a constantly growing flood of those who leave the Jewish state disillusioned and broken, their dreams and hopes cruelly outraged by life.

chapter four

MYTHS

How is a myth born?

From my own anything but pleasant experience, I have learned the secret of a myth's conception; I have watched its rapid growth, darkened by life's authentic detail; its demise, silent and unsung, I have felt. We who once unquestioningly believed now blush and ashamedly avert our eyes, cursing all who abetted us in our faith.

Both in ancient times and in our own, the reason for the appearance of myths is one and the same: the absence of accurate information and the agonizing desire of questing man to realize his ideal, albeit in his dreams. From this originates an impassioned, desperate, and blind faith in his invention or in any rumor lending credence to his hopes.

We Russian Jews invented an Israel of our own; it became the embodiment of those expectations which had remained unfulfilled in the USSR. All the aspirations of our fathers' generation and the Revolution they wrought—freedom of the individual, social justice, humanism, honesty, and love for one's neighbor—all these things, which in Russia had become simply a mirage, were transferred to Israel by the generation of their sons. Belief in these myths could raise up tens of thousands of people to engage in a fight that, in hindsight, seemed meaningless and doomed from the start, uproot them from the places in which they had lived for generations, from the graves of their forefathers, making them, in a single day, dispossessed and defenseless but nevertheless giving them strength to withstand and conquer.

But to what end should they conquer? In order to see the myths elaborated by their wild imagination burst like soap bubbles, leaving them to sink into blank, hopeless despair? Get a group of Jews on their own away from eavesdroppers, and you will see that regardless of whether they had decided to go to Israel or whether nothing was further from their minds, with rapture and childish delight in their eyes, they will begin to take each other's breath away with myths of the "promised land," avowing and swearing that their information is firsthand and that only a Communist agitator or an unabashed anti-Semite can doubt its accuracy.

I myself witnessed the birth of certain myths and, let me be frank about it, played no small part in propagating them.

Myth number one. No one in Israel is apathetic. There every person is ready unselfishly to carry out all that is asked of him if it makes the country grow strong and prosperous.

Well, what do you think? Who would not like to live in a country like that, among that kind of people? Even the most case-hardened individual, the most extreme egotist, somewhere deep in the secret places of his heart cherishes the fragile dream of living in such a blessed place. And this is particularly true of someone living in the Soviet Union, where the official propoganda that is constantly rammed down one's throat affirms that one has all these things but where in fact there is nothing but lies and hypocrisy. So there is after all a country where these things are not just words but truth, and it is the country of my own kith and kin, consequently my country, too—small, full of oranges and lemons, fragrant, like a rich bouquet, with every human virtue—my Israel.

In the days when the first vague stirrings of interest in Israel were being felt, in Moscow Jewish circles, a dear grey-haired old lady, the mother-in-law of a friend of mine, returned home after visiting her sister in Israel. Here was someone who had actually been there. It was an event of such rarity that crowds of Jews—Jews not from Moscow only, but from many towns—began to lay siege to the old lady's tiny, shabby apartment. Like children listening to a fairy tale, they hung on her every word, and she, encouraged by such unexpected attention, talked on and on, ever warming to her theme. With each new telling, she embellished her tale with a ready flood of fresh details.

This is one of her stories, which I can still remember almost word for word.

I arrived in Israel, but there was no one to meet me. Then it turned out that the telegram hadn't arrived. What was I to do? I took a taxi. It was a long way, to another town. Kilometer after kilometer, on both sides of the road, there were orange groves. Israel is way down south, and they're short of water there. They have to water things all the time. On and on we drove. And all around it's oranges as far as you can see. And the little jets of water, going round and round, sending an even spray over all the trees. The taxi driver—he was a Jew from Poland—suddenly stopped the car right there in the road and disappeared among the orange trees. Well, I thought, it's the call of nature, the man couldn't wait. There I sit. About twenty minutes later he comes back. He apologizes and says that he saw one of the sprinklers wasn't working properly. The hose had come off, and the jet was shooting up into the air. So he'd stopped in order to put it right. "Everything's working properly now, and we can carry on." What did somebody else's oranges matter to him? He's a taxi driver; he works for himself. And he wasn't from those parts either. But that's Israel.

Well, that commonplace little tale brought reverential tears to the eyes of the listeners. What a country! And what people! And grandma's yarn was taken into hundreds of homes. I too did my bit, ardently and animatedly, as if I were talking about something really out of the way. Did I for a moment have the time to reflect upon all the other people who had traveled that road in Israel and had also noticed the broken sprinkler? Had they sped by indifferently? The exceptional act of one honest man we transferred in a moment to the whole country, so anxious were we to see beauty in Israel and its people.

The following objection might be raised. You invented a country that didn't exist and are shaken when it doesn't correspond to your fantasy. It is you who are to blame and not Israel. In part, I agree. The sad thing is, however, that Israel turned out to be not only not as good as our dream but scandalously below acceptable standards. We saw so much that was ugly that we scarcely had time to look up between each fresh "discovery."

Here is the face that Israel showed us and how the myth that there is no indifference in Israel looks in reality. I will not quote my own bitter experience. To give a more objective picture, I will cite various people's testimony, just as they gave it to me, bitterly lamenting the wicked irony of fate.

Judith Berelovich (a nurse from Vilna).

I work in the Levenstein Hospital in Ra'ananna. I have more than twenty years' nursing experience in the USSR, which is an adequate basis for comparison. Medical equipment and medicines really are much better here than in the Soviet Union, but, on the other hand, when it comes to the medical staff, the two countries are poles apart and not to the Israelis' advantage. I've been working here for four years and still can't get used to the outrageous indifference Israeli medical personnel show toward their patients. I don't expect I ever will get used to it. Here is one example out of many.

Each morning all our staff have a break. For half an hour, the doctors and nurses closet themselves in a separate room and drink coffee. It happened that a patient, the victim of a road accident, was brought into the emergency department right in the middle of that coffee break. He required immediate treatment. I rushed to the room where the doctors were having their coffee.

"We've still got another fifteen minutes break." The cold indifferent reply was like a blow on the head.

I should mention that, although they had already finished their coffee, no one got up. The remaining fifteen minutes was sacrosanct. No one was interested in the patient.

Alas, indifference and egotism in a doctor, incompatible with his Hippocratic oath, have become part of accepted practice in Israeli medicine.

Ilya Gorilovsky (an engineer from Moscow).

I work near Jerusalem. Our satellite telecommunications station, a miracle of modern technology, has recently been built by the Americans. The staff consists of Israelis. I'm being quite frank when I say that never in my life have I met such a lot of idlers. Without any embarrassment, they conspicuously do no more than they have to. When they see me working (and I work normally, as I've always been used to working), they accuse me of wanting to impress the bosses and ask me whether I haven't realized that because of me they are being made to do more work. With this kind of attitude toward work, I'm not surprised that breakdowns are so frequent. The amazing thing is that the station works at all. I should add that most of its functions are automatic.

Let me give one further example, which to my mind dots all the i's and draws an accurate picture of the social mores deeply rooted in this country.

On one occasion, I came to the station ready for duty. It was Saturday, a nonworking day in Israel, and there were only three electrical maintenance technicians on duty in the whole complex, three young fellows, nongraduate specialists. People like this usually try to make up for the gaps in their education by being zealous in their work. Not so in Israel. During their shift an accident had occurred at the deserted station. Somewhere a water pipe had burst, and for hours water had been pouring into basements and service premises. By the time I arrived, it was already getting close to the powerful 22,000-volt transformers. Water reaching this apparatus could have caused a short circuit and explosion, which would have destroyed the complex worth millions of dollars and, at the same time, would have dispatched to the next world those three luckless technicians who hadn't moved a finger to avert the danger.

When I asked them why they had taken no action during a whole shift, their answer was hideously ingenuous: "Mending water pipes is not our job. We're electricians. That's what we're paid for."

I'm a graduate engineer. I too am an electrician and not a plumber, and I am much older than they. I did not, however, stop to ascertain what was and what was not part of my job. In half an hour or so, I had located and isolated the damaged water pipe; then, using an electric pump, I set about pumping out the water.

I did this not because I wished to cut a figure or astound anyone. Any normal man with an elementary sense of social responsibility would have acted in the same way, and his impulse would have been as natural as breathing. Three overgrown boobies, typical products of Israel, profoundly egotistical and, consequently, amoral also, sneeringly watched what I was doing without even thinking of helping me. And then they went off home without a care in the world.

The engineer Ilyn Gorilovsky has recently left Israel.

The atmosphere in the country is amoral. This strikes not only the newcomer, whose eye is fresh and notes any tiny speck of dirt, but also those indigenous Israelis who have not yet become indifferent to the fate of their country. These are the words of a man well known beyond the borders of Israel, the owner of an art galley in Tel Aviv noted for its unique collection, the millionaire Sam Dubiner:

"What kind of morality can there be in a country where professors and judges, just to have a part of their salary exempted from taxation, have to swear under oath to the Department of Taxes that they have bought books for the purpose of further study, when in point of fact they have never set eyes on those books?"

"How can one speak of morality in this coutry?" asks Svetlana Selyutina, a pediatrician from Minsk, after spending a year in Beersheba before fleeing to Germany.

While I was still in the USSR I knew from "Voice of Israel" broadcasts and rumors which were peddled enthusiastically among Jews of the high standing of public medical services provided in that country, which had the highest concentration of doctors per head of population in the world. It all turned out to be a typical propaganda trick.

I worked for a year in southern Israel and covered every inch of the Negev desert in a Land Rover, visiting agricultural settlements deep in the desert where most of the population are "black" Jews from Africa and Asia. What filth, what unsanitary conditions I discovered there. You can't believe such monstrous conditions exist in the twentieth century. When I examined the children in some of the hovels there, I discovered that most of them had chronic ear infections. These children have puss running constantly from their ears, and no one thinks it worthy of attention. Many of the children had never in their lives been examined by a doctor. The illness had been neglected, and they were in danger of losing their hearing altogether.

I sounded the alarm and demanded that urgent steps be taken. After all, through the negligence of doctors, there would one day be hundreds of handicapped adults in these desert settlements. My fellow doctors greeted my indignation with cold jibes. In their faces I had read the most frightful diagnosis of a doctor's attitude that there is: incomprehensible indifference to their patients, total unconcern about their fate. The most militant of them saw in my alarm unfriendliness toward Israel, a desire to denigrate the country, and they began to spread disapproving rumors about me, explaining my "shabby" behavior by my slightly impure Jewish origins—I had the "misfortune" to be born of a Russian father.

Lydia Lyudkevich (a telecommunications engineer from Warsaw) has been living in Israel for five years and works in Jerusalem in the planning office of the Ministry of Posts and Telecommunications.

I grew up and went to school in Russia, worked in Poland for many years, and I am now able to compare the attitude to work in those two countries with the attitude in Israel. Throughout the world, and in particular in the socialist countries, one can come across examples of an irresponsible, unprincipled attitude to work, but what I have seen at my place of work in Israel is beyond the range of the wildest fantasy.

Fifty people work in our office, or, to be more precise, there are fifty on the roll. All these people regularly draw their salary and arrive at work punctually every day. Only five of them, however, do any work and complete the assignments the office is supposed to carry out. And what about the rest? They openly and unashamedly do nothing. They turn up in the morning, sign on, and disappear about their business until the end of the working day. Five minutes before closing time, they come back, sign off, and, as if nothing were the matter and without any pangs of conscience, leave the office. No one is indignant. No one tells them off. People are used to it. Here it is considered normal.

Lydia Lyudkevich lives in Sweden now.

In my view, this is a very blatant manifestation of concealed unemployment. People who do nothing draw a salary which is, in effect, the dole. They grow used to this kind of life and have no desire for any other.

One could quote countless examples like this. They undermine the exuberance of Israeli propaganda and reveal a depressing picture of human relations. No inflated statistics, no fancy advertising prospectuses can conceal the revolting facts of day-to-day life that one sees eating their way through the gilded façade of official Israel.

Viewed from the vantage point of today, how improbable seems that occurrence from a traveler's impressions of Israel that the old lady passed on when she came back to Moscow. Remember the taxi driver who repaired the water sprinkler in the orange grove? Through his innocuous act he engendered in Moscow great ecstasies among us and provoked the birth of one of the myths about Israel that roam the world in abundance, fogging and causing to spin nostalgic Jewish heads that yearn for miracles.

Another myth current among the Jews of Soviet Russia and passed from lip to quivering lip was the sugary tale of the striking *honesty of the people who live in Israel.* This myth asserts that there are no grounds for lies and deceit in the atmosphere of brotherly, albeit meticulous and exacting, mutual relations which have developed in the country.

I still remember one of the tales illustrating this myth. Recounted in such minute and authentic detail as to render doubt an impossibility, this story made the rounds in Moscow for a long time. The narrators, moreover, would quote a letter received by a Muscovite from a relative in Israel, who, so the story went, was the "hero" of this tale. Having suffered for his dishonesty, he bitterly repented what he had done.   *234141*

A certain person, who had long ago contrived to escape to Israel from the USSR, made up his mind to employ techniques and methods learned beyond Israel's borders in order to carry out certain unscrupulous acts in this country of total honesty. This mysterious someone owned a workshop in Tel Aviv that produced cardboard shoe boxes. Striving to make money by illicit means, this oaf, who was bereft of the moral qualities characterizing the genuine Israeli, resorted to deception. He reduced the size of each box by a centimeter or two, thereby departing from the standard, supposing that such an innocent prank would pass unnoticed and a small amount of not-altogether-honestly earned money would come his way.

In Israel any manifestation of dishonesty stands out like a blot of ink on a sheet of white paper and evokes immediate public reaction. By his act our "hero" degraded the high calling of Israeli citizenship and was promptly exposed by the vigilant state inspectors—young girls in military uniform, zealous and ruthless guardians of the law. He was put on trial, all his possessions were confiscated, and he was ejected from the country in disgrace, a ruined man, barred forever from the Jewish state. And what more terrible fate than that can there be for a Jew?

We gasped. We were moved and could not hide our delight when we heard this kind of story. They spread through the cities of the Soviet Union like wildfire, reaching every single Jewish family and filling people with a sense of legitimate pride in their tiny, far-off national state. Finally setting doubt aside, they made up their minds to go there, whatever the cost, so that at least their children could grow up in this wonder-working atmosphere.

The rose-colored glasses of the Jews who arrived in Israel were smashed to smithereens by the time their owners had taken their first few steps. Here they encountered the flagrant dishonesty that is part and parcel of everyday life and the falsehood and deceit that pursue the new arrival wherever he goes.

No one in Israel, apart from visitors, is surprised or shocked by a fact like this. You have made a business appointment and in order to keep it you travel from Jerusalem to Tel Aviv. You find no one at the agreed meeting place either at the appointed time or later and waste a whole day waiting about. This is a run-of-the-mill occurrence.

In Israel if you do not watch the figures on the cash register very carefully, you can be short changed at the checkout in either a small shop or a huge supermarket. The cashier you catch doing this will not blush or say he is sorry. He will simply fling your money at you disdainfully. If you are spared an insult in the process, you have got off lightly.

To persuade a tradesman in Israel to carry out some household repair is in itself a humiliating problem for anyone with an elementary sense of personal dignity. After demanding an incredibly high price, the tradesman proceeds to do a shoddy job in a timescale acceptable to him and not his client. In so doing he will give the impression that he has done the client a great favor.

You sink in Israel into a miasma of small- and large-scale dishonesty. You begin to rush this way and that, endeavoring to avoid dirty tricks on the part of your fellow countrymen, who cynically regard you—a stranger who does not know the language and is unfamiliar with the ways of the country—as easy and legitimate prey.

At the warehouses in the port of Haifa, the destination of immigrants' luggage sent by sea, you are robbed shamelessly. Not that someone emigrating from the USSR can bring much with him through the fine and clinging filter of the Soviet customs. Even when you have gone through all the formalities and left behind all those possessions you are not entitled to take with you, which amounts to almost everything, you still have no safeguard against robbery at the frontier itself, carried out by local officials and frontier troops on their own initiative.

Irina Feinblum, a doctor from Moscow, was robbed by Ukrainian customs officials after she had submitted to all the due formalities in Moscow and, already stripped of her Soviet citizenship, was on her way to Vienna. In the course of the flight, the plane landed in Kiev and customs officials, behaving like highwaymen, tore from her wrist a bracelet, which Moscow officials had permitted her to take out of the country, and unashamedly appropriated it.

Russian Jews have already been robbed before they arrive in Israel, and the sorry remains of the chattels they have been able to bring with them represent what for a long time will be their only and therefore very precious possessions. But in Israel they do not always manage even to hang on to what is left. Here, in what supposedly is their native country, the final stage of the robbery is carried out, this time not by anti-Semites but by Israelis. The warehouse employees at the port of Haifa descend on the luggage of Russian Jews like vultures and pillage it, unsupervised and unmolested, each one grabbing all he can. The shattered immigrant who discovers his luggage broken and ripped in the warehouse is told unblinkingly that the boxes were smashed in transit and arrived empty. This is what I was told in Haifa, when I was unable to find many of the things I had dispatched from Moscow. Hundreds of other families were "consoled" in the same way.

Quite by chance, a Moscow dentist, Mikhail Gurarii, exposed the trickery of these scoundrels. When he first went down to the port of Haifa to check his luggage, he was shown three broken crates that were quite empty; although somewhat downcast, he accepted his lot. How can one check who stole property on a long journey that passes through several countries. Several days later he went to Haifa to collect the remainder of his luggage. This time they showed him five broken crates, forgetting in their haste that not long before they had shown him only three. There was no further room for doubt: the crates of luggage were smashed intentionally in the warehouse at Haifa and only then were their contents stolen.

Mikhail Gurarii settled in the United States two years ago.

The pillaging in Haifa reached such proportions that a Dutch insurance company, uncircumspect enough to agree in Vienna to insure the luggage of Soviet emigrants on their way to Israel, suffered losses amounting to many millions of dollars and found itself on the verge of bankruptcy.

And so another myth, that of the honesty of the Israelis, was destroyed, leaving behind it a spiritually painful wound.

Vida Olshan, a cabaret singer from Kaunas, has the following story to tell:

"Soon after we arrived in Israel, the famous impresario Giora Godik signed me to a contract. The contract was a good one, sufficient to support my large family, and I plunged wholeheartedly into the work. Concert followed concert. I was well received by the public. I thought myself very fortunate. The Israeli impresario cruelly deceived me, however. He disappeared from Israel, pocketing the whole of my fee. I was left without money and became a target for jibes because of my credulity."

Vida Olshan now lives in West Berlin.

Yuri Kogan, an accompanist from Riga, encountered in Israel the most revolting form of deceit—exploitation of patriotism.

"The impresario Yekhiel Gano included me in a concert tour of French Jewish communities immediately after the Yom Kippur War. We were warmly received by our audiences. Yekhiel Gano suggested to the artists that they waive their fee for three concerts and send all the receipts to the Israeli Army Fund. The artists naturally agreed. We received no payment for three concerts, but the money didn't end up in any fund. The impresario put it in his pocket. The Israeli Embassy in Paris simply confirmed our suspicions."

In our ecstatic discourses we often dwelt on *the moral and political unity of the people of Israel*, how they present an examplary, united front in a world torn asunder by internal contradictions. This also turned out to be a myth. You can hear this particular myth in many of the world's Jewish communities and in Israel itself, even from high-ranking political figures, whose competence and capacity for analysis might be expected to mitigate such flag-waving jingoism.

I shall never forget my talk with the mayor of Jerusalem, Teddy Kollek. He invited a group of immigrants from various countries to his home for a cup of tea. He wanted to hear their opinion of the country and learn what shortcomings a fresh eye might have noticed. I was invited to this tea party and naïvely yearned to open the eyes of this eminent and influential politician to those sinister signs of threats to Israel's existence that seemed evident to me.

He simply grinned in response, his whole aspect making it clear that he had no intention of taking my hasty conclusions seriously. We began to talk about young people, and when Kollek stated that Israel's youth was the most patriotic youth in the world, I asked whether the respected mayor had not been put on his guard by a recent newspaper report about a group of young people called up for military service who had burned their call-up papers as a sign of protest.

"It's an isolated case," said Kollek, dismissing the matter. "In the United States, tens of thousands of young people burn their draft cards or desert in order not to get sent to Vietnam, but no one says America is in danger on account of that."

"Even if a million should do it," I agreed, "America won't be destroyed. She can even permit herself the luxury of losing a war. But not Israel. Israel is like a sapper working in a mine field; one mistake is too many. There won't be a second chance. Israel, unlike any other country, cannot lose a war and continue to exist as a state. Consequently the standards that are applied to other countries are totally inapplicable to Israel."

The protest of a group of young Israelis who refused to serve in the army was a threatening reminder to a still fragile state that had not yet found its feet. The habit of using myth to lull one's conscience and an unwillingness to accept the truth, however bitter, are typical of Israeli society and its leaders. It took the Yom Kippur War to lance the carefully concealed abseses and open certain people's eyes.

What Teddy Kollek had called an isolated case was soon repeated in a more serious form. Two young people, both Sabras (native-born Israelis) fled to Sweden the day before they were due to enter the army, and there requested political asylum, alleging that their motive was that they did not wish to participate in the murder of Arab women, children, and old men. That is what they said, repeating almost word for word the statements of American deserters from Vietnam.

Israeli national morale has taken a catastrophic tumble, but the myths of the monolithic state, like a worn-out record, continue their soothing, soporific lullaby.

The discovery in Haifa of an espionage and sabotage group working for the Syrians was a resounding slap on the rosy cheeks of imagined well-being. The group was made up of both Arabs and Jews, and one of its leading members was a Sabra, the product of a socialist kibbutz and a former Israeli army paratrooper. As they say, that just about takes the cake.

Rust and corrosion are eating away at the fabric of the state, for all to see, but everyone tries hypocritically to look the other way, preferring sweet and soothing myths.

Then, like a bolt from the blue, the Yom Kippur War began to destroy one myth after another, including the myth of the moral and political unity of the Israeli people. An unprecedented event, previously unthinkable, took place: Israeli prisoners of war spoke on Cairo radio and poured filth on their homeland. Even then, no one really wanted to look truth in the face or to ascertain why Israeli youth had lost its former ardent patriotism and become inert and indifferent.

The editor of the Tel Aviv paper *Yediot Achoronot*, Dr. C. Rosenblum, belatedly bewailing the passivity of young people and the anti-Zionism fashionable among them, offered his thunderstruck readers the following "revelation": 20 percent of the teachers in Israeli schools are members of the Communist party, RAKACH, faithful servant of the Kremlin. Need we, he suggests, look further for the reasons?

Of course, Communist teachers are far from being the best mentors for Israeli youth, but are they the entire cause of the trouble? The present-day generation of young Israelis has grown up in an atmosphere of impardonable falsehood, seeing on every hand the abyss between word and deed. Blind nationalistic passions have begun to turn its stomach. The result is lack of faith, a sarcastic attitude toward their fathers' ideals, emptiness, and a tragic sense of impasse.

The most dangerous myth of all, which has already cost a great deal of blood and will continue to do so, was the myth of *the invincibility of the Israeli army*.

In my efforts, more often than not unsuccessful, to expose myths, I have sometimes managed to pin down my opponents with irrefutable facts, but then they would always fling this myth in my face, like a final, quite unbeatable trump card: "But you must admit that our army is the best in the world. You can criticize the state as much as you like, but our army is like the movement of a clock. Everybody admits this, even our enemies."

At that time I still had no knowledge of the Israeli army and was unable to assess its virtues and shortcomings. One thing, however, put me on my guard: the army issues from the state; it is its progeny, and the child could not be entirely free from the defects and diseases of the mother who bore it. There are no miracles. The body is one with communicating vessels; the infection that has stricken one part of it will definitely manifest its ominous symptoms in another.

It is now an open secret that the Israeli army is stricken with the same ailment as the rest of Israeli society. All the phrasemongering about its incomparable qualities, about its exceptional nature and almost magical successes, have ended in a bloodstained soap bubble, which burst during the Yom Kippur War. A newcomer to the country like myself was capable of unraveling the myth and glimpsing the unacceptable truth long before the beginning of the war. And there is no merit here on my part. The truth lay on the surface; you could not get away from it. You simply needed to open your eyes to it, not bury your head in the sand like an ostrich.

As a member of the reserve, I was called up for military service and, along with another soldier, was on night guard duty in Givat Sarfatit, a new residential district of Jerusalem. My partner was Yuri Belyavsky, an immigrant from the USSR and formerly a violinist in the Moscow Radio and Television Symphony Orchestra.

Givat Sarfatit is a hilly district, the highest point in Jerusalem. Part of the territory occupied during the Six Day War, it has been lately developed into a residential area for recent immigrants, most of them from the Soviet Union. Alongside the Jewish blocks of multistory houses, or more precisely, beneath them, nestling at the foot of the hills, are Arab villages; and beyond, visible to the naked eye, lies Ramallah, hostile, lurking, biding its time to take revenge.

The two of us, armed with ancient English rifles dating from the Boer War, went on our rounds through the deserted nocturnal streets of the large district, making quite a good target for an average marksman. This, however, did not disconcert us. In the heart of the district, we discovered (for we were not warned by our officers) huge concrete tanks containing drinking-water supplies and an automatic pumping station, pumping water day and night for the inhabitants of the capital. In dry, torrid Israel, where every drop of water is valuable and constant acts of sabotage are being carried out by Palestinian Arabs, a pumping station and tanks like these become strategic installations of outstanding importance. Their destruction could leave Jerusalem without water for a long time and cause it to die of thirst.

No one was guarding this installation. Anyone, no matter what his intentions, could approach it without hindrance and even enter the open doors of the deserted pumping station, the automatic pumps humming rhythmically and the red lights flashing on the complex control panels. No particular boldness or intelligence would have been needed to bring from the hamlets close by any amount of explosives, calmly place the charges in the station and beside the concrete walls of the storage tanks, set a timing device, depart to a safe place, and wait for the whole lot to go up in the air.

Yuri Belyavsky and I were downcast and spent the period until dawn patrolling this one place, realizing the danger threatening the city if our vigilance lapsed. When we were relieved by another patrol, we did not turn in but went without delay to our commanding officer, Captain Eli Filippovich, and reported the whole matter to him.

He laughed condescendingly when he had heard us out and said that the Arabs hadn't enough brains to think of that kind of sabotage, asserting that the vague presence of a couple of patrols armed with ancient rifles in the streets of Givat Sarfatit was sufficient to stop any saboteur from daring to show his face there.

We could not believe our ears. This was said quite seriously, without any trace of irony, by a veteran staff officer, a paratrooper's badge and a line of military decorations on his chest. What arrogant scorn for the enemy there was in his tone; what irresponsible unconcern! And this man was entrusted with guard patrols in the capital, which even during the "quiet" period between wars was constantly exposed to attack.

Our attempt to speak to other officers brought no relief; the reaction was more or less the same. Our perplexed questions annoyed them. The hostility, rampant in the country at that time, of older inhabitants toward new immigrants, toward the different culture the latter represented, toward their superior level of education, also played its part. At the end of our term of service, in order finally to put us in our place, our officers concocted a "case" against Belyavsky and myself, involving false, trumped-up charges and a hasty trial conducted by Captain Eli Filippovich which led to each of us getting seven days imprisonment. The sentence was actually suspended. We didn't have to go to jail. It was a deterrent designed to teach us not to interfere in other people's affairs.

Belyavsky and I naïvely supposed that questions of state security were just as much our concern as that of our commanding officers. The storage tanks and pumping station that supplied Jerusalem with water were left as before, unguarded and vulnerable to sabotage. We sank into deep dismay. The myth of the high standard of the Israeli army and the competence of its commanders had collapsed before our eyes.

By a sad coincidence our unjust court-martial took place on the ninth day of the month of Av, by the Israeli calendar, Tish b'Av—the most gloomy and sorrowful anniversary for the Jews, the anniversary of the destruction of the Temple, the fall of the last bastion of the Jewish state, twenty centuries earlier, before the onslaught of the Roman legions and internecine strife in Jerusalem itself.

Those trying us that day in a filthy, spit-bespattered cellar in the center of present-day Jerusalem, quite close to the Wailing Wall—those Israeli officers, without themselves being aware of it, had once again destroyed the Temple, but this time in our hearts, the Temple, the symbol of Jewish statehood, which we had tenderly cherished within us and brought here in order to unite our efforts with those of our whole nation and build on the debris of the millennia.

On the ninth day of Av our faith in Israel was finally buried. The final myth in a long line already withered and scattered by the wind was destroyed. We were already fully aware that the legends of the amazing, incomparable qualities of the Israeli army being tirelessly spread throughout the world were a myth—the most dangerous of all the myths spawned by Israel's painted and powdered façade.

The Yom Kippur War, which broke out three months later, only confirmed our worst suppositions. The Captain Filippoviches of the army, with their criminal self-assurance and unconcern, were on the Golan Heights and the Suez Canal, in army intelligence and the General Staff.

They failed to notice enemy concentrations right in front of their eyes, did not prepare the army for defense, and doomed hundreds of trusting eighteen-year-old youths to an inglorious and tragic end. They shocked the Israeli population by the cruel defeats of the first days of the war and demonstrated to the whole world the demise of a long-deluding myth.

chapter five

THE MENDED POT

You can't stick the pieces of a broken pot together; they won't hold. Folk wisdom has asserted this for centuries, and no efforts to prove the contrary have had much success.

The very creation of Israel was a desperate attempt to refute this axion. The present-day Jewish state in Palestine is a pot made up of eighty fragments of differing sizes that have been stuck together (eighty being the number of countries whence the sons of Israel have reached out toward Zion in the twentieth century). A colorful mended pot, to be sure, but a pot with clearly noticeable cracklines yawning dangerously as the glue quickly dries.

Sometimes one cannot understand what it is that unites so many different people, whose flesh and blood has been permeated by the national and even racial traits of those nations among whom they have dwelt for centuries: the classical, biblical type from the Yemen desert with his dark, bronze skin and eyes black as agates; the blue-eyed, snub-nosed, fiery, red-haired Jew from Lithuania; the Georgian Jew, indistinguishable from a Georgian. (I, who have lived most of my life in the USSR, was always amazed when someone from Tbilisi or from Kutaissi, speaking with a thick Caucasian accent, admitted to me in a frank moment that he was a Jew. For me, the external difference between the Bokhara Jew and the indigenous inhabitants of Central Asia, the Tadzhiks or the Uzbeks, is still a mystery locked beneath seven seals.) The German Jews, who fled from Hitler in the thirties and established themselves on the north coast of Palestine, in the resort town of Nahariya, to this day form a closed group. Most of them have still not mastered Hebrew and use only German, a language they adore possibly more than the Germans themselves. In Dimona in the south of Israel, you can see dark-complexioned oriental beauties swathed in colorful saris, the red spot on their foreheads and tiny diamonds, not in the lobe of the ear, but in the side of the nostril. These too are Jewish women, from India or Pakistan. Jews from Morocco look like Arabs, and the grandson of a Moscow rabbi, like a pure-blooded Slav. What is the bond between these people who are so unlike one another? Why do they call themselves Jews? After all, only a fifth of Israel's population are believers; consequently, religion can be excluded as the fundamental binding factor.

The famous French existentialist philosopher Jean-Paul Sartre, in his book, *Anti-Semite and Jew,* affirms that the Jews have survived as a specific community only as a result of external pressure: "The only link holding them together is the hostile scorn with which surrounding nations regard them." Many scholars in both Israel and the diaspora categorically disagree with the French philosopher. They cite arguments explaining the incredible preservation of this nation for thousands of years, while all that is left of the surrounding nations that were its contemporaries is the dust of history and vague references to them in the ancient chronicles. It is not my task to get to the kernal of this argument. I base my case on personal experience and my

own observations and am obliged bitterly to admit that
Jean-Paul Sartre is tragically correct.

We as a nation are grouped, fused, lumped, or bundled
together by the scorn and hatred of those round about us.
While there was no anti-Semitism in the USSR, I felt, not
that I was a Jew, but as though just another citizen of that
country. The first outbursts of officially inspired anti-
Semitism drove us Jews, previously quite unconnected, into
each others' embrace. The common danger fished us out
from the crevices of assimilation and united us into a single
group, bearing, amid the hostility of those who surrounded
us, the mark of Cain. We were obliged to discover our
Jewishness and bore this cross because we had no option. A
sense of human dignity prompted us not to bow our heads
but to come to terms with our new role, to seek and to find
in it a source of moral support and even a cause for pride.

The reality that is Israel—that polyglot, multifaceted,
sometimes quite unmixable, ghastly cocktail called the
Jewish people, a people gathered in from dispersal to their
ancient homeland—this Israel also testifies to the French
philosopher's indisputable correctness. Ever-menacing external danger, the unequivocal threats of neighboring states
to wipe Israel off the map, to hurl her into the sea, unite this
highly unstable entity and hold it together.

I am deeply convinced that if the Arabs were to cease
their threats and conclude a peace with Israel this state
would not endure the concord and, under the pressure of
various mutually incompatible passions tearing it apart
from within, would burst asunder and shatter into the host
of fragments from which it was hastily assembled.

Mending a pot is a waste of time. The assembled pieces
don't knit together, and there are all sorts of sharp edges. In
Israel it is already difficult to conceal the blind enmity and
antagonism that poisons its atmosphere and pushes the various ethnic groups of Jews away from one another. In their
own home, their own state, people from various countries

who for centuries have been persecuted for their Jewish origins bristle with hostility toward one another, employing in their fratricidal internecine strife arguments and methods of their former persecutors.

"Any healthy, human seeds (with whatever charge of Zionism they may be furnished) when planted in this soil, poisoned by the venemous hatred of one Jew to another, will perish," says I. Yudin, a repatriate from the USSR, communicating his unexpected discovery through the pages of the newspaper *Tribuna*. In the same newspaper his former compatriot, Leonid Gelfand, states gloomily:

> The Jews in Israel don't get on at all well and seem ready to play all kinds of dirty tricks on one another.... The word "Jew" does not exist in Israel without some kind of epithet, e.g., a Rumanian Jew, a Moroccan Jew, a Russian Jew, a Georgian Jew, and so on. Sometimes it is dropped altogether, viz., "a Rumanian thief," "a Russian drunkard," and what is said about Turkish Jews is unprintable. On occasions I have heard the following appellation: *schwartze khaya*—"black animal."

Such are the ominous cracking sounds emitted by this brittle pot, stuck together with the spittle of Zionism. Such is the atmosphere of real ethnic tension between groups in Israel's Jewish population, although the authorities deny it until they are hoarse. Even when things went as far as the sadly notorious murder in Migdal-Ha'emek, the authorities' first reaction was to reject an ethnic motive for the crime.

This is what happened. In a small development town in Galilee, inhabited mainly by immigrants from Morocco and where in recent years repatriates from Russia have been settled, extremely antagonistic relations grew up between the two ethnic groups. One public holiday, when some Russian Jewish young people gathered for a party, a handful of "Moroccans" burst in on them, and in the ensuing fight a young man from Riga was killed. He had only recently arrived in the country and was on leave from the army, visiting his widowed mother in Migdal-Ha'emek. This murder caused such a flare-up of hostility that on the following day hundreds of people from both Russia and Morocco poured into the streets armed with whatever was at hand, and it looked so much that a bloody pogrom would ensue that police reinforcements had to be sent to the town to break up and keep apart the inflamed opposing factions.

Outbursts of hostility between ethnic groups shake Israel constantly. The older inhabitants have grown used to it; but such occurrences stop the newly-arrived immigrant in his tracks. Hardly had passions in Migdal-Ha'emek time to cool before Ashdod came close to large-scale bloodshed. The pretext was the groundless, insulting dismissal from the port of several dozen stevedores, immigrants from Georgia. These men and their families, who did not know the language and were unfamiliar with the customs and ways of the country, were left without a livelihood, and when they poked their noses into the doors of various institutions in search of support against arbitrary dismissal no one wanted to listen to them. They were laughed at, mocked, and sent off the premises.

The Georgian Jews went on a hunger strike outside the Ashdod council offices. Their wives and children joined them. Day after day beneath the blazing sun, these people, driven into a frenzy, continued their hunger strike in full view of the whole town. Did their anguish move Jewish hearts? Not in the least. The worthies who had come from other countries—Morocco, Iraq, Poland, Hungary—were also fellow Jews, but they had reached Israel from other crannies of the diaspora much earlier than their Caucasian kinsmen. They did not hide their disdain; they gloated at the sufferings of the Georgians and jeered them, not merely stopping at offensive and disgusting epithets that not every anti-Semite would dare to employ.

Then came the explosion. The turbulent Caucasian temperament and the feeling of ethnic isolation brought out on to the streets of Ashdod every single Georgian Jew. Barricades appeared. The smashing of glass in shop windows was heard. The ominous stench of a pogrom, this time Jews against Jews, hung over the town. The frightened shop-keepers hysterically demanded that troops be brought in and that the "filthy Caucasians" be pacified with gunfire. Even the newspapers got a taste for Georgian-Jewish blood and joined the racist chorus. A miracle in the person of the wily and resourceful minister of transport, Shimon Peres (now prime minister), prevented the most shameful carnage, and for a long time the newspapers, which could not forgive him for depriving them of the pleasure, frightened their readers by suggesting that now that the "Georgians" had sensed their impunity, there would be no stopping them cutting every throat in Israel.

The tiny state, choking in a circle of enmity, is divided into dozens of far-from-friendly communities on the basis of geographical origins. To this day, Israeli Jews settle in districts and towns on a community principle. Most of the "Bulgarians" live in Yafo, the "Germans" in Nahariya, the "Rumanians" in Hadera, the Bokhara Jews in Beth-Shemesh, the "Georgians" are concentrated in Ramla and Lod.

But the highest and most impassable racial watershed, which divides Israeli society into two fiercely warring camps, is the color of one's skin: on the one hand, the Jews from Europe and America; on the other, the Jews from Asia and Africa: the Ashkenazim and the Sephardim—the white Jews and the black Jews. Even the single Judaic religion could not build a bridge from one camp to the other. In Israel one striking fact, which officially confirms this racial watershed, is taken for granted: the existence in the country of two chief rabbis—the Ashkenazi Shlomo Goren and the Sephardi Avadi Yosef. Before the one God, the nation which created monotheism draws a shameful line using the yardstick of the Jews' eternal foes, the racists, to divide compatriots and coreligionists.

The Sephardim now account for more than half the population of Israel, and, being much more fecund than the
Ashkenazim, they will soon enjoy an overwhelming majority. Their prominence is especially noticeable in the army,
where already more than three-quarters of the total number
of Israeli soldiers is furnished by the prolific Sephardi
families. In the not too distant future, the only Ashkenazim
left in the armed forces will be those in positions of command and in the Air Force, where a high level of education
is required.

Apart from the color of their skins, an economic factor
deeply divides the Ashkenazi and Sephardi communities of
Israel, turning them into irreconcilable enemies. The vast
majority of wealthy Israelis and almost the whole middle
class are Ashkenazim, while in the poor districts like Hatikvah in Tel Aviv or Qatamon in Jerusalem only Sephardi
Jews live. According to official figures, of the 132,000
families eking out a beggarly existence, scarcely unfit for
human beings, the great majority are Sephardi.

How did this glaring social injustice arise in a new country, created within the memory of the present generation in
an almost empty area from several floods of mass immigration? Who is responsible for this?

Of the immigrants arriving in Israel between 1948 and
1972, 51.3 percent came from the African and Asian countries; the remainder came from Europe and America.
Twenty percent of the Jewish nation now live in Israel,
compared with 6 percent during the first years of the country's existence. Of those who settled in the country between
1948 and 1972 almost 60 percent were fit for work and 30
percent were under the age of fourteen. It is not without
interest that out of the overall total only 50 percent of those
who came from the Asian and African countries were em-
ployable as opposed to 72 percent of those who came from
Europe and America. The average age of an immigrant settling in Israel is around twenty-five.

There are very many reasons that have led to the unjust social demarcation of the Israeli Jewish population. Some are objective, and some must rest in their entirety on the conscience of Israeli socialists who, either alone or together with others of their ilk, have governed the country from time immemorial—since long before the creation of the state itself.

For the most part the pioneers of the Jewish colonization of Palestine were Ashkenazi Jews from the Russian Pale of Settlement and from the ghettos of Eastern Europe. Before 1948 and the foundation of the state of Israel, a single strong Ashkenazi community formed in Palestine, which naturally acquired all the key positions and created in the space of several generations the fairly sound economic basis for a tolerable existence and even prosperity.

Then an Aliyah of Jews who had survived the catastrophe of nazism came to Palestine. These too were Ashkenazim, hapless and destitute, but these hundreds of thousands of Polish, Czech, Hungarian, Rumanian, and Bulgarian Jews did not form a stratum of poverty in the Israeli population. Apart from their natural gumption and extremely high level of professional and educational training, their economic renascence was facilitated first and foremost by the celebrated German reparations—pensions for life and compensation for property stolen and destroyed by Hitler and his followers—which began to be paid to surviving Jews with Teutonic precision by the government that succeeded the Nazis. As a result, this group of Ashkenazi Jews also quickly got on its feet, opened shops, workshops, even factories, and became part of the petty and middle bourgeoisie. They had nice apartments, sometimes even villas, and they owned their own cars, something which in the 1950s became the yardstick of economic prosperity.

Soon after the founding of the state, the Sephardi branch of the Jewish nation also came flooding back into the land of their ancestors. During the years of dispersal, they had lived in the Islamic lands of the Middle East, North Africa, and

Asia. One hundred twenty-five thousand fugitives came from Iraq, thirty-five thousand from Turkey, thirty-two thousand from Libya (from a total Jewish population of thirty-five thousand), thirty-five thousand from French North Africa. During the famous "Operation Flying Carpet," more than forty thousand Yemenite Jews, knowing nothing of European civilization and in terms of development stranded in the period of the fall of the Second Temple, were transported to Israel by air from the torrid deserts of the Yemen.

The Sephardi Jews, the so-called "blacks," from the very first assumed the status of hapless paupers in comparison with their firmly established Ashkenazi brothers in the historical homeland they had at last inherited. They arrived from semifeudal, underdeveloped countries emerging from colonial status, and they bore all the birthmarks of the frightful backwardness of those countries: mass illiteracy, large families, lack of professional training and productive skills, chronic illnesses, resignation to a lack of rights, and, flowing from these things, sapped initiative and creativity.

This wave of immigrants was a most serious test for Israel as a state and for the Zionist socialists as a ruling clique, and they failed resoundingly, showing the first and ominous signs of their social and political bankruptcy.

The large Sephardi families were herded into temporary dwellings that soon became permanent, settlements of hastily built huts—ma'barot—and there, to this day, districts of dire and terrible poverty have flourished—hotbeds of insanitation, drug taking, crime, and prostitution. In wretched little rooms where once two people lived, now three times as many members of these rapidly growing, fecund families crowd together. Twenty-five thousand youths neither attend school nor have a job. They loaf about the prosperous Ashkenazi districts with nothing to do but swell the ranks of gangs of petty thieves and robbers. Thirty-thousand young girls from those same districts are the crudely tarted-up, scruffy prostitutes who "adorn" the pavements of

Israeli towns. Take a look into the cells of the large number of prisons Israel has inherited from the former administration of the British mandate and you will discover that most of the Jews who view the world through prison bars are those same Sephardim.

The Israeli government has thoughtlessly and ruthlessly condemned this group of Jews to poverty and a wretched, vegetating existence because, for reasons of "socialist principle," it declined categorically to distribute equitably the generous capital investment—offered as an incentive to the economy by Jewish businessmen from all over the world—create sufficient jobs, and teach its not-quite-white brethren trades or productive professions. The Jews from Asia and Africa were herded into new ghettos, condemned to demoralizing inactivity, and, finally, corrupted by wretched, humiliating handouts, which reduced these people to the situation of beggars and members of a grey proletarian mass.

The small, economically prosperous Ashkenazi family has its offspring taught in the best schools and then, of course, sends them to university without counting the cost. It will even send them abroad. These are the families that supplement Israel's reserves of doctors, lawyers, engineers, and teachers. Their children inherit shops and factories or cosy, well-paid jobs in government service. Even in the less spectacularly successful families, the children are equipped with family professions and the inherited incentive to work.

In the Sephardi families, however, the younger generation grows up in completely different conditions and receives a different heritage. Children struggle through school for only a few years and then drop out, preferring the streets with all their dubious attractions. They do this with the tacit consent of their illiterate, backward parents and the indifferent neutrality of the Israeli public. It is rare for one of these children to reach the university and only a handful breaks through into high society, which is extremely disinclined to admit "coloreds."

One need only recall the scandalous elections of 1973. The office of president in Israel is symbolic. He is a purely decorative figure, having no influence on the life of the country, even less than does the monarch in England. Not even this token position of a figurehead could be yielded to the Sephardim. Since its conception Israel has been governed by Ashkenazim, who use various permitted and unpermitted tricks to manipulate at elections the votes of the menacingly growing Sephardi majority. And yet you might think that God himself had ordained that the Sephardim should be offered the powerless presidential throne to still their passions and assuage, albeit temporarily, with this token, which incurred no obligations, the awakening interest in politics among the "colored" community. At first it looked as if this was what would happen. The ruling coalition nominated two candidates, a "white," Ephraim Katzir, and a "black," Itzhak Navon. The gratified Sephardim demonstrated noisily in support of their candidate and anticipated triumph. Many Ashkenazim too regarded the election of Itzhak Navon as just. Antagonism, however, had bitten so deeply into Israeli society, and hostility toward the "coloreds" was so deeply rooted among the ruling elite that the wise statesmen of the socialist leadership sounded the retreat. To the total shock of the Sephardi community and the embarrassed perplexity of the rest of Israel, Ephraim Katzir became president of the Jewish state.

An abyss, foul and frightening, cuts into two unequal parts the fragile body of Israel, which has not had time to grow to strength and maturity. The communities confront each other with hackles raised. The abyss shows no signs of closing, but yawns wider every year, begetting monstrous offspring damaging to the state. The "Black Panther" movement, borrowed from the American blacks, enjoyed ardent support among young Sephardim. It finds an outlet, however, in demonstrations which are loutish, not constructive, redolent of riots and permeated with intense and unreasoning spite toward their Ashkenazi "brothers."

I remember an occurrence that happened soon after our arrival in Israel. We recent repatriates were living temporarily in the Ulpan village of Mevasseret Zion, close to Jerusalem. Three dark-skinned young fellows, Sephardi Jews, introducing themselves as "Black Panthers," dropped into our club to talk to us. We, the temporary inhabitants of the village, Ashkenazi repatriates from Europe and America, went to the club, quite interested and anticipating a closer acquaintance with indigenous Israelis, whose fellow citizens we were so reverently becoming.

It was then, in the club, that I and many of my friends, who had only recently set foot in the "Holy Land" of Israel, got our first whiff of the nauseating stench of Jewish internecine strife. These three semiliterate and totally uncouth "Black Panthers" told us—we who had not yet recovered from the suffering and insults inflicted upon us by anti-Semites in the countries where we had formerly lived— with provocative, loutish impunity that if we went to live in the apartments that Sokhnut [the Ministry of Immigrant Absorption] had offered us (and which we had bought with our own money), if we did not give them up free of charge to the Sephardi Jews, then they would cut all our children's throats and thus redress the balance of justice.

I would not have believed, even from my closest friend, an account of the "discussion" I witnessed in the Ulpan club at Mevasseret Zion. Heaping threats on our heads, the "Black Panthers" departed from the club in satisfaction and left us alone with our somber thoughts.

Another incident I witnessed throws further light on this situation. It took place in the army during the Yom Kippur War. Two-thirds of our company were Sephardim; about ten of us were immigrants from Russia, most of whom had received a higher education. On one occasion, the company commander sent for us "Russian" soldiers and told us that a "Moroccan," i.e., a Jew from Morocco, had got completely "stoned" on drugs and was, therefore, a danger to himself and to those around him. He was almost out of his mind; he needed to be disarmed and arrested, for, according to the captain's information, he had a knife in his possession.

We did not even pause to wonder why the captain had chosen us for this "mission" and not Sephardi Jews, of whom there were plenty in the company. The Sephardim would simply not have obeyed the Ashkenazi officer's order, directed against a fellow Sephardi, even if he had been a criminal meriting stern punishment under martial law. Three of us executed the order, disarmed the addict, and quelled his resistance. Naturally, in so doing, we ruffled his hair a little. The other Moroccans then surrounded us threateningly while the white Jews in the company took our side, so the company was sharply divided into two groups seething with reciprocal hostility, and we almost had a vicious bloodbath on our hands. We had not sensed the danger and allowed our captain to thrust us into the abyss of racial hatred between Jews, which even at a time of mortal danger like the Yom Kippur War had not closed up.

It is hard to believe, but "mixed" marriages between Jews of the two communities in Israel are surprisingly rare. They amount to only 12 percent of all marriages. While in the U.S.A. almost 40 percent of Jews marry non-Jews.

The diverse and multicolored kaleidoscope of Israel's Jews culminates in the completely black Falashas—also Jews, who come from Ethiopia. These men and women from equatorial Africa until recently wore loin cloths instead of clothes and lived the life of an isolated tribe in the jungle, differing from their Negro neighbors in no essential way, save for their fervent confession of Judaism and the fact that like Jews the whole world over they concluded each prayer with the traditional "Next year in Jerusalem."

Now their dream had come true, and they had landed in the fiery furnace of Jewish ethnic hostility, the color of their skins and their Negroid features acting like oil on the long and fiercely burning flames.

At least the Falashas are considered Jews. The arrival in Israel from America of the first group of Black Israelites, who belong to a Judaistic sect but are otherwise unconnected with the Jews, provoked an open scandal. These "black brothers" settled in Dimona in the south of the country as Jewish repatriates, proclaiming that they and only they were the real Jews and that all the rest of the inhabitants of the country were false descendents of Abraham. They stated that they would alter the land of Israel to suit their own tastes. They also issued a warning: that the Negroes of America had received a "voice from heaven" bequeathing to them this land flowing with milk and honey and were preparing to emigrate to Israel en masse.

A joint letter to the newspaper *Tribuna* with the expressive title, "You Sow the Wind...," signed by E. Friedman, S. Finsel, N. Friedman, T. Fischer, and others, evidences the horror occasioned by this news.

We have come from a country where the classics of Marxism and Leninism were invoked to convince us that there was no such thing as a Jewish nation. Did we really need to fight our way over all manner of obstacles to our native land in order to hear from a black "prophet of Israel" one and the same thing?

We are confronted by the fact that this horde will emigrate to Israel, insofar as their leader, Ben-Ami Carter, has already informed us that most Negroes in the U.S. are "Israelites." If today we admit to our house some hundreds of Negro families, on what basis can we tomorrow refuse entry to the remaining fifteen million?... Why is it that Minister Pinhas Sapir is disturbed because in twenty-five years time to every fifty-five Jews in Israel there will be forty-five Arabs? He closes his eyes to the fact that tomorrow we shall have a situation where for every million Jews there will be six or seven million "descendents of Yehuda" or "Israelites," to put it plainly, blacks; and Golda Meir, when she gets up in the morning, need have no doubt that for every Jewish child delivered during the preceding night a thousand picanninies have been born.

Today fifty families of French repatriates have left Dimona. Tomorrow not one family of the western Aliyah will come here when they know about our "charming neighbors.". . .

We are only one step away from the time when, after the Negro "Israelites" and the Ethiopian Falasha Jews, which have been hastily appended to the list of Jewish "close relatives," we shall have African tribes of "Yehudahites" aspiring to come here, Eskimo-"Levites" or a motley selection of hippie-"Cohens." One can easily imagine the scene at Lod airport when a half-naked cannibal family applies for residence rights on the grounds that their father ate a Jew the previous week and therefore has Jewish blood in his veins.

The ominous signs of racial conflict are vividly portrayed by the newspaper *Tribuna* in an article called "Dynamite in Dimona."

The city fathers of Dimona meet everyone who, for one reason or another, comes to the town. They tell them about the black Yehudas and conclude with the warning: "This is dynamite that sooner or later will explode." The mayor of Dimona, Itzhak Peretz, and his deputy, Israel Navon, sum up as follows: "From the point of view of urban development and the solution of social problems, this is problem number one.". . .

The head of the Negro "Israelite" community, Ben-Ami Carter, has great power over his flock. There was a time when he used to invite foreign journalists to press conferences and inform them that Israel was a racist state that practiced discrimination. Quite recently he invited a large group of people to a talk, which took place in the apartment of one of the "Israelites" in Shkhunat Ganitsakhon. Before the talk began, he took off his everyday clothes and put on his best—a green robe, a black scarf, and a knitted green cap. "We are the black Israelites," he declared. "Virtue is our creed, and we have in our hearts love for every man. Most blacks in the U.S. are Israelites. We have come here at our heart's bidding to build a realm of justice. This is our native land, and here justice must hold sway. We have lived in slavery in the U.S. for more than four hundred years. Our forefathers were taken by force from the golden shores of Africa, and since then our slave masters have done all that they could to beat our culture out of us.

But from grandfather to father, from father to son, from lip to lip, the memory of our past, the memory that we are Israelites, has been transmitted. You know that we have come here in order to sweep out all the filth from this land. We have returned to our native country to tell people how they should live. This land is not like other lands. It is the Holy Land. God has commanded that this land should be ours, and you must understand this. Many here have no faith in God at all. Tel Aviv is like New York. The sacred river Jordan is polluted. We shall remove all industrial sites from its banks. I am here in order to herald a new epoch for you and show you a new way. We are not simply Jews; we are Israelites. Jews are just the descendents of Judah. The Jews are not a nation. There is only God, the Lord, Abraham, Isaac, and Israel."

One further rift divides the Israeli nation yet more deeply, sending fresh cracks across the surface of the hastily mended pot called the Jewish state. This is not the color of one's skin, not the ethnic problem, which alone is sufficient to destroy the progeny of the fathers of Zionism. I am thinking now of the hostility and the confrontation between the religious minority and the atheist majority, of the clashes leading to protracted government crises and to serious, sometimes incurable, spiritual injuries, inflicted upon people who sincerely believe in the state of Israel and wish to become its citizens.

Religious circles, for all their small numbers, wield great strength and, to a significant degree, regulate the flow of charity money from abroad. Consequently, Israel's socialist rulers, although atheists, retreat before them step by step, thereby still further intensifying the potentially explosive atmosphere inside the country.

Regardless of their attitude to religion, citizens of Israel are deprived on Saturday, the only nonworking day, of the opportunity of using public transport, and those who do not have their own car—usually the poorest section of the population—are obliged, willy-nilly, to observe the religious commandment and spend that day at home.

An atheist, the foe of any religion, cannot contract a civil marriage but is forced to act against his conscience and seek the blessing of a rabbi. Neither can he be buried in his own country without the intrusion of a member of the clergy.

The concessions the government has made to the rabbinate and the kowtowing it indulges in have reached such proportions that in Jerusalem, in the ancient quarter of Mea Shearim, a fanatical religious sect, the *Neturei Karta* [guardians of the city], demonstratively refuses to recognize the state of Israel and, consequently, its laws. These orthodox Jews do not pay taxes, do not serve in the army, and periodically hold rather wild demonstrations—in short, they violate the basic principles of law and order. The government puts up with this, pretending not to notice what is happening.

Religious fanatics, not only from this sect but ordinary adherents of orthodox Judaism, sensing their impunity, take more and more liberties. They can get away with anything, even instances of common or garden-variety gangsterism.

It is widely known that believers are opposed to pornography. Most nonbelievers, too, are not exactly ecstatic about the stifling, filthy ooze that creeps from the windows of the pornographic book shops. They also protest and endeavor to combat the delusion of the age. Such a combat, however, has its standards and rules. Two students of a yeshiva [a religious seminary] were so inflamed with wrath against the sway of pornography that they broke into a shop called Eros one night with cans of kerosene and set fire to it. The ensuing blaze almost destroyed whole blocks of houses in Tel Aviv, and only the self-sacrificial courage of some "atheist" firemen kept the roofs over the heads of hundreds of people.

The young arsonists with "peot" fell into the hands of the police and were deservedly put behind bars. That, however, was not the issue! The religious leaders, instead of censuring the unseemly activities of their erring sheep, raised their voices in their defense and the authorities got cold feet. A religious festival was approaching, and the president of the country, Zalman Shazar, in order to earn forgiveness from the rabbinate and mollify its anger, took an unprecedented step and demonstratively visited both the criminals in their cell and celebrated the festival with them rather than with the country as a whole.

The celebrated discussion about *who is a Jew* has already rocked the country for many years, perplexing sensible people.

It is like a dormant illness that each time erupts with fresh virulence. "More governmental crises have been caused by the question 'Who is a Jew?' than by any other issue," writes Ruth Bonam in the newspaper *Nasha Strana*.

Sometimes rapprochement between believers and nonbelievers begins to seem possible,... but there are also periods of uncompromising politicization of religion, and then one wants to take up arms for the fundamental right denied to our citizens by the religious community—the right to have a family....

Not everyone has been lucky enough to be born of a Jewish mother, and, therefore, not everyone "fits" the Halacha's definition of a member of the Jewish nation.... Anger is of no avail. On the contrary, it exacerbates the struggle between the two camps, the struggle which Ben-Gurion feared more than he feared the Arabs, the Russians, and economic collapse all rolled into one.

A. Kleiner, an immigrant from the USSR, expresses his amazement in the pages of the same newspaper:

When the Soviet newspapers published the news that the racist law "Who is a Jew?" had been passed in Israel, I, like the vast majority of Jews in the USSR, regarded this report as just another libel on the Jewish state. When I got here, I discovered that this law really existed. What are you doing? Surely you must realize that in the main Jewish communities of the world, in the USSR and the U.S., there are hundreds of thousands of mixed families who are doomed to assimilation? Surely it is our duty to save these families from assimilation and return them to the Jewish nation? Surely you can see that you have blocked their way to Israel with this law; you are cutting off the Aliyah and pushing these families into assimilation? Where are your Jewish heads and your Jewish intellects? Do you have any love for the Jewish nation? Do you care about its continued safe existence?

Bodeful black humor emanates from the *Nasha Strana* article "With God's help" by G. Tseplikovich:

If the Messiah were suddenly to come today and the resurrection of the dead were to take place, it might well be that a considerable number of those Jews who died in the concentration camps and ghettos would turn out to be illegally resurrected and not entitled to a wretched Teudat Ole [an immigrant's certificate in Israel]. Then, their second coming to the next world would be accompanied by further torments: they could not be buried in a Jewish cemetery or have the kaddish, the prayer for the repose of the dead, read over them. The question of whether it would be necessary to annul the service of prayer already conducted on their behalf on days of remembrance, would long be discussed in the Israeli chief rabbinate, and its decision would depend entirely on the authoritative opinion of Rabbi Soloveichik of Boston.

Such were the sadly amusing thoughts which went through my head during the throes of our government giving birth to this law.

Even the pope cannot dream of such great might as that of our rabbinate. And if he could he would not use it, as he would not wish to forego the title of God's representative for all Catholics and be transformed into the representative of a single political party, as has happened with us.

Many Russian women and their Jewish husbands brought up their children consciously to regard Israel as their homeland. These women come to our country proud on their children's behalf. The children themselves, however, who have lived in fear and sometimes even gone to prison for their "seditious" convictions, are not Jews, for only their father is a Jew and their mother did not change her religion.

One can only change what exists. What if these mothers had no religion? What if they did not believe in any kind of God?

Only a tiny ruse can save the situation. In order to become members of our family, these women, God protect them, must not tell the truth. They must begin with a lie. They must say that they have thought through the tenets of the Jewish religion and come to the conclusion that this religion is the best in the world. Consequently, they wish to renounce their own (which they haven't got!) and accept instead (instead of what?) the very best.

From the commercial standpoint it is a profitable maneuver. There is no other way. The Halacha says that a Jew must be born of a Jewish mother; the father does not count.

Let us take a short excursion into history. Whence did this truth emerge? After all, our Torah states that heredity is transmitted by the line of the father; be it priestly rank ("Cohen") or the matter of the inheritance of property. Even the Messiah had to be born of the house of David, i.e., of his father's, not his mother's, line. The fact of the matter is, however, that two thousand years ago, when the Romans attacked our territory, we had then as we have now our own state and priests too, but not our rabbinate.

The sages of that time, discerning that in the society of Roman warriors our women started to get pregnant (whether this was the result of rape or whether it came about by mutual consent is unimportant in this particular case), were afraid that the existing law of the Torah might fragment our nation, and in order to preserve the nation they embarked upon a compromise (and therein is their sanctity). They said that a child born of a Jewish mother was a Jew, but they did not say that a child born of a Jewish father was not a Jew. . . .

I would not like my thoughts to be interpreted as an attack on religion. I want to come to the defense of all that we have that is holy. I want us to stop trying to deceive God, who is my God too. I don't want my God dragged into political intrigues. I don't want my God to become the God of a single political party.

The domination of religion in a country where most of the population are atheists deforms our existence, destroys lives, and leads to tragedy. N. Gutin recounted in the newspaper *Tribuna* the sad story of the love of an Israeli girl and a young Swiss Christian, who wished for his fiancée's sake to become an Israeli citizen and accept Judaism but who was brought by the rabbis to attempted suicide:

"It turns out that we live in a country whose laws are capable of putting a civilized man in an impasse. The motives which direct the acts of our officials are incomprehensible to a normal man. The workings of our institutions and departments run contrary to elementary human logic.

Can it be, that we who have created and who endure all this are normal civilized people?

The pot, in which the Zionist fathers are concocting a single nation from the dozens of ethnic groups of diaspora Jews, boils and bubbles. The steam builds up beneath the clamped-down lid, the pressure increases, pushing menacingly against the flimsy walls, no more than a multitude of shards of an ancient vessel, smashed two thousand years ago by the Roman legionnaires, which have been stuck together.

chapter six

ISRAEL AND THE DEATH OF THE RUSSIAN JEW

The resolution of the General Assembly of the United Nations on the partition of Palestine and the creation of the state of Israel struck a blow against one of the largest Jewish communities in the world—the Russian Jewish community. It was a painful blow, one that knocked it off its feet and did not allow it to get up again. The disintegration of that most colorful collection of three million Jews, the last guardians of a national culture and national traditions, was catastrophically hastened. This disintegration was irreversible, excruciating, and bloody.

In my view, there were two reasons that led to the directing of this blow at the Russian Jews.

The Soviet Union, conducting the imperialist policy inherited from the designs of the former czarist regime, crudely forced her way into the Middle East, sniffing out bases and strong points anywhere it could find a foothold, in order to commence full-scale expansion into this alluring area of the planet's surface. Awakening from lethargy, the

Arab nations raised the green banner of Islam and avoided godless communism like the plague. Consequently, the Soviet Union put its money initially not on the Arabs but on the Jews, and, to the pique of Great Britain, actively supported the idea of creating a state of Israel. At the time of the first Arab-Israeli war, Jewish military formations were armed from Soviet arsenals, and in all the international forums the USSR zealously defended Israel's right to exist.

The Soviets, however, did not manage to achieve their main aim of establishing a foothold in the Middle East. Israel sensibly declined to take the fatal step in her dangerous love affair with the USSR, which would definitely have culminated in occupation and all the consequences flooding therefrom, and would, on no account, agree to make bases available to the Soviet Union. On the contrary, she sought protection from the West. The "ingratitude" of the tiny Israeli David provoked the wrath of the Moscow Goliath, who unleased an explosion of anti-Zionism in the guise of unmitigated anti-Semitism upon Soviet Jews.

The second reason behind the Kremlin's mass attack on the Soviet Jewish population—an attack that commenced soon after the creation of the Israeli state—was the authorities' fully justified apprehension that Israel would evoke a renaissance of Jewish national consciousness to the detriment of Soviet patriotism, and, moreover, that it would awaken among Soviet Jews the age-old yearning to emigrate to the land of their forefathers. In a country hermetically sealed off from the outside world by the Iron Curtain, this was impermissible sacrilege. The authorities saw an appreciable danger to themselves in the awakening of such feelings: they could serve as an example that would infect the other small nationalities, inhabiting the USSR in profusion, and shake perceptibly the foundations of the multinational empire. Time has shown them not to have been altogether wrong in their presentiments. This is why, in answer to the formation of the state of Israel, a signal was given in the Soviet Union to institute official, government-inspired anti-Semitism, which descended on the heads of the unsuspecting Jews like a bolt out of the blue.

This gloomy period of stunning hypocrisy spanned the youth of my own generation, which had been reared in the principles of internationalism and was altogether alien to the ideas of racism and enmity between nations. The upshot was that we Jews in the Soviet Union suffered the most incredible losses in the struggle which grew up around the state of Israel. If in the ancient lands of Judah the victims were counted in hundreds, then with us, far from Palestine amid the snows of icy Russia, thousands and tens of thousands perished. Jews were exiled to Siberia and killed not only for their Zionism or sympathies with Israel but simply because they had been unlucky enough to be born Jews and to land in the jaws of the rampaging Moloch of Russian anti-Semitism.

This bloody wave, which has rolled on, its force unabated, from that time to the present day, burst over the backs of my generation with particular pain and devastation. It will only be exhausted when the last Russian Jew has perished. The Jewish Question can be resolved either according to the Hitlerian model or through complete and total assimilation or perhaps by a combination of these two equally foul methods.

Recounting this drama as its witness and victim, I shall make little use of statistics, figures, or newspaper articles. It is my view that personal experience and observation serve better to illuminate this somber picture and can capture, as in the crystalline prism of a drop of water, the sufferings of millions. Their sufferings are not now at an end but continue as they gaze into the future with agony and dread.

And what a good life we had before all this happened! How cloudless the sky of our childhood! Happily ignorant of who we were and of the weighty sins that had lain upon our race since long before we were born, we explored the world about us under the Russian sun, which smiled down both on us and on the graves of our forefathers in the Jewish cemeteries, as old as the world itself.

I clearly remember prewar days in Russia. One of the most attractive features of Soviet power was the nationalities policy conducted throughout the gigantic territory of the former czarist empire, whose population spoke more than a hundred different languages. Russian great-power chauvinism, which had roots centuries old, was boldly and, at times, quite cruelly eradicated. The spirit of enmity between nationalities was being exorcised, and a feeling of friendship between the representatives of various peoples, of equality and brotherhood, was persistently nurtured, particularly among the younger, rising generation.

In the remotest corners of the land, the cultures of tiny national groups were reborn, and where before there had been no written language one was created.

It is, after all, a known fact that there was an article in the Soviet criminal code that levied a sentence for up to two years for insulting a man's national dignity. And this article was most rigorously applied against any person who dared to lay hands on the holy of holies—friendship between nations.

The results of this policy were most amazing. I was a pupil in a Russian school. My classmates included Jews, Russians, Byelorussians, Ukrainians, Tatars, and right up to the outbreak of the war none of us was aware of any distinctions between us. We felt that we were citizens of the same country, to which we were proud to belong, and never even thought about our national origin. Each knew his native language, but Russian united us and was gradually becoming our own language.

Some of us had longer noses and some of us had shorter ones. There were some with larger cheekbones and others with smaller ones. Some had dark hair, while others stood out because of the flaxen color of theirs. None of these things, however, were regarded as ethnic or national characteristics but as the personal, individual traits of a particular person.

It is true that even then, before the war, all the Jewish schools had been closed. But this passed unnoticed. The Jews themselves were drawn toward the Russian language, behind which loomed the majestic edifice of Russian culture. The younger generation quickly became assimilated, and no one saw anything at all sinister in that.

After all, we still had a Yiddish literature with excellent poets and prose writers, theatres, led by the Moscow State Yiddish Art Theatre, dominated in its turn by the gigantic figure of Solomon Mikhoels. Jewish songs were performed on the radio, and there were even special broadcasts in Yiddish. The main thing was, we all sincerely believed, that the bright future of communism was being built, after which time national problems would wither away and the whole world would become a single nation, united and full of love.

A very accurate indicator of the disappearance of national distinctions and the triumph of the idea of friendship between nations is the mixed marriage. Before the war these marriages were taken as a matter of course. No one viewed them askance. They were, on the contrary, welcomed and encouraged. They were something fashionable and a reflection of the spirit of the age. As a result of this, today in Russia there live millions of people, by now already grown men and women with families of their own, whose mother or father was Jewish. It is true that in their passports they are registered as Russians, but all the misfortunes now descending on the Jews of the USSR concern them deeply and have put them into an agonizing moral dilemma. Whose side are they to take? Should they join the victims and share the unenviable fate of their Jewish cousins, or should they skulk behind their Russian passports, deny their origins, and break all ties between themselves and their Jewish kin?

Now, after so many years have passed, I no doubt tend to idealize the prewar period in Russia as an amazing time of the most harmonious relationships between representatives of various nations. Of this otherwise ghastly period, with its mass executions, prisons and concentration camps full to overflowing, ubiquitous informers, and spirit of treachery and betrayel, one bright recollection has remained in my mind: complete national equality, the precious feeling of brotherhood in both joy and adversity.

Already by the end of the Second World War, the first sinister cracks had appeared in the multinational edifice that is the USSR. In accusing whole nations of betraying the interests of the state during the period of German occupation, Stalin committed one of his most monstrous crimes: he deported from their traditional homelands to Siberia and slow extermination every Crimean Tatar, Kalmyk, Chechen-Ingush, as well as every Greek and Bulgarian who lived on Soviet territory.

A man was declared a criminal and set outside the law, regardless of his behavior or individual merits, simply on the basis of his nationality. This was patent genocide; moreover, it was genocide on a large scale, carried out with extreme cruelty and without any right of appeal.

Officially, as before, friendship between nations was sung as the unshakable basis of the Communist party's policy. In fact, however, prison trains were bearing these wretched people to the back of beyond, to sickness and death in the freezing cold of Siberia and the torrid heat of the Kazakstan deserts.

But this was only the beginning. Soon afterwards, at a triumphant celebration of the day of victory over Germany in 1945, Stalin raised a toast to the health of the great Russian nation, unequivocally singling it out from the company of nations of the USSR. The signal for a shameless campaign of great-power chauvinism had been given. The bacchanalia began. It was crude and in bad taste and aimed at the basest human emotions. In a country that was the home of more than a hundred nations, the Russian people were extolled as the best, the most intelligent, and the most industrious. And what about the others? A coy silence was maintained on that subject. And if anyone dared to speak, he was forthwith accused of bourgeois nationalism and punished as a very dangerous criminal.

The Russian land, Russian daring, Russian beauty. These were the only things about which songs and poems were written, and the Ukrainians and Armenians, Tatars and Uzbeks, Lithuanians and Estonians were forced to sing them and declaim them. This was all the radio noised abroad and the only message that was screamed from the newspaper headlines—in Ukrainian, Armenian, Uzbek, and the other languages of the USSR.

This infatuation with all things Russian went to bizarre and even absurd lengths. The newspapers, the radio, lecturers on their platforms, without batting an eyelid, vied with one another in proving the superiority of Russian science over everybody else's. It was no longer Marconi who had invented the radio, but Popov; not Edison who had invented the electric light bulb, but Yablochkov; not Stephenson who had invented the steam engine, but Polzunov. Every discovery in the world was ascribed to the Russians alone, and floods of such latter-day discoveries poured down on the immature minds of the young and the dazed and discouraged members of the older generation.

Sometimes the word *Soviet* was coyly substituted for the word *Russian*. And then everything Soviet became the best, the most advanced, the most progressive. And the people, that same Soviet people, that were best of all, responded with bitter irony, with such catch phrases as these:

The Soviet midget is the tallest in the world.
Soviet paralysis is the most progressive.

But when one particular nation is declared to be the best of all, there is naturally the need for its antithesis, the worst nation of all, that scapegoat who can be blamed for all woes and anathematized as the source of all ills. The victim was not hard to find.

The Jews.

There were 3 million of them. By a miracle they had survived the bloody slaughter perpetrated by the Nazis during their wartime occupation of the western regions of the USSR, the former Pale of Settlement. These 3 million people were loyal to the Soviet regime; indeed, they were in no small measure to blame for its coming into being and becoming firmly established.

The sledge hammer of hatred fell upon three million heads—for the failures of Soviet policy in the Middle East; for being sympathetic toward Israel (in fact, merely for intimating the possibility of future sympathy); for a letter sent from Israel or even from anywhere abroad.

The nation was found on which was heaped the blame for all the tribulations of the Russians and, at the same time, those of the Ukrainians, the Tatars, and the Uzbeks.

With the knowledge and at the instigation of the Central Committee of the Communist Party, with the assistance of press, radio, and administrative measures, there began an official, unbridled persecution of the Jews. Like everything in Russia, it knew no restraint. Thus began the agony of a whole nation, millions of people, guilty of nothing more than being unlucky enough to be born Jewish.

It was forgotten that the Russian Revolution, which had brought the Communists to power, had had a significant number of Jews among its leaders. No one remembered any longer that it had been the Jews more than any other nationality of the czarist empire who, through their wholehearted belief in the ideas of universal equality and brotherhood, had given their lives in the Civil War, raved in delirium caused by typhus, gone without food until their bellies were swollen, and all for the sake of the triumph of communism.

In Minsk, where I was studying at the university at that time, there stood in Gorky Park a simple unpretentious memorial to the heroes of the Civil War. It was a fairly low, wooden pyramid crowned by a metal, five-pointed star. It was erected on the common grave of four high-ranking Red Army officers who had fallen during the fighting with Pilsudski's Polish forces in 1920. Two division commanders and two division commissars: all four names on the grave were Jewish.

The memorial stood for more than twenty-five years. By a miracle it survived even the German occupation of the town. After the war, however, when the persecution of the Jews began, the memorial was unobtrusively removed and the grave mound leveled. The names of these heroes were committed to final oblivion.

In the town where I was born there was a street quite near ours called Hirsch Lekert Street. When I was still a child, I knew, as did all my contemporaries, that this street had been named in honor of a Communist revolutionary who had been foully murdered during the Civil War. When the Nazis occupied the town, they tore down from the houses the signs which mentioned Lekert's name and called the street by its pre-Revolution name, Semyonovskaya. After the Nazis were driven out, the street was naturally renamed once again, but the name of Hirsch Lekert was not restored to the signs. Lekert was a Jew. And the street, on which, incidentally, Jews for the most part lived, was renamed Moscow Street.

Even names like Uritsky and Volodarsky, major revolutionary leaders who happened to be of Jewish descent, were removed from squares, factories, and works. Yet these were men who had long been dead and had once been buried with full honors.

Every mention of Jewish heroism during the years of the Second World War was expunged, and all kinds of rumors and fantasies were circulated concerning Jewish cowardice and treachery—Jews deserting, trying to avoid mobiliza-

tion, and sitting out the war deep in the home front, shel-
tered behind the broad back of that honest genuine patriot,
the Russian soldier.

Never a word was said about the tens and hundreds of
thousands of Jewish young men and women who had not
waited to be called up but had volunteered for active service
because that was what their hearts had told them to do. Not
a word was said about the two hundred-fifty thousand officers and men who did not come back from the war to their
Jewish families but were left behind in anonymous mass
graves on the Volga and the Dnieper, the Danube and the
Vistula, the Oder and the Spree. In percentage terms, the
war cost the Jewish population more dearly than any other
nation of the USSR. And this is setting aside the more than 1
million women, old men, and children who were destroyed
by the enemy in the territories he occupied.

No one in the USSR today knows about the heroic deeds
done by Jews during the war. A studied silence is preserved
about the fact that ninety-three Jews were awarded the
highest Soviet military honor. Proportionally, there are
more Jewish *Heroes of the Soviet Union* than from any other
ethnic group in the USSR, including the Russians.

Everything possible was done to ensure that the memory
of this should disappear. The propaganda machine had but
one end in view: to discredit the Jews, to blacken their
name, to present them to the Soviet population as monsters,
on whose conscience were all the sufferings and woes both
of the Russian people and of the country's other
nationalities.

The existence of the state of Israel and the concomitant
possibility of Jewish solidarity precipitated the fight against
"cosmopolitanism" and the worshipping of the West. Jews
were accused of every known sin, and monstrous antipatriotic actions were laid at their door. The pages of the newspapers were littered with Jewish surnames. If a Russian sur-

name was mentioned, then the first name and patronymic was at once supplied, from which the reader could instantly conclude that the accused was no other than a Jew.

After the press treatment, after the stormy meetings and gatherings where anti-Semitic hysteria was artificially whipped up to fever pitch, came the administrative measures. Jews were demoted and dismissed. Hundreds and thousands of people—scientists, writers, artists, high-ranking officers—were sent to the concentration camps of Siberia without either investigation or trial. Jewish newspapers and theatres were closed.

Solomon Mikhoels's tragic death heralded the beginning of the open campaign of anti-Semitism in the USSR. Mikhoels was such a famous figure and his name was so well known beyond the confines of Russia that the Soviet state security agencies dared not arrest him. Instead, it preferred some kind of charge against him to destroy him in the way in which it had disposed of thousands of other people.

Solomon Mikhailevich Mikhoels was a Yiddish actor and director of genius, who in the talent-rich Soviet Union was the equal of Stanislavsky and Nemirovich-Danchenko. There wasn't a single educated man in Russia who had not heard of Mikhoels. His fully deserved fame was crowned by his being awarded the distinguished title of *People's Artist of the USSR*. He had a chest full of medals and decorations. He was a recipient of the Stalin Prize. His name was one of the constellation of names that the Soviet government flaunted in the international arena to demonstrate the achievements of its nationalities policy. He had created the Moscow State Yiddish Art Theatre and until the end of his life (and the end of the theatre coincided with Mikhoel's own death) was its head. The auditorium was always full to overflowing whenever the great artist appeared. The non-Jew, the Russian spectator who did not even know Yiddish, delighted in the genius and mastery of his acting.

The brightest and most colorful personality in Russian Jewry, he was used by the government when it suited its

interests as a bait or a screen in matters of special importance to the state. During the Second World War, he headed a
delegation of Soviet Jews to the United States of America,
and the fervent, impassioned speeches he made there played
no small part in increasing the flood of material assistance
to the Soviet Union. Mikhoels did a great deal; to build up
the USSR's prestige abroad. He was elected president of the
Jewish Anti-Fascist Committee of the USSR. He participated
in various international organizations, uniting the best
forces of world culture in the fight against reaction and
nazism.

The Soviet government used the great artist's charm and
dynamic, bounding energy for its own selfish purposes, but
his authority on the world stage grew to such an extent that
it went rather beyond what the Kremlin had planned.
Mikhoels became a symbol of Russian Jewry; it was necessary to eliminate him before an attack on the Jews could be
launched. Mikhoels's days were numbered. He was doomed
to perish. It was only necessary to find a way of removing
him which would not result in an international scandal.

The town of Minsk, the capital of the Byelorussian republic, was the place where he perished. Before the war, hundreds of thousands of Jews had lived there. During the occupation, the Nazis had shown particular cruelty in their
dealings with them. By an evil irony of fate, the assassin's
hand caught up with Mikhoels in the very place where the
smell of the massacred Jewish population's blood hung yet
in the air above the heaps of still warm ashes.

I remember that day very clearly. It was a cold day of early
spring. The damp wind was chasing the brick dust through
a waste of ruins and rumbling across the metal sheeting of
caved-in roofs. That was how Minsk, one of the most heavily damaged cities in the USSR, looked then. One could
walk for kilometer after kilometer and not come across a
single undamaged house. There were few passable streets,
for they had been blocked by fallen masonry, and people
made their way over the hills and heaps of rubble, wearing

paths with their feet among the chaotic masses of stone, concrete slabs, and convulsively twisted iron girders.

A dead city, a city of graves, a city of ghosts. And outside it, buried hurriedly in antitank ditches, lay the bodies of more than one-hundred-thousand executed Jews who used to live there.

But the town lived on. In any old building, made fit for human habitation heaven knows how, lectures were read to students of the university. I was one such student.

The huge building of the opera and ballet theatre was one of the first to be restored after the war. This was the last theatre that Mikhoels visited in his lifetime. The multistory Hotel Byelorussia had been built on the site of buildings destroyed by fire, and for many years it was the only hotel in the town. This was the last hotel in which Mikhoels stayed.

Mikhoels came from Moscow as a representative of the State Stalin Prize Committee. He was to assess the performance of the local opera theatre, which was in the running for this prize. He was greeted and received like an important, honored guest. Photographs of the great artist were published in the newspapers. A spate of banquets and receptions at the highest level were held in his honor.

The remnant of the Jewish population—those who had survived the war—were especially jubilant. The Hotel Byelorussia was besieged by hundreds of people. People waited for hours on the streets in order to shake Mikhoels's hand or simply to look upon a living miracle.

That cold spring night in 1948 was for him a fatal one. Only in the morning did the town learn of the evil deed. It was unbelievable, and the mind recoiled from it. Mikhoels had been murdered barbarically and with inconceivable cruelty. His mutilated body was discovered in the middle of the road near the Byelorussia. His skull had been smashed in with a blunt instrument; his crushed body bore the marks of the wheels of an automobile, which had been driven over it several times.

Life at the university shuddered to a halt. Without any order from the rector, studies ended spontaneously. Students and professors, in sorrowful groups, crowded the corridors, lecture rooms, and the library. Horror and bewilderment gripped everyone. Many rushed off to the mortuary of the Municipal Hospital, where the body was lying, but access there was restricted.

I remember a conversation in the university library between two rather deaf old professors, both admirers of Mikhoels. They had been allowed into the mortuary and were now exchanging impressions in loud voices as the hard-of-hearing are wont to do. They were the first people I heard reject the official version, that there had been a motor accident. The most superficial examination of the body bore witness to premeditated murder.

Soon the authorities circulated a new official version: the murder had been committed by unknown criminals. And then a fresh swarm of puzzling questions made everyone's head spin. What was the motive for the murder? Robbery? Nothing had been taken from the deceased. Even his watch was still on his wrist. Was it a maniac who had gone on the rampage? This too was dismissed. The crime had been committed in the center of the town not far from government buildings that were under heavy police guard. And the street itself was one of the few in the town that was lit at night by electricity.

Little by little the dreadful suspicion began to creep into people's minds. It seemed so monstrous that no one wanted to believe it at all. But more and more people began to whisper it. More and more faces grew somber, and people hid their eyes in shame and horror.

The authorities, however, clearly forseeing the possibility of such speculation, went through the whole cynical farce of a state funeral with full honors and hypocritical speeches. When Mikhoels's body was taken through the town to the station, whence the funeral train set out for

Moscow, thousands of people poured out on to the streets to bid their favorite artist a final farewell. Tear-stained, shaken men and women clustered among the ruins or climbed up into the occasional surviving trees of the town to get a look at the closed coffin. One old man sat unsteadily on the branch of a tree, and with hands numbed by the cold wind played on a violin a sad Jewish melody.

Jewish hearts, besides their sorrow, held a premonition of impending misfortune, of a fate to be shared by the whole nation Mikhoels had celebrated with the brightness of his talent.

Their premonition was fulfilled.

Only several years later did I learn the details of Mikhoels's death. I happened to meet a man who had been working in the Minsk NKVD at the time of the actor's death. By the time we met, he had already been thrown out of the NKVD for being Jewish. He admitted to me in a fit of gloating, vengeful frankness that he himself had taken part in the preparations for the Mikhoels's operation, and I sensed the absolute truth not only in the facts he revealed to me but particularly in the tone in which he spoke. He spoke dully, in a matter-of-fact manner, without stressing any particular word, as one might talk about an ordinary assignment that had been gone through over and over again. Moreover, everything that he said tied in absolutely logically with the facts that everyone knew and only filled in the blanks which had evoked at first bewilderment and subsequently suspicion.

Mikhoels had not come from Moscow to Minsk alone. He had been accompanied on the trip by the editor of the journal *Teatr* [theatre], a man called Golubyev, who was not a Jew but a Russian. He was an inconvenient witness and so shared the fate of Mikhoels.

They both lived in one of the best rooms in the Byelorussia and were apparently friendly with one another, so when the telephone rang at midnight and an unfamiliar voice, claiming to be an employee of the Party Central Committee, invited Mikhoels to an urgent government meeting and said that a car was already waiting outside, Golubyev did not allow him to go alone.

They went downstairs together. A car was actually waiting for them in the deserted street. Two men got out of it, obligingly flung the door open for Mikhoels, and tried to convince Golubyev that since he had not been invited there was no point in his going. Mikhoels and Golubyev insisted that they would go together.

The car drove about two hundred yards away from the hotel and stopped. The two men threw themselves upon Mikhoels and Golubyev, smashed in their skulls with wrenches, threw the bloody corpses out into the roadway, and then drove backwards and forwards over them several times. The car then drove off.

As a matter of fact the authorities never got round to announcing that the criminals had been caught, even for appearance's sake. This seems hardly surprising, since they were employees of the NKVD, the same people who were conducting the so-called investigation.

Mikhoels was removed. The authorities achieved several aims at a single stroke. World public opinion was taken in by the official version of his death. The funeral with full honors put the finishing touches to hoodwinking progressive public figures in various countries. It was now possible to deal with the rest of the Jews without compunction about choice of methods. Mikhoels's death was a blessing for the authorities. It paralyzed the Jewish population of the USSR, and any action thereafter could surprise no one.

Both Yiddish theatres, the one in Moscow and the one in Minsk, were closed. The actors were fired and left without any way of earning a living. The theatres were closed quietly, without announcement, so that the authorities did not have to look for a pretext or to explain the motives for their action.

The cynicism of Soviet policy on the Jewish Question is unparalleled. To illustrate this, here are a few examples of which I know, not second- or third-hand, but from my own experience.

The Minsk Yiddish Theatre, although inferior to the one in Moscow, had in its company many gifted artists, and its tours of many Soviet cities enjoyed great popularity. For the Jews of Byelorussia, it was the only center of their national culture. The best-known actors of this theatre—Sokol, Trepel, Aronchik, Sonkin—were their idols.

After Minsk had been liberated from the Nazi armies of occupation, the theatre personnel returned from Novosibirsk, where they had been evacuated at the beginning of the war, and the question of a building arose. The city was in ruins. There was not even a trace of the prewar building.

At first the Byelorussian Theatre gave them a home and, once or twice a week, made its stage available to the Jewish actors. This could not go on for long, as it interfered with the normal working of both companies, and after insistent requests from the Jewish public the authorities came to a cunning and uniquely insidious decision.

Still standing among the ruins of the town were the well-built brick walls of the central synagogue. There was, of course, no question of rebuilding it. All around, parishioners were footing the bills for building and repairing both Orthodox and Catholic churches, but the Jews of Minsk were categorically denied permission to build synagogues. The authorities suggested giving what was left of the synagogue to the Yiddish Theatre. No resources were made available for building operations; the Jews would have to do their own collecting if they wanted their own theatre. This was unprecedented; all theatre buildings in the USSR were being built and restored at state expense, and only in the case of the Yiddish Theatre was a discriminatory exception made.

The Jews agreed without complaint. With unheard-of enthusiasm, volunteers collected money from the population.

People who after the war had eked out a beggarly existence gave their last kopeks. Many of them, when they had finished their day's work in the factory, came to the building site and, without any payment, carried bricks, mixed concrete, and painted walls. They still had no apartments of their own; their families were huddled together in wretched hovels. But for them, the building of the theatre was a matter of the highest importance.

And from the ruins arose a beautiful building with a colonnade, a large stage, and a roomy auditorium. The first presentations in the new theatre were a celebration for both actors and audience.

The celebration did not last long, and the hangover was a bitter one.

The Yiddish Theatre was closed and the actors dispersed. A talented company, which had taken decades to form, simply disappeared. The names of the great actors were heard no more. Some, wandering from one casual job to another, were lost from sight; others died. All that was left of the theatre was a memory.

And what was the fate of the fine building, which had been restored with Jewish hands and Jewish money? It was given to the State Theatre of Byelorussia. And when this happened, no one burned with shame, no one felt any pangs of conscience. It was all part of the order of things.

I encountered a comparable instance in the town of Bobruisk, not far from Minsk. The greater part of the population there was Jewish. Among them were many religious Jews. For a long time they begged the authorities to allow them to build a new synagogue in place of the one destroyed by fire during the war. At first the authorities refused to give an inch; then suddenly and very obligingly they agreed and even made a site available for this building on one of the best streets in the town. This at first perplexed and depressed the Jews, but having thought the matter over they interpreted such kindness as a sign of more favorable winds, of a softening in the policy of the state.

The money was quickly collected. The building was put up by the best bricklayers, painters, and decorators, all of whom, of course, gave their services free. Every believer worked for a number of days on the building site. The synagogue was decorated with loving care. A few services were held.

One fine day, believers coming to the synagogue were met by a closed door, to which two Russian workmen were nailing up a sign—*State Archive.*

Just so. The building, which the Jews had built, had been taken from them and handed over to an official institution, without a single kopek being repaid. Most important of all, however, the believers were left without their sanctuary. The Orthodox and Catholic churches in the town went on functioning normally.

Yet greater cynicism was manifested in the matter of perpetuating the memory of those members of the Jewish population who had perished at the hands of the Nazi invader.

Surely everyone in the world has heard of such harrowing places as Babi Yar in Kiev, Trostyanets in Minsk, Ponar in Vilna. Hundreds of thousands of Jewish old men, women, and children—the innocent victims of nazism—rest there in huge trenches. The earth above these frightful graves was leveled; there is no reminder of the tragedy enacted there.

There is a lot of talk about war victims in the Soviet Union. Memorials are erected on mass graves. Flowers are laid at the feet of obelisks. But the Jews are segregated even in death.

The relations of Jews who perished and representatives of religious communities have gone from one department to another. With tears in their eyes, they have begged permission to erect memorials over the graves. And not at state expense, but with money they themselves collected. Everywhere they received a blank, unqualified refusal. It is true that in certain towns the Jews were permitted to collect money and deposit it in the state bank, which is where the money has remained to this day. The people concerned were quite simply swindled. Since no permit was issued for such a building and since no one person deposited the money, the money remains unused and unusable.

Nowhere are there any memorials. The anonymous mass graves are overgrown with grass and scrub. The earth has subsided and fallen in. Even on the sad anniversaries of these Nazi executions, relatives are not permitted to gather at the graves.

In Kiev, so as to eradicate once and for all from man's memory any recollection of the Jewish victims of nazism, multistory dwellings were built at Babi Yar right on top of the bones of tens of thousands of people. But this act of blasphemy and barbarism by shameless anti-Semites reaped its reward. I am an atheist. I do not believe in God and the power of the Almighty. But I was shaken by what happened at Babi Yar. Two blocks of apartments built on these bones soon collapsed, burying those who had dared to go and live in them.

In the USSR even dead Jews are persecuted, to say nothing of the living. With each passing day, the Jews began to feel even less at home and even more terrified in a country where they themselves, their grandfathers, and their great-grandfathers were born. Their motherland had turned into a wicked stepmother.

In the streets, the now-fearless hooligans began to insult and humiliate the Jews. Children at school felt themselves rejected by their former friends. In the universities and institutes of higher education, under any or no pretext, the doors were closed to Jewish students.

The turbid waves of anti-Semitism, however, continued to sweep across the Soviet Union. There was the notorious trumped-up cases of the Doctors' Plot. Thousands of people found themselves behind bars. Tens of thousands were fired. Hundreds of thousands sat at home in terror, afraid to show themselves in the street any more than was absolutely necessary. In the cellars of the Lubyanka in Moscow, the whole flower of the Jewish intelligentsia was destroyed. Famous poets and writers such as David Bergelson, Perets Markish, Leib Kvitko, and many, many others had a bullet put in the back of their necks, and their earthly remains buried heaven knows where. There were no trials.

Events were approaching a tragic denouement. An act of genocide on an unprecedented scale was being prepared. The whole of the Jewish population was to be deported to Siberia. Long columns of freight cars, identical with those that but recently had rumbled along the black trails to Auschwitz, Maidanek, and Treblinka, drew toward the places where most of the Jews lived.

Only a miracle could stay the criminals' hands. The miracle happened. Stalin died. With his death, many plans were suspended, including the plan to resolve the Jewish Question. In the heat of the battle for power, Stalin's heirs for a time seemed to have forgotten about the existence of the Jews, and people breathed more freely, emerging with difficulty from the state of numbness in which they had spent the preceding few years. Bright spots of hope even emerged—that all would change for the better and that the Jews would be restored to a place of equal rights with others.

But these hopes were not destined to be fulfilled. Anti-Semitism was by now deeply embedded in people's hearts. The Jews were slighted as before, even without orders from above, just because people in a position to slight felt like slighting. The personnel departments of institutes of higher education and commercial undertakings sifted through their personnel and got rid of Jews whenever convenient. It is perfectly true that, even so, many continued to hold quite good jobs, but this was simply attributable to the fact that industry, science, medicine, and the arts were experiencing an acute need of highly qualified specialists with initiative.

And it was simply uneconomic to manage without the services of the Jews altogether. Jewish brains and capable Jewish hands were building the nation's ballistic rockets, splitting the atom, making Russia one of the great powers.

Every Jew, however, wherever he worked, experienced a keen sense of uncertainty about the morrow. After all, as soon as the opportunity arose to replace him with another specialist of the same caliber who happened to be Russian, he knew that his days were numbered.

The Party propaganda machine had mastered one particular rule—to write about the Jews only what is bad or negative, and if it should happen a Jew did something noble or heroic about which it was impossible to keep quiet, then every effort should be made to conceal the hero's nationality.

A typical instance of this kind of thing was the Kursk Affair, which was portrayed throughout the land in a film entitled *An Echo of the War.* The Soviet press wrote a great deal about this event.

This in fact was what happened. Many years after the war was over, in the large industrial city of Kursk, some construction workers unearthed a huge German bomb weighing about a ton, deep below the ground. This rusty monster had been resting there since 1943, and there was a danger of it exploding at the first careless contact. A whole housing area, some factories, and a stretch of railway line were threatened.

As a result of the alarm being raised, thousands of inhabitants were evacuated from the threatened area to safe places, the factories were closed down, and rail traffic was halted. A team of bomb disposal experts with a captain in charge came to Kursk with all speed. These hitherto-unknown people soon became the heroes of the hour. At risk of their lives, they brilliantly carried out the job of rendering the bomb harmless and saved the city from incalculable damage. The captain in command of the bomb disposal squad acted with particular distinction.

The heroes' photographs appeared in every newspaper in the Soviet Union. They received decorations. As for the captain, it was reported that before the incident in Kursk, he had disarmed two thousand unexploded mines, shells, and bombs. And since this squad included soldiers of various nationalities, the press and radio lost no time in proclaiming that their epic deed was proof of the triumph of the Soviet nationalities policy, a shining example of the friendship of the peoples of the USSR.

Everything would have been fine had it not been for one irritating detail. The commander of the bomb disposal squad, Captain Gorelik, was Jewish. A ruse worthy of a bare-faced cheat was resorted to. On a group photograph of the heroes, where the nationality of each soldier was mentioned, Gorelik was simply described as Captain Gorelik. Soon a film was made and appeared on the screen, depicting the events at Kursk. A Russian actor played the part of Captain Gorelik; he was given another name—a Russian one.

Subsequently a joke was launched, which was not altogether unconnected with these events: A performance will be given by the musical ensemble Friendship between Nations, which includes the following performers: Ivanov (Russian), Kazachenko (Ukrainian), Dumbadze (Georgian), Rabinovich (accordian).

If a Jew breaks a world record in a sporting event, plays an important part in putting out a fire, or makes a significant discovery, and it is impossible to hush up the fact itself, then the man's nationality is hushed up. But if a Jew does something unseemly, then all attention is bound to be focused on his nationality.

Where was all this leading? In the first place, the Jews were developing an inferiority complex; their minds and personalities were being monstrously distorted. Many began to be ashamed of their nationality and to hide it from other people, changing their names and forenames to Russian ones; if they could manage it, they changed their nationality too. People like this clutched at assimilation as to a lifeline—not altogether reliable in Soviet conditions of lawlessness but better than nothing.

Others looked toward Israel. That tiny country, far away and shrouded in mystery, became for a time a guiding star that shone down upon Soviet Jews through the gloom of humiliation, insults, and fear.

We now come to one of the most complicated problems that faced Soviet Jewry. Although humiliated and persecuted in their own country, they were also categorically refused the right to leave it. It is all but impossible to leave the Soviet Union for a foreign country, impossible for all— for the Russians, for the Tatars, for the Jews. The Declaration of Human Rights, passed by the United Nations and hypocritically signed by the Soviet Union, is in fact regarded as a worthless piece of paper. The population of the USSR is not familiar with it. On the only occasion that it was published, in an obscure journal known only to a few people, Article 13, which mentions the right of everyone to leave their own country, was brazenly omitted.

Even in terms of the complete denial of rights, which prevails for all peoples in the USSR, the position of the Jews is unique. They have neither their own language nor the semblence of statehood, and they, as distinct from other nations, are subjected to overt discrimination against their nationality. On the other hand, they have, as a further distinction from the other peoples of the USSR, their own national state outside the frontiers of the Soviet Union, the state of Israel, which is ready to receive them and grant them citizenship.

The way to Israel, however, is completely sealed off. Until recently only in a very small number of isolated cases, predominantly the old and the invalids, by dint of unbelievable humiliations and tribulations, obtained the longed-for visa.

I suppose that people in the West, however hard they may

try, cannot imagine all the inhumanity and refined sadism a Jew in the USSR must go through when he has stated his desire to emigrate to Israel.

These are the stations on the road to Golgotha through which every man who has expressed the wish to leave the country must pass.

First of all, there must be an official invitation from the country to which you intend to travel. This invitation, moreover, is only regarded as valid if it comes from a close relative. In the absence of such an invitation, the case will not be accepted for review.

Let us suppose, however, that you have relatives in Israel. You have to let them know that you want them to register the invitation through the proper channels and send it off. Perhaps you think that this is the easiest thing in the world? Just write a letter or make an international telephone call. Please don't forget that you are writing or telephoning from the Soviet Union. Every letter that goes abroad is checked by the censor, and a large proportion, particularly if they are going to Israel, disappear without a trace. An international telephone call will be listened to and will frequently be cut off at just the moment when you are saying things that the authorities don't care for.

You write one, two, three letters, telephone a few times, and eventually, thank God, your cry is heard. This is just the first and tiniest step forward. The invitation has still got to get to you. It is dispatched, but a month passes, then another, then a third, and still you do not receive it. Once again you look for an opportunity to let the people in Israel know that they should send a second invitation. They send one. Once again, having crossed the frontier of the USSR, it disappears. While you are getting nervous, searching your letter-box every day and writing complaints to the post-office, the officials of the State Security Service (KGB) are grinning, sitting in their offices and adding all your invitations to the file of the case already opened in your name. I, for example, was twice sent invitations I never received. I knew people who were sent five letters and still did not get what they were waiting for.

All the same, by a miracle, sometimes in the most inconceivable way, the invitation reaches your hands. This is where the most difficult business begins—trials through which not everyone is capable of enduring and holding his ground.

Apart from the invitation, in order to submit an application to emigrate, one needs a reference from one's place of work or study and the written permission of one's parents, if they are still alive, signed and sealed by a senior Soviet official in the place where they live.

The man in the street cannot imagine what this means.

You yourself are obliged to go to your place of work and ask your superiors for a reference to append to your application to leave for Israel. As soon as you mention a foreign country, and in particular Israel, your superiors' hair stands on end. They, of course, refuse categorically to give you the reference. Nor is this all. From that moment onward you are declared a hostile element. A general meeting is called of the whole staff with whom you work, and in front of everybody you are assaulted in foul language and made the target of the most unbelievable accusations. Then, on the first pretext that presents itself, you are dismissed from work. Exactly the same thing happens to your wife and to your children too, if they are students. Students are automatically expelled from their institutes, and a young man so excluded is forthwith called up into the army and dispatched for two years to some remote place in the vicinity of the Chinese frontier.

Your family is already at the center of a full-scale tragedy before a single step has even been taken toward your desired aim. As soon as you are out of work, you are in danger of being declared a vagrant and a parasite under Soviet law and of being subjected to administrative exile in places not so far off—perhaps somewhere in the Siberian taiga, where, separated from your family who are left without any means of support, you chop down trees for a pittance. In the Soviet Union this is called "educating through work." In order to avoid this kind of fate, you search feverishly for any kind of work, even that which demands minimal qualifications and is very poorly paid, simply to avoid a pretext for administrative measures. Two of my comrades in Moscow, both with families to support, one a distinguished engineer and the other a film director, worked for a year as postmen for the tiny wage of sixty rubles a month. This miserable income is not even sufficient to feed one person.

If you did not get the reference, the authorities may not accept the rest of your documents. When I was fighting a running battle to get my reference, one of the most important men in the Soviet cinema industry, who was supposed to sign it, admitted in all honesty that he had received instructions from above not to give it to me.

You land in a vicious circle. You sell your last remaining things and are reduced to a state of extreme nervous and physical exhaustion. You humiliate yourself, you go down on your knees, and after tribulations lasting for a year or sometimes two, you become the possessor of the wretched reference—a slip of paper on which is written that you worked in such and such a place from such and such a year to such and such a year. And that's all. You have borne all that anguish simply to get hold of this putrid scrap of paper.

Your sufferings, however, are far from over. You still have to get the permission of your parents. As a rule, old people, who are living out their last years, don't want to move away from the place where they have spent most of their lives. The very fact that their children are going away and won't even be able to attend their parents' funerals is in itself tragic. But it is even more frightful for the parents to be left in hostile surroundings and to have to listen to the oaths and curses directed at their crazy children. The parents are scared stiff of signing the form of consent demanded of them because, if they do, their children's actions will become generally known and they could well themselves become a target for the persecution and insults of their fellow townsfolk.

Let us suppose, however, that the parents were sufficiently understanding and courageous to sign the form of consent. It now has to be witnessed in an official institution of the town where the parents live, so we have a repetition of the business of the reference. Everyone you ask refuses to witness the form of consent. In my own case, for example, people refused outright even to discuss the subject, first of all in the housing administration and subsequently at a police station. With great difficulty and after much coming and going, I managed to get my parents' signature witnessed in a notary office. (Notary offices, by the way, were soon afterwards instructed not to witness this kind of document.)

By the time you have got together in a bundle all the bits of paper you need, you no longer bear any resemblance to a human being.

You now have in front of you the most important and usually insuperable obstacle—OVIR, the visa and registration section of the Ministry of Internal Affairs of the USSR, the government department that actually issues exit visas.

There are branches of OVIR in all the major cities of the Soviet Union. In recent years there have been fewer and fewer tourists to be seen in them and an ever-increasing number of Jewish faces. The Jews have literally laid siege to these departments. They have been going there for years, and even when they are driven away they come back again.

The officers from the Ministry of Internal Affairs who work in the visa section make no effort to conceal their hostility to the Jews. Whoever you were before you put in your application—a famous actor whose portrait appeared on posters, or a writer whose books had previously been read with interest by those same officers—the treatment is the same: disdain, boorishness, and insults. No account is taken of age or sex. It is as if you were prisoners in the hands of a warden; everybody is treated in the same way. And this is quite natural. These, after all, are officers of the self-same

Ministry of Internal Affairs that is responsible for guarding prisons and concentration camps.

There is, however, a difference. After a long and unpleasant acquaintanceship with OVIR, I have the impression that the officials of this institution were chosen for certain special qualities, one of the most important of which is sadism. Yes, sadism is precisely what I mean. What I observed cannot be described in any other way. Among the Jews I chanced to meet at OVIR, there was one married couple, Rita and Dan Borshchevsky. They were young people. He had begun his higher education and was then employed as a worker. She was an engineer and a translator from Japanese. They hadn't been married very long. Rita had a six-year-old son by her first marriage and was then in the final stages of pregnancy with her second child.

They had been trying to get permission to emigrate for so long that they had almost forgotten how long. Their case was being handled by a female official of the visa section, a certain Akulova [*akula* in Russian means "shark"], who was a captain in the Ministry of Internal Affairs. Her name was one which made many Jews in Moscow shudder when they spoke it. She reminded me, not only in her character and behavior, but in her appearance too, of the notorious Nazi war criminal, Ilse Koch, who tortured women in the German concentration camps and acquired infamous renown for making ladies' handbags from human skin. Ilse Koch's photograph had stuck in my mind, and when I saw Akulova I felt at once their physical likeness—cold, fishy eyes, thin lips like worms, heavily curled hair dyed white.

She derived enjoyment from insulting people. She took particular delight in venting her feelings on women. Rita Borshchevsky became one of her victims, and it is a miracle that I am not using the word *victim* quite literally.

When, at the end of their whole ordeal, the Borshchevsky family was finally given permission to emigrate, Akulova was responsible for issuing their visas. This was the coup de grâce she dealt the Borshchevskys.

The visas were already lying ready on Akulova's table, when, for the umpteenth time, Dan Borshchevsky came to see her in order to find out whether or not permission had been given. Akulova stated to him that they had been refused permission and that the decision was final. As soon as he had gone, however, she at once phoned Rita, his wife, and demanded that she come at once for her visa.

This pregnant woman, weak and ill not only because of her condition but also on account of frequent encounters with Akulova, dragged herself across the whole of Moscow to OVIR. Akulova greeted her with a smile of serpentine cunning.

"You have been granted permission to emigrate to Israel," she said, and seeing how Rita's face lit up, added in a businesslike voice, "but your son's been refused."

The seven-month's-pregnant woman slumped unconscious on the floor. Akulova emptied a decanter of water over her face, and when Rita opened her eyes said, without a tinge of remorse, "I was joking. You've all been given visas." And she thrust them at her as she lay on the floor.

Here is the real face of this Soviet woman called Akulova, a captain in the Ministry of Internal Affairs and a Communist. The Moscow model of Ilse Koch. The only difference between her and Ilse is that she hasn't yet got her instructions to make ladies' handbags from human skin. She would do them just as well.

Major Zolotukhin of the Moscow visa section, Lieutenant-Colonel Kaiya from Riga—one could quote a long list of these sadists in the uniform of the USSR Ministry of Internal Affairs. This is the kind of mincer you have to go through if you think of leaving the Soviet Union.

There is a further, not unimportant, obstacle that awaits you in the visa section. Every person over fifteen years old must pay 900 rubles, i.e., a thousand dollars at official exchange rates, for his exit visa. Where can you get that amount of money? There may well be four or five people in the family who are over fifteen, making the sum four or five times as big. No exception is made even for the very old; moreover, when the latter leave, their pension earned over their whole working life is automatically discontinued.

Now let us do a few simple sums. The ordinary engineer or doctor in the USSR earns on average 100 to 150 rubles a month. With prices at the existing level, this is barely enough to make ends meet. There can be no question of saving. With such a miserably low level of earnings, the average Soviet family is unable to pay this ransom to the visa section. Let us suppose, however, that one sold all one's goods, got help from one's relatives and friends, or even, if worst came to worst, the money you couldn't yourself raise was simply collected by your fellow Jews.

This, however, is where the familiar denouement begins. You are not even invited to the visa section for an interview but are simply informed dryly over the telephone that you have been refused permission to emigrate to Israel. No explanations of reasons and motives are given. Furthermore, you are reminded that if you take it into your head to make another application all the papers have to be collected and completed all over again.

People spend ten to twelve years getting permission to leave. One Moscow man named Khatsernov had one child when he first put in an application but was father of five children by the time he left for Israel.

That's the way it is, so if you, dear reader, are weary of reading this long drawn-out story, then just think for a moment how it must seem to the people who are living through it.

One needs to possess great stubbornness and will power in order not to give in. One needs to believe fanatically that for you this is the only way and there is no other. And without doubt one needs to possess great courage. Soviet Jews were not short of stubbornness nor of courage either.

Harmless accountants who in their daily lives wouldn't have hurt a fly, housewives who were entirely wrapped up in never-ending worries about children, food, and clothing, students who with no small difficulty had broken through the cordon of discrimination and got into a university—they were the people who took up the cudgels and openly challenged Soviet power for the first time in its history.

In Soviet conditions all forms of protest are unthinkable. Street demonstrations are forbidden, and the press, which is in the hands of the government, will publish nothing that is not to its taste. Written complaints vanish without a trace into the bowels of the bureaucratic machine.

Quite spontaneously, without any organized plan or campaign, simultaneously in various cities, the Jews discovered their way to fight. From Moscow and Leningrad, Kiev and Odessa, Minsk and Chernovtsy, by routes known to God alone, angry and indignant letters of protest and pleas for help to men of goodwill were sent out to the West. There were both individual and collective letters, with the names and home addresses of hundreds of signatories.

This was a cry of despair from many voices. It was the cry from hearts reduced to the state when terror disappears and all possible retribution is disregarded.

These letters seared the hearts of readers of the Western press and came over the wires like a nightmarish cry. Enlightened public opinion was troubled. Demonstrations of solidarity and support began to take place in the West. With amazement the world learned of, and began to discuss, the terrible fate of Soviet Jewry and of the heroic, unparalleled struggle going on in the USSR.

The battle gave birth to its own heroes. A man from Riga called Grisha Feigin, whom no one had heard of until then, took a step that ruffled the feathers of the unflappable Soviet government. This former army major and Second World War veteran, holder of eight decorations and medals, returned all these prizes to president Podgorny as a sign of protest. This was something quite unprecedented. When the shock wore off, the authorities could think of nothing better to do with Grisha than to lock him up in a lunatic asylum. A mighty wave of protest, which rolled across the whole world, forced them afterwards to retreat and set him free.

Alla Milkin, a nineteen-year-old student and member of the Komsomol, proved to be a girl of surprising boldness. She typed a number of copies of her petition to the delegate of the All-Union Komsomol Congress, in which she asked them to help her exercise her legal right to emigrate to Israel. She stood at the gates of the Kremlin, and, until she was arrested, handed them to every delegate that came past. This too was something quite new in the Soviet Union.

Naturally, the Soviet press kept quiet and didn't say a word about these incidents. The articles in the press were simply more anti-Semitic than before. The Western press and radio, however, did not keep silent. The truth about the fight the Jews were putting up found its way through the wall of jamming to the inhabitants of the USSR. Hundreds and thousands more people, liberated from habitual terror, opened their lips, which till then had been mute. Fresh strength was infused into the ranks of the fighters.

The attempt of the abashed authorities to stage a propaganda counterattack looked pathetic. A press conference of so-called representatives of Soviet Jewry was shown on the television screens. With difficulty, they had managed to scrape together a score or two of nearly senile old men, forced them to revile their own people and the state of Israel and praise up to the skies the great life lived by Jews in the USSR. What was squeezed out of them sounded so insincere, and the feeling that they had been forced into doing it was so strong, that even the Russian viewer turned his back on the television in disgust.

A struggle began, the end of which, even today, is not in sight. A drama started to unfold whose denouement will be very tragic.

The most active of the Russian Jews began to believe in Israel when they had lost all faith in Soviet power. The creation of the Jewish state loosed upon them the persecutions of the Russian anti-Semites, made them pariahs in their own country, second-class citizens, targets for taunts and jibes. Their only way out was to pin their hopes on Israel, and instead of the USSR, they publicly claimed as their motherland this distant country that they did not know. With the resolve of men and women who can retreat no further, they stormed the Iron Curtain.

They did not then suspect that there was no way forward for them either. They could not have visualized in their wildest dreams Israel's hypocritical role in the dirty game of international politics centering on the Russian Jewish problem. They believed, they idealized Israel, they prayed to Israel, and this undoubtedly gave them strength to withstand the enormous strain of the struggle.

Events unfolded with incredible speed. Letters of protest to the Soviet authorities, not anonymous but signed by dozens and hundreds of people, such letters as had previously seemed unthinkable, were sent to the Kremlin. Copies of them reached the West by secret routes, and there the columns of the newspapers were dotted with the names of the protesters. People overcame their fear of the secret police, which until then had petrified the whole country. As they went to prison, they hurled down the gauntlet to their judges.

A glorious epic had begun, a page in the history of Russian Jewry amazing in its moral beauty and mass heroism, equal in pathos to the uprising in the Warsaw ghetto. It was, as I now realize, a last soaring flight, a final surge of passions, on the eve of the agony that the Jews, and first and foremost the Russian Jews, had already entered.

The twenty-fourth of February, 1971, when twenty-four Moscow Jews for the first time in the whole history of Soviet power dared to take a defiant and desperate step, was like the ninth wave of this storm. Close to Red Square, by the walls of the Kremlin, in the very lair of their oppressors, they occupied the reception hall of the Supreme Soviet of the USSR, went on a hunger strike, news of which instantly reverberated around the world, and presented the authorities with an ultimatum, one point of which was the demand that Jews should be permitted freely to emigrate to Israel.

That day brought the first victory. For the first time the authorities yielded, and state commissions were formed to deal with the problems of Jewish emigration. Precisely from that day, it was no longer a pathetic trickle of the ailing and the elderly who came to Israel but a torrent of young and energetic people, at the rate of about three thousand per month.

After the first hunger strike there were a series of others. The example caught on. There was tinder-dry kindling in plenty. Only a spark was needed. Ten days after us, 160 Jews from Riga, Vilna, and Kaunas occupied the Supreme Soviet in Moscow. Then a further 50. There were sit-ins and demonstrations in Latvia, Lithuania, the Ukraine, and Georgia.

But the resistance of the authorities, once they had recovered from the first shock, grew at the same rate, and repressive measures began to increase. Trials, whose purpose was to intimidate Soviet Jews, took place in Kishinev, Riga, Leningrad, and Odessa. Dozens of Jewish men and women were thrown into prison or put for long years behind the barbed wire of the concentration camps. At the same time, however, hundreds and thousands were actually leaving the USSR and, like souls escaping from the nether regions, headed for Israel, that unknown but desired country.

When they reached Vienna, the remote approaches to the promised land, their first contact with Israeli officials was like a blow between the eyes.

This is the testimony of Mikhail Talisman, which I quote from the Israeli Russian language newspaper *Tribuna.*

Vienna. Mid-1971. A plane of repatriates has arrived from Russia. At the airport a lanky fellow meets them and blurts out:

"And where do you think all you lot are off to? You think everything's fine in Israel?"

Concluding thus:

"If there was anywhere to go, I'd leave Israel myself."

The new-fledged citizens' hot flush of enthusiasm quickly cooled down. They were trampled on roughly and unceremoniously. A flood of bitter and dramatic letters poured from Israel to the USSR, revealing the disagreeable truth, begging people to pause and reconsider before it was too late. It was then that the final act of the tragedy of the Russian Jews began. Through sheer momentum, the flight from the USSR still continues, later to be translated into flight from Israel. Where? Into the unknown. It is here in Israel that Russian Jews have their last shoots of national consciousness blighted and are thrust toward assimilation.

The Moscow engineer Ilya Zilberberg, a bold fighter from the earliest stages of the struggle, was the author of one of the most famous protest letters in the world, in which he mercilessly exposed Soviet anti-Semitism and stated for all to hear: "Protest and national consciousness grew within me simultaneously. In me anti-Semitism did not engender terror and the urge to adapt, but pride and interest in everything Jewish."

Ilya Zilberberg lasted less than six months in Israel. His pride rapidly evaporated, and his interest disappeared. He went to live in London, taking his small children with him, and now those children chatter in English, never having learned a single word of Hebrew.

Lyuba Bershadsky was once a celebrated, active participant in the struggle for Jewish emigration, one of the first twenty-four to proclaim in an appeal to world opinion the awakening of Soviet Jews. When she, who had spent many years in Soviet concentration camps, made a tour of Europe and America, Jews feted her like a national hero.

Where is she now? This quite elderly woman fled surreptitiously from Israel to escape from her debts and, for more than a year now, has been beseeching forgiveness of the Soviet authorities and begging them to allow her to return to Moscow to a humiliating and sterile existence.

In what pathetic farce the heroic drama ends. How many broken lives! How many tears the world does not see!

And how do things stand in Russia? Those millions of second-class Soviet citizens, having learned from the example of the ones who left that Israel does not offer a way of escape, now seek salvation from increasing anti-Semitism by demonstratively turning away from their Jewishness as if it were a plague. For them, assimilation is the final chance to survive physically. The number of mixed marriages grows rapidly, and the children of these marriages shun their Jewish parents.

The once glorious Russian Jewish community, which gave so many great men to the world, is in its final death agony. Having withstood the czarist pogroms, miraculously survived Hitler's crematoria, and stubbornly resisted destruction for many centuries, it has begun to disintegrate and rapidly dissolve among the other nations of the USSR. And this occurred from the very moment when the state of Israel was created in Palestine. Contrary to the wishes of its creators, Israel has become not a regenerating ferment for the Jewish nation but a catalyst hastening the process of its disintegration.

chapter seven

ISRAELI SOCIALISM IN PROFILE AND FULL FACE

Wherever socialism, in the name of the common man and in his name only, wends its way in triumph, its fanfares drowning the barking guns of public and private executioners, it has its individual traits. Each socialism has a face of its own, different from that of the socialism next door.

Once someone even proclaimed socialism with a *human face*. Yes indeed! What will they think of next! In Czechoslovakia. In the brief days of Dubcek's "Prague spring." It was a challenge, one in the eye for some other socialisms, Soviet socialism for example, Hungarian, Polish, and German (east of the Elbe) socialism. The implication was that if Czechoslovakian socialism had a human face, their socialism had some other kind of face, more like an animal's snout. No one was going to stand for that. So the tanks went into Prague, wiping the human likeness from the face of Czech socialism and imprinting their own features upon it.

Even Hitler was building socialism—national socialism. To this day grandmothers use its visage to frighten naughty grandchildren.

For more than fifty years they have been building socialism in the biblical land of Palestine. It too has its own face—not a completely Jewish face, but clearly Israeli.

Old men, among those who came here at the beginning of the century and lived through a host of hopes and disillusionments, delight to regale us latter-day Israelis with the following cautionary tale:

"Once upon a time in Russia before the Revolution, the Social Democrats split into two factions, the Bolsheviks and the Mensheviks. They broke off relations and even became enemies over their differences as to how socialism—the happiness of humanity—should be built. The Bolsheviks got the upper hand, and the surviving Mensheviks fled from Russia to Palestine. What Bolshevik socialism brought to Russia you can read in Alexander Solzhenitsyn's *The Gulag Archipelago.* If you want to know what the former Mensheviks did in Palestine, take a look around you."

As the saying goes, we Soviet Jews have forgotten more about socialism than the rest of the world ever knew. After all, we were born and grew up to the tattoo of socialist drums and for a long time believed that it was the one and only political system humanity needed to make it completely happy. Then we fled from that system. All eyes were upon us, for everyone knows that you do not swap riches for rags. We did, however, only to discover that in blessed Israel they were building socialism too. We jumped out of the frying pan into the fire. Soon there will be nowhere to escape to—socialism has become so overly fashionable.

I address myself to all those who have a hankering to build socialism in their own country: talk first with us and hear what we, who have had our fill of paradise, have to say. If that doesn't put you off, God help you! Build to your hearts' content. It is the right of every man to build his own prison with his own hands.

Any kind of socialism, no matter what face or mask it may assume, has quite a lot in common with its fellows. The similarity of methods and techniques used by socialists to acquire power is striking. Did you notice, dear reader, a number of extremely similar events taking place at about the same time, admittedly in various countries?

Let us tax our memories and think back. It is the beginning of the 1930s.

In Germany Hitler's National Socialists arranged the Reichstag fire, blamed their political opponents, unleashing upon them the wrath of the nation and herding them behind the barbed wire of the concentration camps, and assumed absolute power in the country.

In December 1934, the assassin Nikolayev, sent by Stalin, shoots Kirov, one of the Soviet Union's most popular leaders. Invoking the "righteous" anger of the people, Stalin began on a hitherto unknown scale to wreak retribution on everyone of whom he disapproved. Hundreds of thousands were executed, tens of millions put behind barbed wire. The person responsible for these events, the puppet Nikolayev, was of course executed, as were those responsible for his execution. Thus the executioners of the executioner were dispatched to the next world and all the evidence destroyed, along with any possible opposition to Stalin. With a firm and ruthless hand, Stalin began with those left alive, who long remained dumb with fear, to frame the gleaming edifice of socialism.

These analagous events resounded through the whole world, bringing countless misfortune to humanity. Naturally, not many people noticed that something similar was happening at about the same time, not in Leningrad or Berlin, but far off in the Middle East.

On the beach at Tel Aviv one summer's night in 1933, another shot rang out. The following morning, the whole Jewish community of Palestine was shaken. Haim Arlozoroff, the most eminent and popular member of the Socialist party leadership, had been killed. Without any investigation the socialists' enemies, Jabotinsky's Zionist Revisionist party, were accused of causing his death. This took place on the very day before the elections for the ruling body of the Jewish Yishuv (the Jewish community in Palestine). The disgraced Revisionists, on whom lay the stigma of the murder, lost the election, and Ben-Gurion's Socialists effectively paved their way into office, which they have held until quite recently.

Since 1934, a lot of water has gone under the bridge. The British have left Palestine. The state of Israel has been in existence for nearly three decades, and in almost every settlement there is a street named after Arlozoroff. It has long been clear to all that the Revisionists were not to blame for Arlozoroff's death. A whole arsenal of underhanded tricks was employed to conceal the truth: suborned witnesses, the mysterious disappearance of persistent truth-seekers, the removal and substitution of police documents. To this day, however, the Israeli Socialists desperately resist any move toward an objective investigation.

The handwriting is similar, is it not? In Germany, in the USSR, and in Israel. They even acted at almost the same time, as if they were drawing on one another's experience and trying not to drag their feet, so as not to sully, God forbid, the banner of socialism.

What is the face of Israeli socialism like? It is a special kind of socialism, unlike any other, although it shares many family characteristics. Although socialists were long in power in Israel, both the socialist and private sectors coexist in the economy, and sometimes this symbiosis leads to the most unexpected and, more often than not, deplorable results.

Judge for yourselves. Whatever bad things one can say about the Soviet and East European type of socialism, it does have attractive sides. At least medical treatment and education are not paid for out-of-pocket. In socialist Israel, as in certain capitalist countries, both must be paid for privately and, in the cases of quite a lot of people, are either fairly inaccessible or outrageously expensive.

On the other hand, the whole cultivated assembly of socialism's negative features blossoms profusely in Israel: inefficiency; state bureaucracy, the bane of all that lives and is creative; lack of interest on the part of the workers in high productivity and the end product of their work; embezzlement, which is a widespread and permanent feature; corruption on a national scale; and, flowing from all this, political passivity and indifference on the part of the bulk of the population.

A friend of mine, formerly an economist in Moscow and now pursuing that same profession in Israel, defines the face of Israeli socialism as follows: "It consists of two halves. The negative sides of socialism have been adopted and so have the negative features of capitalism. The two forms of economic management—private and state—dwell side by side in the one economic organism, creating at their meeting point a most propitious environment for unpunished corruption and misappropriation, which have become a real disaster for the country."

The following example is absolutely typical and will elucidate what I have in mind. Engineer K. arrived in Israel from Russia at about the same time as I did. He is an energetic and very able man who occupied a quite important position in Moscow and gave up everything for the sake of his dream—to live and work in his own Jewish state. For a specialist with his qualifications, the opportunities to find work here were extensive, both in Tel Aviv and in Haifa, the most desirable cultural centers. Brimming over with enthusiasm and a fervent desire to serve his new native land, he himself voluntarily went to work at the end of nowhere in the Negev Desert, where the life was hard and, because of the climate to which he was unaccustomed, sometimes intolerable. This is not a man to whine or complain. He spoke to me because he was seeking advice and not because he wanted to expose anyone. He works in a state-owned factory, which for many years has been running at a loss, like most of the enterprises in the socialist sector.

What a fantastic state of affairs! Two factories producing exactly the same product. Ours belongs to the state; the other is a privately owned company. They have a high level of profitability; we're continually losing money. Every year the state supplements our income to the tune of millions of ILs [Israeli pounds], while the private firm is taxed at an incredibly high rate and in part subsidizes us, the dependents. Nevertheless, the private firm, almost stifled by taxes, remains profitable, and we can never manage without state hand-outs.

I'd thought previously that such bad management could only flourish in the Soviet Union. Now I realize that the state sector in the Israeli economy has far outstripped the USSR.

No one asked me to do this, but for my own information I carried out a time study. I took a watch and checked and noted down the amount of time in the course of a full day the average worker is occupied in useful work. I couldn't believe my eyes. It was two-and-one-half hours in a day, and he was being paid for a full shift.

My amazement, and subsequently my indignation, made me an odd man out at the factory. People began to look askance at me. My perplexity was spoiling these people's quiet lives, who with their charity-case and loafer psychology had got used to being paid for doing nothing.

Then open conflict broke out. We had to carry out certain work on the high tension cables that supplied the factory with power. Power at the factory was my responsibility, and there was no way of keeping anything from me in that department. For carrying out this work a contract for the sum of four hundred thousand Israeli pounds was concluded with a private contractor. I was presented with an accomplished fact. Not suspecting that anything was wrong, I did my calculations for the whole job on the basis of the rates prevailing in Israel. The difference in totals was striking. Their figure was four-and-one-half times greater than mine. The cost of all the work was 90,000 IL. The private contractor was putting 310,000 IL into his own pocket—and not just his own. A lot of people were involved in this fraud, from employees of a state-owned factory to the officials of government institutions under whose jurisdiction and supervision it came.

I traced the chain from bottom to top and recognized the familiar features of the bribe-taker and the thief. They tried to buy me off. I was threatened and seriously feared for my life, but I continued the investigation. I could not do otherwise. I hadn't left the USSR and traveled to the end of the world in order to live apathetically and breathe the stench of theft and corruption. There is plenty of that kind of thing in the Soviet Union. But there at least people are afraid. Sooner or later retribution catches up with the scoundrels. Here it is done almost openly. It seems almost to have become tacitly accepted as normal behavior. And no one is afraid of having to bear the responsibility. In Israel such pranks are not punished.

It only remains for me to add to the sad story of Engineer K. that he didn't manage to get anywhere. Anyway, it would have been laughable if he had come out on top.

I must mention here a major case of fraud in the Sinai's Abu Rudeis oilfields, which were captured from the Egyptians during the Six Day War. There, assets worth many millions of Israeli pounds were misappropriated by a slick group of operators headed by a millionaire named Friedman. The Israeli press almost choked over the sensational revelations. The scandal shook the walls of parliament. One minister was forced to resign (it is true that he was reinstated quite soon afterwards; after all he was a Socialist, a member of their own party). And that was the end of it. The huge losses were written off, and Friedman struts about at liberty, continuing to live on a grand scale, eating his way through his ill-gotten gains.

I saw him on the highway from Tel Aviv to Haifa in a luxurious American Cadillac, and he looked calm and self-assured. The person who pointed him out to me was one of those who had uncovered the whole shady business and precipitated the scandal. He looked far from calm and self-assured. Trying to expose those shysters had caused him so much suffering and distress that when he saw Friedman in the Cadillac he seemed somehow to cringe, as if he were trying to avoid notice in his cheap, aging car.

And what about the late, lamented Bar-Lev defense line on the Suez Canal? Several contractors reportedly became millionaires working on the building of this "impregnable" line of defense, which was breached like a sheet of paper

during the Yom Kippur War. How many people lined their
pockets and made their piles on that? Then it was all paid
for with the lives of hundreds of soldiers.

Such frequent and enormous misappropriations in such a
small country would have been enough to bankrupt any
other country, even a larger one! The pages of the newspapers abound in reports of one fraud after another that the
police have exposed.

People thieve and rob all over the world, not only in Israel, but I am sure that nowhere does there exist such a
propitious atmosphere for swindling as here. Lack of supervision and bad management, the hallmarks of Israeli socialism, make it smooth sailing for practitioners of fraud.
The permanent opportunity to make good what has been
stolen with the money of the world's Jews permits the socialist government not to worry unduly and to concentrate
on one thing—holding tight to their ministerial portfolios.

One of the most important levers for hanging onto power
is the trade unions, the General Federation of Labor in Israel, Histadrut, which is closely linked with the socialist
parties. These trade unions are as unique as the state itself.
This is what Dr. I. Tseitlin writes in the newspaper *Tribuna:*
"Phenomena such as the power of Histadrut in the economic sphere (industry, banking, insurance, trade, transport, etc.) enslave the country's ordinary citizens, who see
in Histadrut not their unbiased defender but one of the
country's chief employers."

Hevrat Gaordim (the General Cooperative Association,
Histadrut's economic section) owns 13 large conglomerates,
1,712 smaller companies, and has a joint holding in 150
others, including the main shipping company Zim and the
airlines El Al and Arkia. The sum of Histadrut's holdings
represents 25 percent of the gross national product. The
capital assets of the trade unions in industry exceeds 10
billion Israeli pounds. The number of people working in the
whole Histadrut network at the end of 1972 was 233,000.

I have abstracted these figures from the June 1973 issue of

the monthly magazine *Mi*, published by the socialist party Mapam, closest to orthodox Marxism of the Israeli socialist parties.

The Israeli socialist trade unions, while continuing to wave the red flag, have become a blatant exploiter of the workers. They speak out demagogically in defense of the workers' interests only in those cases which concern a privately owned enterprise. Then, they egg on the workers to strike, thus taking care of their competitors in the private sector and reducing national life to a state of chaos.

M. Rabinovich makes the following comments in the pages of the magazine *Doma* (March 1973):

We who have come from the "socialist paradise" have had direct experience of the lies and pharasaical hypocrisy of those who herald the building of a "just society," social equality, etc., etc. We have the right to warn our nation to beware of mellifluous phrasemongers, irresponsible prophets bearing slogans that become pitfalls for the unwary....

Is this social experiment, unprecedented in scale, of the running of enterprises by the trade unions themselves, justified? Is social progress being achieved in these enterprises—the improvement of working conditions, workers' profit sharing, and participation in management?

In Histadrut's enterprises, profitability lags behind, productivity is lower, and conditions are frequently worse than in privately owned enterprises. The sluggishness and clumsiness of the bureaucratic apparatus in these trade-union-owned enterprises act as a brake on the country's industrial development. Their inability to equal privately owned eterprises in dynamism and resourcefulness has led to the government being obliged to turn to private investors.

But even today Histadrut makes the development of private industries complicated, and even now conditions have not been created in which it would be more advantageous for foreign Jewish entrepreneurs to invest capital in our country's economy than it is for them to give it hand-outs.

In an excess of self-flagellation the leader of Histadrut, its secretary-general, Yitzhak Ben-Aharon, a member of the Central Committee of the Socialist party, makes the following admission, and I quote: "We plunder public funds in order to create a class of wealthy people.... Those who stand close to the till get rich. No one can get rich in this country without the permission of the government. And that permission is given by two or three people."

You'll never put it better than that, Ben-Aharon, as long as you live.

The port of Ashdod has become the personal toy of the dockers union. Their chief, Iogoshuah Peretz, looks and acts just like a gangland thief, and his fellow Moroccan stevedores bow to no one in their admiration for him. The police guards at the dock were Moroccans also and adept at looking elsewhere as the place was robbed blind. Eventually, in the summer of 1975, the authorities fired these guards, and the robberies stopped immediately. When this handsome, simple, semi-educated demagogue, Peretz, came to the port, the new guards, who were Moslem Druzes, asked him for his papers, for they were new and did not personally know the uncrowned king of Ashdod.

How he screamed! Like a madman. But the guard insisted upon seeing his documents. Peretz telephoned his dockers and called a strike. After all, his humiliation must be paid for. A one-day strike, costing millions of Israeli pounds— which the government paid to the various shipping companies—was the result. But, what's the worry? The money came from the coffers of American Jews. And that will teach them to anger Iogoshuah Peretz.

The government put Peretz on trial. On the day of the trial, another one-day strike was called. Peretz gave his men a farewell speech. "If I am convicted," he said sweetly, "burn down the city." He was given a small symbolic fine, which was promptly paid by Histadrut in an attempt to pacify the vindictive union boss.

In that same summer of 1975 a singular incident occurred which, though unrelated to the Ashdod strike, is equally suggestive of the power wielded by organized fraud and corruption over the government's efforts to control illegal activity. Israel is a country of small shopkeepers; thousands and thousands make their living selling all manner of merchandise to the public. Some are rich and some are poor, but they are all alike in that none of them keeps books. They pay tax on their earnings only as their consciences tell them— this may be one-hundredth of the real tax.

The government, being eternally hungry for taxes, finally lost patience and passed a law forcing all shopkeepers to keep records. Seeing in this law an end to their highly advantageous tax situation and their excessive profits, the shopkeepers of Israel called a general strike. Shops closed all over the country, threatening to bring life to an abrupt halt. This was too much; the government relented, withdrew the law, and allowed the shopkeepers to return to their former habits.

Enmeshed in hypocrisy, the rulers of Israel publicly fling filth at one another. They keep passing the buck, and life in the country creaks on its way, like a cart with ungreased wheels, along the winding, rutted, pothole-filled road to socialism.

In Tel Aviv, the foul-smelling slum district of Hatikvah ["hope"] coexists with Savyon, where villas, each one richer and more elegant than the next, bask in palm groves like those outside Florida's Miami Beach.

Of the 614,000 urban families in Israel, 132,000 Jewish families (and this amounts to more than half a million persons) live either on or below the poverty line. Sixty-nine thousand families (300,000 persons) are crammed from three to seven in a single room. Just think about those figures! According to official standards and figures, every third Jew in Israel festers in poverty.

From the streets of Qatamon there emanates a stench of drug addiction, prostitution, and crime that spreads across the whole face of Jerusalem.

In the palm-lined avenues of Herzliya and Caesarea, the progeny of the new-fledged millionaires on their pampered thoroughbred mounts ride gaily in the same cavalcade with eminent Socialist party officials.

These are two faces of Israel.

Closer acquaintance with life in Israel leads to more and more discoveries, each one more surprising than its predecessor. The crown of local socialism, the object of its pride for many years, the kibbutzim, quickly lose the glossy plumage of the brochures if one delves beneath the polished surface.

It is not for me to judge. Perhaps in earlier days, when the process of colonizing the land was going on and the pioneer spirit of the first settlers was still alive, this was a sensible and progressive way of organizing agriculture and defending the frontiers at the same time. I have no wish to cast doubt upon the courage and heroism of those who drained swamps, who died of malaria, who erected the first dwellings and plowed the first furrows in the desert. That generation fulfilled its task of laying the foundations of the state.

But if those nameless, righteous heroes were today to rise from their graves, look upon Israel, and see what their sometime-glorious kibbutzim—once the school of Jewish agriculture, the crucible where social rejects from the villages of Eastern Europe were forged into worker-peasants—had degenerated into, they would not believe their eyes and would curse those who disturbed the peace of their graves.

What do people know about the kibbutzim, and what impressions of them do members of the hosts of delegations and tourist groups take away to the rest of the world? What kinds of legends subsequently enjoy currency among the gullible, both Jews and non-Jews?

O Lord, having heard of these wonders, how one wants to turn one's back on everything—the noise and bustle of the city, the constant, plaguing worry over one's daily bread, the education of one's children, the intolerable nervous strain imposed by modern civilization—and go to the kibbutz where...

everyone is equal and all live together in a single large family;

there is no money, no cult of the golden calf, and all are free from the base sentiments engendered by filthy lucre;

each works according to his abilities, according to his strength, in the open air, gazing on a landscape that rejoices the eye, and receives just what he needs for a modest healthful life;

mothers are liberated from the burden of caring for their children who, straight from the cradle, are taken to a special nursery building and who, in the evenings for an hour or two, are returned to the mother before returning to the supervision of trained nannies and nurses;

once children have attained their majority they live separately from their parents and grow up quite unlike them;

having worked his stint in the fields or on the farm, the kibbutz member can dedicate the remainder of his time to satisfying his cultural needs, having at his command movies, the theater, television, the reading room, and, of course, his personal library in a cosy little apartment, as like all the others as peas in a pod.

Paradise. The best that the world's socialists have achieved in practice, after so many unsuccessful and bloody experiments. Oh how splendid it would be to go there and behold true socialism, beautiful no longer in theory but in reality. To savor its fruits.

Let us then take a bite of this rosy fruit and look into its heart.

Good heavens! How unlike the poster everything is! And how on earth can this be called socialism? It is pure capitalism and, at that, capitalism that has turned somewhat sour.

The kibbutzim have long been transformed into group exploiters and recipients of charity. These vaunted socialist enterprises, zealously supported by the government, enjoy enviable tax advantages at the expense of private-sector farms, which are taxed at twice the rate. The kibbutzim are solicitously showered with a golden rain of grants and subsidies.

Only when one knows this can one determine the worth of all the advertising trumpery—the theatres built in the kibbutzim, which are every bit as good as those in the cities, the swimming pools and the like—all of which is bound to be shown to the stunned and uninformed visitor.

The kibbutz collectively exploits hired labor like any thoroughgoing capitalist and pockets the surplus value. Almost all building works in the kibbutzim, including the erection of the celebrated theatres and swimming pools, are carried out by the hands of hired laborers, Arabs and Druzes, who are paid at the lowest rates and are completely beyond the pale of the social services. Seasonal work in the fields and plantations, in particular the gathering in of the harvest, is carried out by drawing on a large amount of outside labor.

In recent years, many kibbutzim, in an effort to maximize their income, have begun to set up industrial enterprises and relegate to the background agriculture, which was initially the reason for the birth of the kibbutz movement. Many workers from neighboring towns are employed in these small and profitable factories, and the kibbutz, in the capacity of employers, pay them a monthly wage. According to data published in the magazine *Mi*, 60 percent of those employed in kibbutz metal-working, furniture, and food factories are hired workers.

Nor is this the whole story. Even the day-to-day work of serving the kibbutz members themselves—the communal kitchen and dining-room work, the community laundry, etc.—has also begun to be handed over to hired workers. And it is here where exploitation assumes its most refined and unexpected forms.

Quite often in kibbutz dining rooms, I would meet waitresses and kitchen hands of a non-Jewish ethnic type. They were girls from Germany, Denmark, Sweden, or France, foreign tourists, who, having had their curiosity aroused by advertisements about life on a kibbutz as a model of social justice, had been inveigled into having a free holiday in one. They arrive in Israel in hordes, on cheap charter flights run by almost every airline in the world, and cheerfully settle down in the kibbutzim. Above their heads is the southern sky. There are even some palm trees. They actually are fed free of charge and given a place to sleep, but . . .

But for all this, one has to work . . . and work also without payment. Work as a dishwasher or waitress, a laundress or a milkmaid. And there is no turning one's nose up if one is sent out to work in the fields.

You must agree that it is a very well-conceived scheme. In this day and age to have people working for nothing, just for their food and shelter, is usually much more complicated. Here, however, it is all simple and straightforward.

Where, then, is the vaunted justice and socialism? Exploitation and acceptance of charity satisfy the modest needs of a microscopic section of the population (5 percent in all), living in tiny settlements in the bosom of nature.

It is no accident that young people who were born and grew up in kibbutzim have begun to desert them in fairly large numbers and make for the towns, eloquently rejecting the road chosen by their parents, leaving the old folk to end their days in the communal kibbutz dining rooms drinking cups of tea bought with American money.

Ruth Zilberberg of the Israeli Ministry of Finance Economic Planning Bureau has published an interesting piece of research, which shows that the number of people living in Jewish agricultural settlements has declined sharply in recent years. Whereas in the mid-1950s 80 percent of the Jewish population of Israel lived in the towns, that figure has now reached 90 percent.

Young people leave the kibbutzim in the same way as in Russia they flee from the collective farms. Large deep cracks furrow the façade of Israeli socialism.

The question then arises: Why does the government

watch over the kibbutzim with such care and sustain them in every way? Are they highly profitable and essential in dealing with the problem of the country's food supply?

Here too the facts do not accord with the rosy propaganda pictures. As the Minister of Agriculture Chaim Gvati, himself a kibbutz member, was forced to admit, 55 percent of the fodder required by Israeli livestock farming is imported from abroad. How is that for a start! The milk and meat produced in the kibbutzim turn out to be rather expensive. What is the point of importing fodder, most of which becomes manure. Wouldn't it be better to buy the end product from abroad? It might well be cheaper.

So the tinsel of propaganda slips away and a somewhat seamy reality is left. As before, however, the kibbutzim are advertised throughout the whole world as the shop window of Israeli socialism, and the government fusses over them as if they were a beloved child. Why is this?

At this point we come upon a rather serious discovery. The kibbutzim are absolutely essential to the Israeli ruling socialist block because they long ago became a well-regulated incubator, supplying reliable and dedicated people for senior positions in all spheres of the state apparatus. In the army, the police, the trade unions, and in parliament.

This is particularly obvious in Israeli embassies in foreign countries. The down-to-earth kibbutz member in his favorite "apache" shirt, completely foreswearing the tie, for him a symbol of bourgeois degeneracy, stands out against the background of polished diplomats, always dressed in accordance with protocol. Then you see how strong the network of secret political commissars is in Israeli institutions.

Moreover, the kibbutz diplomats' shunning of their colleagues' bourgeois way of life is largely verbal. In Paris, in Bonn, in London, in Washington, they enter their costly automobiles with a degree of enjoyment and live at public expense in elegant apartments in the most highly respectable districts. And when the period of service abroad is over, they take returning to the kibbutz very hard and go to almost any lengths to obtain fresh appointments in the decadent capitalist world.

In the Israeli army most of the officers, right up to the top brass, including pilots and paratroopers—the whole core of the war machine is staffed by kibbutz members. Officially, the army is apolitical and its officers do not belong to any political party, but this is simply a version for simpletons circulated by the powers that be. The young men who have grown up in the kibbutzim are from the cradle imbued with socialist ideology, and when they become officers they remain loyal as long as they live, not to Israel but in the first instance to their parents' political party.

It is, therefore, no accident that the whole of Israel is convinced that a military takeover in the country is unthinkable. The kibbutz officer class acts as a bridle on the army and will never direct its guns at its own party chiefs. This fact was recently made public by General Ariel Sharon, one of the most able soldiers in Israel and one of the few non-Kibbutzniks and nonsocialists to achieve a position in the army high command. Although during the last two wars he has become a legend in his own lifetime and a favorite of the whole army, the path to the supreme military appointment, that of chief of the General Staff, is completely closed to him.

Kibbutz members sit at desks in ministries, heading the celebrated Israeli bureaucratic apparatus, which in its stultifying qualities is second to none in the world. It is they who have engendered and firmly implanted in the country the institution of protectionism and individual petitioning, which has become the prime mover in every field, from getting a job to obtaining a license to open an enterprise in the private sector. The result of this is that one cannot take a single step in Israel without protection.

It is not only officials who afford protection but also old men sitting out their retirement in the kibbutzim. I myself, on the advice of my friends, was obliged to make use of their services in order to achieve some sort of solution to a trifling problem that had got completely bogged down in the bureaucratic apparatus. You are taken to see a grey-haired but still quite alert old man in some kibbutz in the Valley of Jezreel or on the shores of Lake Tiberias, where the old boy is meticulously washing dishes in the communal dining room or peeling potatoes in the kitchen. The old fellow is bound to be wearing an "apache" shirt, which has almost become the party uniform. In the shade of the palm trees as you drink a cup of free kibbutz coffee together, you anxiously unfold your troubles to him. He looks at you as if you were a foolish child, dials some Tel Aviv or Jerusalem number, and five minutes later the problem is settled.

After all, this same old boy formerly wore out the seats of his pants in innumerable ministries, or he may have been a diplomat or a general. In a word, he ruled the country, and now his protégés, whom he turned into first-class bureaucrats, are everywhere. The old fellow can do anything. He can give orders to a minister, and the latter will not object. The old boy will keep his influence until the day he dies, and in his declining years, through the medium of protectionism, he will continue to weave the socialist net in which the whole country flounders inextricably.

The kibbutzim are incessantly turning out fresh supplies of neatly fitting cogs, and with them the party fills the spaces in the government machine. With the help of these cogs, the socialists rule the country. They rule sloppily and without skill, sometimes simply unwisely, but they will not give their power up to anyone without a fight, even if the fate of the country is at stake.

Socialism as a whole, and in particular its Israeli variety, contains a deep infusion of hypocrisy. It is not only the people suffering from political color-blindness who swallow the bait of its advertising propaganda. In a vast quantity of books and articles about Israel, in the travel notes of visiting journalists or voyagers, there is one particular attribute which one is fed up of hearing about, which always crops up, and which this author himself has witnessed.

I went to visit a kibbutz, where I was touched by the sight of Jewish peasants toiling in the fields. Overwhelmed with impressions, I was led gently by the hand into a communal dining room with a thousand places, where all the dwellers in this particular village are fed free of charge with vitaminized, high-calorie kosher food. I also ingested some of this food, nor did I have to pay. Sitting drowsily after my ample meal, my gaze lighted upon the waiter who was clearing away the dirty dishes from the table, and a persistent thought began to bore into my brain: I had already met this man with the meekly averted gaze, dressed in the white jacket of a waiter. After a gentle sounding, the waiter too confessed that he had met me previously, even naming the date and place of the meeting. But of course! It was X, the Israeli minister! I had been at a reception he gave the previous day in Tel Aviv. Minister and waiter in one person! How democratic! This is genuine government by the people!

This minister is a member of a kibbutz and from time to time is obliged to forsake his ministry, to return to his native kibbutz and, like all its other members, not to shun menial work, if only for a day.

Even a man of such broad experience as the Slovak writer Ladislav Mnacko swallowed the phoney bait. He was at one time a member of the Central Committee of the Czechoslovak Communist party, broke with that party because of its intolerable hypocrisy and lies, and after fleeing to the West, spent a period of time in Israel. In his book on Israel, which was circulated illegally among Jews in the Soviet Union in hand-written copies, he related to his readers in the most affecting tones an almost identical story about a minister-cum-waiter, and I recall what a sharp and gripping impression it made on us in Moscow. Israel seemed to us to be a Garden of Eden, where all the dreams of humanity about equality and justice had been realized, and genuine socialism—not the spurious variety of which we had had more than our fill in the USSR—had triumphed.

No, this is not a lie. Israeli ministers actually do, from

time to time, come down from the capital in their luxurious government cars to their remote kibbutzim and demonstratively, for all to see, spend an hour or two peeling potatoes or washing down dirty tables to the accompaniment of the affecting sighs of ecstatic lady tourists and political morons. I myself have seen the then Minister of Agriculture, Chaim Gvati, thus engaged in the kibbutz Yif-at and even Yigal Allon, in his kibbutz on the picturesque shores of Lake Tiberias. They come to their kibbutzim as once the gentry visited their country estates; and, having posed for the benefit of the watching public with a towel over their shoulders in the communal dining room, they enjoy a free holiday in the bosom of nature, receive foreign visitors, and provide for them such feasts as would have been beyond the means of a wealthy feudal lord.

I have observed that ardent socialist Yigal Allon not only in the kibbutz dining room with a dirty towel over his shoulder, but at a high-society ball at the New York Hilton, where he seemed reasonably at ease in his superbly tailored dinner jacket among a crowd of American millionaires— theoretically speaking, socialism's most detested class enemies. That warrior of socialism Yigal Allon did not seem in the least inclined to sink his proletarian teeth into their throats. On the contrary he warmly embraced the sharks of capitalism one after the other. The richest Jews of America had gathered in the ballroom of the Hilton—those who are stigmatized by the socialist orthodox as the vilest enemies of the workers, as exploiters and bloodsuckers—to toss the odd million dollars into the socialist cap taken round by Yigal Allon. They were giving generously to poor Israel.

There was neither socialist nor capitalist in that company. There were just Jews. The national spirit hovered beneath the crystal chandeliers and above the tables, groaning with the fat of the land. The proletarian socialist Yigal Allon, who prides himself on not having a cent's worth of personal property on his conscience, Max Fischer, the Detroit financier, and Jack Greenberg, the oil king from Colorado, were here all full of brotherly love for one another.

I was at that ball and to this day my tiny son plays with the blue-and-white silk ribbon bearing my name that adorned my chest in the Hilton hotel, giving evidence to my temporary inclusion in the company of the elect.

I witnessed the sleek hands of these men of fabulous wealth unfalteringly signing checks for millions of dollars, vying with one another, as if they were at an auction sale, as to who could give the most to his poor Israeli brethren.

I sat at the same table and ate steaks from the same salmon as their wives, young and old, on whose necks sparkled diamond necklaces, each of which was worth enough to feed the population of a whole Israeli town.

I looked at the sycophantic smiles of professional beggars on the faces of the Israeli representatives, from the deputy prime minister of the socialist government downwards, as, setting class and party pretense aside, they licked up the crumbs from the golden platters of American capital. Then, for the first time, I was transfixed by a horrifying thought: this was national socialism of the highest order, however monstrous and absurd this label might seem when applied to a Jewish state.

Let us consider this soberly and without emotion. Let us remove the trappings of verbal tinsel and look at what is within. We must not be put off by frightening words. Gas chambers and genocide were no more than the barbaric means to achieve an end—the building of socialism for a single elect group of people—the representatives of the German master race.

In preaching his own brand of socialism, Hitler put the interests of the German people above everything else and robbed and plundered other nations. The German National Socialists used the hands of the Wehrmacht soldiers to achieve this. Israeli socialists unashamedly rake in money from other nations, bloodlessly and without cannibalistic impulses, using the hands of wealthy members of the local Jewish community.

I must immediately make one reservation. I disagree completely with those who, in vain attempts to denigrate Israel, accuse it of fascism, who compare the attitude of Israeli soldiers toward the local population in the Arab territory they control with the bestial acts of the Nazis in the countries they occupied. The efforts of Soviet propaganda in this regard are particularly strenuous. And there are certain people in the West who mask their out-and-out anti-Semitism with anti-Zionism.

I have been a soldier in the Israeli army, both in peacetime and during the Yom Kippur War. As a member of the Israeli forces, I have spent quite a lot of time in the Arab territory occupied during the Six Day War. Not once have I either seen or heard of a single case of impolite behavior toward the local population on the part of the soldiers. On the contrary, the Israeli army, unlike other armies, makes a point of behaving correctly and courteously in occupied territory. This sometimes leads to bizarre happenings, inconceivable in any other country, and as an example of this I include the following personal reminiscence.

One night during the Yom Kippur War our platoon was put on the alert and moved into some Arab settlement near Ramallah in Samaria. The major in charge of the operation warned us that according to information received a group of terrorists was hiding in one of the houses. We arrived at this house in a number of vehicles. The major and two soldiers went to the door. Then something happened which would have brought a wry smirk to the lips of a soldier in any army. You probably think that they began beating on the door with rifle butts and kicking it in with the toes of their boots? You must be joking. The major knocked politely, and, when after a long silence someone on the other side of the door finally deigned to reply, he apologized in embarrassment for the late call and requested that some soldiers be allowed to enter the house. After the search was over, without any terrorists being found, the major spent a long time asking the householders to excuse him for having disturbed them. The major's sensitivity, the fact that he waited patiently outside a closed door until the householders got around to unlocking it, could have cost us dearly if there really had been terrorists in the house. However, even the danger of being thus repaid for soft treatment does not alter the Israeli psychology.

No, there is no fascism in Israel. But there is no end of national socialism, and this I intend to prove.

Where does Israel get the money to build its socialism? Where does most of the money for state and party projects come from ? Even a child in Israel knows that it comes from abroad, from the world's Jews, in the form of charity and loans.

By the way, Israeli socialists stubbornly resist the offers of Jewish businessmen to invest capital in the country's economy. Who is going to permit foreign capitalists to exploit Jewish workers, to make profits from the sweat of Jewish toilers? The Israeli socialists prefer to accept money only in the form of a gift.

The Jews of the United States, Canada, Australia, Argentina, France, and the United Kingdom give many hundreds of millions of dollars a year. What do these millions represent?

In the main they are the surplus value the Jewish capitalist receives as a result of "exploiting" the American, South African, or Argentine worker. This is not kosher money; from the point of view of orthodox socialism it is unclean, and for representatives of a "workers" party to accept is indisputably a sin.

The money is accepted without blushing, however, and like professional beggers, the Israeli socialists berate the bestower and demand more and more. Why should they worry about the working class of other nations in the sweat of whose brow this money has been acquired? Not even a flush of embarrassment tinges the socialist cheek.

Is this not national socialism, which sets its own national interests above everything else?

The Israeli exploitation of Arab labor is carried out on a gigantic scale. Arab workers are brought in from the occupied territories; precise figures are not published, but on the basis of such fragmentary data as gets into print, the number of Arabs brought daily to work in Israel is well above fifty thousand.

Every morning at dawn, from Nablus (Shechem), Hebron, Bethlehem, and Gaza, hundreds of trucks move toward the "green line"—the 1967 frontier. In the back of them in serried ranks sit Arabs, their white headdresses fastened round their foreheads with black agals. They work on almost every building site, in many plants and factories, on vegetable and fruit farms. They surface roads and plant trees. They empty the garbage and carry loads about on their backs.

In contrast with Europe, building work in Israel is not highly mechanized. Cheap Arab manual labor is more profitable than imported machines, particularly now that fuel costs have soared. Without these swarthy hands, which are accustomed to blazing sun and the hot Khamsin wind, the Israeli economy would long ago have given up the ghost. Arab labor is highly advantageous and is the basis of the profitability of many enterprises. One can hazard a judgment as to the situation of these imported workers on the basis of an extract from the article "Today in Beersheba" published on 24 February 1974, in the "semi-official" newspaper *Nasha Strana*. The author Meshulam Ed writes: "At a conservative estimate, there are about three thousand Arab workers employed in Beersheba, mainly on building sites. Many of them work for private contractors, who do quite well out of them: they underpay the Arabs and deprive them of their social rights. As a rule these contractors employ a few Jews in key positions."

Further on the author quotes the words of the director of a large plant employing twelve hundred Arabs. The director admits that he receives orders from above to hire as many Arabs as possible because one does not have to pay so much attention to formalities as when dealing with Jews. This kind of solution to economic problems fits in quite comfortably behind the socialist façade.

I do not think that anyone will want to argue with me when I suggest that the celebrated discussion about *who is a Jew,* which has been torturing the country for so many years, smells of primitive racism a mile off, and which in a Jewish environment after the tragedy of the six million, seems blasphemous and unbelievable. The atheist socialists yield one bit of ground after another to the religious lobby, which though small in number is powerful and enjoys influential support outside the country.

This faction makes people of today, of the electronic and space age, live according to the ancient laws of biblical times. A child born of a non-Jewish mother is obliged to submit himself to a religious rite in order to be counted as a proper Jew, which for someone of atheistic views is humiliating.

A non-Jew, even if he is a member of a Jewish family, is treated with disrespect even after death. He may not be buried in a cemetery. Such is the case with one of Israel's most famous heroines, Waltraute Lotz, whose memory is thus desecrated by religious bigots. She was of German origin and the wife of Wolfgang Lotz, himself half-German, half-Jewish, and an Israeli citizen. For many years she worked in Cairo on behalf of the Israeli intelligence, supplying Tel Aviv with very valuable intelligence information. Eventually the Egyptians managed to break her cover, and she and her husband were imprisoned. By a miracle she escaped capital punishment but languished in jail for many years. When she was set free, she returned to Israel, where, although still quite young, she died as a result of the ordeal she had undergone. In socialist Israel no graveyard space was available for her burial. Her blood and her origins were inappropriate.

I cannot even bring myself to make any comment.

Once upon a time, when Sholem Aleichem was alive, in the golden days when Jewish national life flourished in the numberless shtetels of the Pale of Settlement—in the plains of Poland, Byelorussia, the Ukraine, and Bessarabia— among the various trades and crafts followed by Jews in order to feed their ever-hungry families, there was one, that of begging, which was considered no more disgraceful than any other. This was not an amateur occupation but a profession, one handed down from generation to generation. Every shtetel had its beggars and scrupulously, as if it were paying an extra tax, supported them from the cradle to the grave ... and then their children and their grandchildren. It never entered the head of the shtetel beggars to do any useful work. Why? The alms given by soft-hearted Jews fed them no worse and often more amply than the miserable earnings of a tailor or a carpenter. The beggars did not consider their profession humiliating. On the contrary, they paraded their rags before a crowd in the street with pride and openly scorned the worn-out workers whose bounty they magnanimously accepted.

Even Soviet power, which severely persecuted parasitism, could do nothing with the shtetel beggars. The Jews continued to feed them, and they, just as if they were at work, went the daily round of their territory, exacting tribute from every home.

In the shtetels of those days, begging was not just a profession but a psychology and a philosophy, and, sad though this might be, is still one of the Jewish traditions that along with various others has survived to the present day, while there is little trace of the shtetels themselves and the very image of the Jew has altered irrevocably.

One does not know what criteria guided the state of Israel in selecting from the national treasure house what to preserve for the future and what to renounce. The sense of humor, one of the most precious Jewish qualities, was carelessly tossed aside, but begging both as a profession and a psychology was taken up with alacrity to lend strength to the young state's arm.

Socialist Israel became the legal heir to the traditions of the shtetel beggars. This disreputable occupation has been established on a national basis and is serviced by the most modern system of telecommunications and computer technology. Thousands of Israelis in the central apparatus and an even greater number abroad, in almost all the countries of the world, do exactly the same thing as their forefathers did in the dusty shtetel streets. They are no longer in rags but in smart suits. They do not go barefoot but travel in magnificent automobiles, and they do not demand from Jews a few cents for some food but millions and hundreds of millions of dollars, sufficient for the upkeep of a modern state with a population of three million and a large and extremely expensive army.

The Jews of the diaspora, however remote the nook where they have sought shelter, will nevertheless be unearthed by Israel's tribute collectors and be forced to part with a proportion of the contents of their purse. The beggars of today with their diplomatic passports do not stand on ceremony. They appeal to national feelings. They reopen spiritual wounds with the threat of anti-Semitism, and, if that is not enough, they pave the way into people's pockets with crude pressure and take recalcitrants by the throat.

While taking part in this kind of pouncing on Jewish purses in the United States, I myself landed in some curious situations. I remember in one little town in Pennsylvania the money collector and I were making for a jeweler's shop in order to relieve its Jewish proprietor of a little cash, but when he saw us through the window he locked himself in and fled by the back door.

In another place the collector accompanying me spent a long time getting some money out of an old Jew, the owner of a small scrap-metal foundry. In full view of the Negro workmen crowding around us in the workshop, the collector belabored the grudging, perplexed Jew with every insult under the sun, pointing his finger at me and calling me a national hero, in whose presence this little man should burn with shame. The foundry owner, in the same kind of greasy overalls as his workers, his eyes running and inflamed by the heat from the smelting furnaces, defended himself, meekly mentioning his two daughters who were at college and whose education he had scarcely sufficient money to pay for.

The psychology of begging has permeated the whole Israeli state structure and poisoned it from within. Here, as distinct from any other country, they do not save money and do not count it. If there is not enough, the world's Jews will toss them some more. Nobody could care a fig about anything. They live from one hand-out to the next, clinging to the flowing udder of the Jewish milch cow.

This psychology has killed creative stimulus and questing zeal. Every day in Israel projects offering great advantage to the country are destroyed. Valuable suggestions promising certain financial return are dismissed. Why bother? After all, money can be obtained without even working for it, without taking any risks or troubling one's bloated brains.

Socialist Israel has become one enormous charity case hanging round the neck of world Jewry or, to be more accurate, living off the workers of all those countries where Jews live. Dependence has crept like leprosy into the soul of every individual Israeli, corrupting him morally, turning him into a parasite. It is no accident that the most active and productive element of the population inevitably flees the country.

Any Sabra (any Jew born not in the diaspora but here in Israel, in the land of his forefathers), as soon as he has learned to read, sees on the walls of his kindergarten or his school or the hospital innumerable tablets with one and the same text but with a variety of different names. These tablets explain unequivocally to the young Israeli that the kindergarten he attends, the school where he sits at his desk, the hospital where he had his glands removed, were built with money given by such and such a family from Cleveland or Johannesburg. Each room in these buildings, each corridor, is dominated by the humiliating little plaques bearing the name of the bestower.

Later, the young Israeli citizen sees those same tablets in the university and the vocational training school. Even when he goes into the countryside, in every little grove he stumbles upon a memorial plaque that sears his eyes with the name of some Jew beyond the sea whose money paid for the trees being planted there in memory of his late mother or mother-in-law, who sleep their last sleep in a cemetery in New York or Brussels.

It is not surprising that the clot of an inferiority complex starts to form in his bloodstream. His initiative is sapped and a degrading, yet calm and unrebellious, feeling of dependence begins to permeate his being.

And wherever he works, on whatever rung of the social ladder that fate may place him, he will at best be an official who drinks too much coffee, smokes too many cigarettes, and sleepily awaits the end of the working day. He is spiritually castrated, and castration is untreatable.

Perhaps one can point to this as the most serious result of socialist government in the ancient land of Palestine, and it also represents the main reason for the rapid disintegration of a quite recently created state.

And this happened in the same state where, according to the researches of Israeli attorney Berman, more than *$40 billion dollars,* in different forms of *donation,* has been given from abroad—more, in short, than was contributed to all Western European countries under the Marshall Plan.

chapter eight

DEAD SOULS

M y friend called to see me in his aged, battered Peugeot. This man is one of the few that our family has got to know well in Israel. The friendship was made easier by the fact that he knew Russian, although not all that well. Russian, however, was the native language of Tamara, his wife.

He had met Tamara in Moscow thirty years before and brought her to Palestine, where their children and then their grandchildren were born. By the way, as far as the grandchildren are concerned, I should be more precise: they were born not in Israel but in America. But more of that later. It is worth going into further detail about my Israeli friend. He merits it; moreover, he is very typical of the country.

His face is the typical face of a Jew from a Polish *shtetel*: fair-haired (this one can deduce from the remaining hair around his wide bald patch) and grey eyes, containing the glimmer of eternal sorrow, beneath upward-thrusting heavy brows, like the pitches of a roof. A perpetual kindly smile, reaching out to everyone, never leaves his full, childlike lips. He is big-boned and thick-set. You can tell that his ancestors were draymen somewhere in Volhynia or Podolia.

The kindness and honesty of this man are indescribable. Of such as he, people say in Russia: "They use the likes of him for carrying water." That is to say, such people are ripe for exploitation by anyone who feels so inclined. He is a man who never says no. He is always ready to run and help someone, even if you wake him up in the middle of the night. He genuinely suffers if for reasons that have nothing to do with him he cannot console or aid someone. His wife is the same sort of person.

It goes without saying that being possessed of altruism like this they have not made much money in Israel. They have been used to carrying quite a lot of water! They worked in a kibbutz in the scorching heat of the Bet She'an Valley; then when his wife, being a nothern woman, fell ill from the unaccustomed heat and aged in the space of a few years, they moved to place near Asqelon. Hence once again they plowed the land, milked the cows, and would possibly have remained farmers had it not been for the wars, one after the other. He was called up for each one and was always an inconspicuous but very necessary soldier. The family toiled away on the sun-parched earth, running the farm without the help of a man. Somehow in snatches he managed to get an education and reached the rank of major in the army. He went into the reserve, and, as quite a mature person, almost a grandfather, he graduated from the university. In late middle age he moved to Jerusalem, whence he set out to the Yom Kippur War with his tank regiment. Tamara saw their son off to join the paratroopers in the Golan Heights. Thank God they both came back alive.

If there is anything good in this country, then it has been created by men like this friend of mine. There are very few of them left in the Israel of today, boiling like a cauldron, rent apart by squalid passions. The ideals of the pioneers are now openly derided, and the urge, contracted from abroad, to make money, has broken down the frail shoots lovingly tended by the pioneers' hands. These people are like tiny oases in an arid desert whose sands advance inexorably and are on the point of engulfing this last source of life-giving moisture.

So my friend called to see me in his aged shabby Peugeot, with its suspiciously rattling engine and bumper fastened to the patched-up body with bits of wire, grinning from ear to ear with his brows arched in curiosity.

"Get ready' We're going for a picnic!"

"What kind of picnic? Where?"

"Get ready! You've got five minutes! The car's waiting. I haven't switched the engine off."

He was always looking for some way of entertaining us and would have done anything to add some color to the first days in our new home and strengthen the unstable love for Israel in our hearts. He had now hit upon the idea of carrying us off with him to this picnic with his comrades, old warriors like himself, cart horses such as go on working until they drop in the shafts.

"You'll meet some real people," he cried with enthusiasm, permanently scorched by the Palestine sun, the smile shining from every wrinkle of its surface, and his brows reaching up to a sharp point until they became the two pitches of a roof. "This is really Israel! And as for the rest, you can keep it."

That was his only opinion. To be more precise that was what he wanted to think. In fact, the rest was the genuine, authentic Israel, and in it my friend and his comrades looked like extinct birds that had flown in from heaven knows where. We new arrivals in the country could not help noticing this, but trying to change his opinion was a waste of time. And was it worth upsetting him?

We drove out of Jerusalem in a long column of nearly a hundred vehicles, and while we were traveling through the streets of the city among the flood of brand-new limousines and station wagons, our old jalopies, preserved heaven

knows how by their thrifty owners, were in such contrast as
to look like museum pieces that had been brought out for an
airing. Both the cars and their owners were museum pieces.

We joined the highway and raced off deep into Samaria,
Arab territory occupied during the Six Day War. Somewhere there, according to my friend, was a pleasant shady
wood where the advance party had already set about roast-
ing a lamb. We traveled through occupied territory where
we were completely alien, past Arab villages with turquoise
blinds in the windows. Barefoot boys and women in black
with bundles on their heads followed us with their glances,
which, even in the sun's heat, sent a chill down our spines.

No one cared much for us here—there was little ground
for doubt. Two jeep-loads of soldiers in their green berets,
one in front of, and one behind, the column, covered both
sides of the road with the barrels of their machine guns,
guaranteeing our safety in the event that Arab antipathy
toward us assumed a more acute form than mere scornful
glances. Then we reached the wood, with the smoke of the
campfire, the smell of roast lamb, bottles of orange juice
passed from hand to hand. And songs—songs of days gone
by when a nation was born in battle; the songs of Palmach
and Haganah—unpretentious, simple, and moving. Tears
came to the old warriors' eyes, broken down old war horses,
whose fighting days were over. Nowadays no one had any
use for them, and to everyone else they were a blight on
the landscape. They themselves took in the visage of mangy
old horses among the polished automobiles in this egotistical consumer society of the country that, when they were
laying the foundation stones, they had conceived so differ-
ently.

The isolation was sad and excruciating. Beyond the grove
of trees lay the stepped, bare white rocky slopes, spurs of
the Judaean Hills, among which Arab villages lurked
malevolently.

Here, amid the submachine-gun security, a fifteen-year-
old girl, while horsing around with the soldiers in one of

the jeeps, snapped a pair of handcuffs on her wrists. The handcuffs—brought along in anticipation of a clash with the Arabs—snapped shut, and the soldiers had no key to open them. The keys had been left at the command post, so we had to travel to Jerusalem before the girl could have the handcuffs removed. Of course, handcuffs are needed; they are always needed here.

The column set off back past those same somber, withdrawn villages and blank, estranged glances. In the first vehicle, like a dreadful and sickeningly unpleasant symbol, sat a tear-stained Jewish girl, surrounded by soldiers, her outstretched hands pinioned by the handcuffs.

My friend, never down in the mouth, sat at the wheel of the car, eyebrows never still, trying to cheer us up with stories of the people we had met. I interrupted him to ask him about their children. After all, to judge by their age, they probably had grown-up children, but for some reason they were not there at that unhappy picnic.

"Children," his brows rose to form a sharp wedge. "All the children are far away." And his eyes twitched in regret, as if the wind had blown some sand into them.

It turned out that the same thing happened in almost every family. The son or daughter, once they had spread their wings, broke away from their family and at the same time from Israel too. The fathers, overcoming inconceivable obstacles, had agonizingly made their way here from the lands of the diaspora, to a bare country in which they and their young wives were destined to encounter hardship, deprivation, sickness, and perhaps a bullet. With a stubbornness that made their heads ache, they had learned an ancient language, which for centuries had been reckoned dead, and used it to proclaim to the world that after two thousand years they had regenerated a Jewish state in Palestine. The children who had been born here, proudly named Sabras, the fruit of the cactus, soft and sweet within but outside prickly and hard to handle—the first generation of

Jews not to know the sidelong glances of anti-Semites—had fled whence the fathers had come, trampling their parents' hopes and deriding their impractical and irrelevant honesty and idealism.

These men and women had no descendents in Israel. Their posterity was beyond the sea, once again speaking foreign languages, elbowing and pushing their way toward another national cake and from time to time slipping a little hard foreign currency from the sweet life abroad to their luckless parents.

My friend has a beautiful daughter. I have seen her photograph. She and her husband went to Los Angeles and there made themselves a comfortable little nest, in sharp contrast to their parents' home. Both grandsons were born in America, and when they were brought to Jerusalem to show to grandpa they could not find a common language. The grandsons' native language was English, and grandpa and grandma made them smile when they spoke Hebrew.

This happens in the families of the old warriors who gave their children an example of altruism and love for their country. Imagine the situation among the petty bourgeoisie, forming the bulk of the Israeli population, for whom everything is valued in terms of money, and not just money but hard dollars. From among them there is a never ending, ever increasing drain of young people going abroad.

Both my friend's daughter and her husband are now the possessors of precious American passports, but under Israeli law they and their children, who were born abroad, will remain citizens of the Jewish state to the end of their lives, even if they never set foot there again. In official statistics, which demonstrate to the whole world the constant growth of the Jewish people in their historical homeland, these four bogus citizens, and hundreds of thousands of others like them, will, in the form of impressive figures, delude the public, the sociologists, and even the United Nations.

The law of return, which was passed in order to gather all Jews to the land of their forefathers, offers the country's citizenship to anyone who expresses his desire to have it, as soon as he gets off the airplane at Lod airport. He may leave the country forever that very day, but he will retain his citizenship even after his death. There is no way of getting rid of it.

In 1972 as a result of this situation, the Jewish population of Israel was nearly 3 million. According to unofficial figures, in the United States alone there are about a quarter of a million Israeli passport holders. There are about fifty thousand of them in Canada and about the same number in Germany and in England. All told, throughout the whole world there are not less than half a million.

These are people whom Israel has long since lost but whom she stubbornly continues to regard as her own, bragging exaggeratedly at every street corner about her well-being and the impressive growth in the number of Jews who live there. The situation is the same as with Chichikov, the hero of the immortal epic *Dead Souls*, by the Russian writer Nikolai Gogol. Long ago, in the time of serfdom, when the number of peasants a landowner possessed was the measure of his position in society, when peasants were bought and sold like cattle, a certain confidence trickster, by the name of Chichikov, made a tour of the estates of provincial nobles and offered them an unusual deal: he was buying dead souls, i.e., lists of dead peasants. It is true that he bought them for a song, but, after all, nobody had made an offer on them before. When he had bought up a huge number of long-deceased individuals, Chichikov became the owner of whole villages of dead peasants, and, feigning that they were alive, he quickly progressed in society, assuming a position appropriate to the number of serfs he possessed on paper.

At the present time Israel owns half a million dead souls,

and their number increases like a snowball rolling down hill.

New immigrants from the countries of the free world settle in Israel for a variety of reasons. Perhaps they are lured by the enticing promises of those who recruit on Israel's behalf or are uprooted from the places in which they lived by manifestations of anti-Semitism. They may succumb to a paroxysm of religious sentiment or have suffered a series of reverses in their personal life. Whatever the reason, they scarcely have time to set foot in the land of the Bible and be presented with their new passport, bearing a menorah (a seven-branched candlestick) on its cover, before they sober up and flee whence they came, warning others not to make their mistake.

In Jerusalem I had a neighbor, a French Jew from Marseilles. In France, he had been extremely well-to-do, owned a large amount of property, and success had crowned his business ventures. The Six Day War turned his head. He became suffused with a feeling of national pride, recalled the wrongs done to him by French anti-Semites, persuaded his family to accompany him, and got ready to leave. It goes without saying that a move from one country to another is fraught with serious problems. This Marseilles Jew was obliged to sell all his possessions at rock-bottom prices and to get rid of his house for half its value. The sum resulting from these various sales and the capital he had managed to accumulate in earlier years he took to Israel. He settled in the ancient capital and, walking on air, did the rounds of all the historical by-ways, shed a tear of fulfillment by the Wailing Wall, and, bit by bit, began to get involved in business, continuing those preoccupations which in Marseilles he had enjoyed with such success.

All was not the same, however. Here he encountered on every hand practices which were in glaring contradiction to the standards of business practice that had prevailed in his earlier life. People deceived him. They broke their word. He got bogged down in red tape like a bee in a honeypot. The money he had brought with him melted and disappeared. With unbelievable rapidity he drew close to total ruin.

It was then he came to his senses. Robbed of almost every last thing he possessed, he fled the country and returned to Marseilles. Mercifully he had retained his French passport. These are the words he said as we parted: "You're better off living with anti-Semites than with anarchists."

Both he and all the members of his family will figure for all eternity in Israeli statistics as citizens of the Jewish state, and if any of them is so imprudent as to happen to show his face in Israel he will be assessed for taxes like any other citizen and called up into the army in the bargain.

If you talk to officials about a case like this or in general about new immigrants leaving the country on a large scale, you will provoke the same indifferent, stereotyped answer, devoid of bitterness and emotion.

"There's nothing new to us in that. All told, from each of the previous waves of immigration, only 10 percent remained in the country. Yet we managed to survive. We even set up a state."

"Oi vey is mir!" one feels inclined to say, as the Jews did in days gone by when they were at a loss for a reply.

It is true that only a very small number of people from each wave of immigration actually stay in the country and settle down. They are either incorrigible idealists who are prepared to wear their families out in the name of the idea that has taken them over, or they are ne'er-do-wells who have no luck wherever they are and feel that among their own kith and kin they will somehow keep their heads above water, that the sense of Jewish solidarity will save them from being allowed to go under. Both the one and the other are not the best material for building a state, particularly in such uniquely complex conditions.

Gifts, talents, efficient and energetic people are washed out of the soil of Israel and swept away. The atmosphere in the country is not conducive to that kind of personality. The productive people begin to feel stifled and to lose confidence in their powers; and they flee, anywhere to get away, swelling the number of dead souls in the Israeli statistics.

Once they are free from the mortifying grip of Israel, these souls soon revive and, with the passports of other countries in their pockets, again spread those wings that had forgotten how to fly. Thereafter, their names are murmured respectfully by those who have been less lucky, as examples of a head-spinning, fairy-tale career.

A fugitive from Bulgaria slogged away in Israel for a year or two as a taxi-driver before saying "to hell with it all!" and skedaddling to America. Now he is the richest man in Florida, and the deposed king of Bulgaria, Simeon, considers it an honor to be invited to his table. Not long ago this fortunate fugitive from the Holy Land paid a triumphal visit to his fellow citizens, sending a tremor of envy and excitement through the whole country. He decided to celebrate his son's bar mitzvah by the Wailing Wall in Jerusalem. To this day, people with nothing better to do rack their brains trying to calculate the colossal sums of money he spent impressing everyone and how many crowned heads and persons of high rank he had flown in by private airplane in the capacity of accompanying dignitaries.

Why make a secret of it? In his heart of hearts, every Jew cherishes the hope that one day, just as happens in the fairy tales, he will find a millionaire relation. I found one not in a fairy tale but in reality. He really is a millionaire, living in Milan and having houses in Lugano in Switzerland and in Cannes on the French Riviera. He is the owner of a large international company with interests in America and even the Soviet Union. He had arrived in Italy from Israel twenty-five years previously, with $50 in his pocket. In Israel he had vainly attempted to make a modest success of his life.

And then there is Mashulam Riklis in New York, a star of the world of business, who seemed to soar up by magic, a

Sabra, who to this day speaks English with a thick Israeli accent. One could quote hundreds of examples of this kind of success. But these latter-day millionaires, of whom nobody would have heard if they had stayed and vegetated in Israel, are only a small part of a much larger problem.

The Jewish state has lost and continues to lose tens of thousands of fine specialists, acutely needed at home, who have blossomed and managed to manifest their talents only in foreign parts.

And what are the talents that have passed through Israel as they might an inhospitable courtyard and now feed other cultures with their richness, bringing them fame and honor?

Fifteen years ago a young man came to these shores, one of a whole flood of Jewish immigrants from Algeria. He had already taken his first steps in filmmaking in the *Maghreb* ["the West"; here it means Libya, Tunisia, Algeria, and Morocco]. In his historical homeland, he went vainly from door to door offering his gifts and his talents. No one wanted to know. Indifferent, Israel passed him by. He went to France. His name is Claude Lelouch. The whole world now knows this most talented director and his films, *Un Homme et une femme* and *Vivre pour vivre*, have woven fresh laurels into the already rich crown of French cinematic art.

Sabras, the hope and pride of the state, foresake Israel in teeming shoals. They were to show the world the new kind of Jew, free from the complexes of the diaspora, courageous and hard working, for whom money was nothing, an empty sound, when compared with the interests of the Jewish state. These young people were to embody the Zionist fathers' dream of a Jewish working class and peasantry, created from the descendants of the *Luftmenschen*, the "men of air," the shopkeepers, the small-time brokers, Sholem Aleichem's marriage brokers, second-hand dealers, peddlers—that *lumpenproletariat* that filled the ghettos and the shtetels of the Pale of Settlement.

Take a walk along Fifth Avenue, the street containing New York's most expensive shops, and typical Israeli speech, the indestructible Hebrew accent, cannot fail to attract your attention. The voices come from inside the shops.

For heaven's sake do not make the same mistake as I. At first I thought that these were the customers' voices. I took them for a noisy crowd of Israeli tourists that had spread the length of Fifth Avenue and was storming the shops, looking for souvenirs to take home. Not so. The Israelis were not buying. They were selling. In almost every shop, lurking behind the counters, were robust young men with that provocatively independent look that immediately gives away the Sabra. In their thick Hebrew accent and their noisy Eastern style, they vied with one another in pressing goods on the customer—from expensive furs to Sony batteries. I walked from one end of Fifth Avenue to the other, and it seemed to me that I was not in New York but on the Dizengoff Road in Tel Aviv.

Fifth Avenue is the sorry embodiment of the collapse of the Zionist idea. The Jewish small traders, after two thousand years spent wandering along other people's streets, finally acquired their own state, where, from the cradle, they instilled a respect for physical labor into their children and grandchildren. These children and grandchildren, however, flee as fast as possible from their eccentric parents to alluring foreign parts, and there they return to the not altogether respectable occupation of their forefathers, so anathematized by the Zionists—small trading.

I talked to many of these slick, rather insolent Fifth Avenue shop assistants. With the occasional exception of those who came to Israel as babes in arms, they are Sabras. There are even some who lived for a long time in kibbutzim. Most of them have done army service in tank units or as paratroopers. They speak of Israel with an ironic sneer, as they might about a half-baked member of the family. They are

ecstatic about America. Some of them already have a
passport with an eagle. Others hope to get one in five years
time. The inviting prospect of marrying well gleams ahead.

"Will you marry a Jew?"

"What does it matter so long as she doesn't look like a
crocodile and her old man's got plenty of money."

One of the fraternity, broad-chested with the hands of a
blacksmith's striker and a mane of black hair done in the
modern Afro style, explained to me his credo, standing by
the window full of tape recorders and transistors and not for
a moment taking his quick eye off the customers:

> To live in Israel you need to be either an idealist or a madman.
> Isn't that so? And I, thank God, am neither the one nor the other.
>
> Israel has the most revolting climate in the world. To be able to
> endure it, you need to believe very deeply in something, or you
> are an idiot.
>
> Israel has the most vicious tax system. Yet salaries are misera-
> ble. Who's going to put up with that? Only an idealist or a cretin.
>
> In Israel more likely than not you'll end up with a bullet in your
> head or die from some other unnatural cause. Who wants that to
> happen? It's no choice at all.

This taunting, scornful attitude toward the idealists who
have preserved the last crumbs of spiritual purity is a completely run-of-the-mill phenomenon in Israel today. Russian
immigrants of the last Aliyah, who fought their way to Israel
and who bore in their hearts a burning charge of Zionist
idealism, were met with a bucket of cold water. In this consumer society, deeply corroded by pragmatism, the voices
of such idealists struck a sharp discord. People in general,
and in particular Sabras, looked at them as if they were
stricken with the plague, or fools.

Old men from previous generations of bankrupt Zionists,
whom no one here takes seriously, endeavored to console us
by explaining that the Sabras were a modest people, reserved, who had no use for pathos and high-sounding
words, but underneath the surface. . . And then there would
begin the fables and the inventions about these Sabras to

which we had credulously lent our ears when we were still in Moscow.

It may well be that Sabras do not care for high-sounding words, but what a Sabra says without any pathos across the counter of a radio shop on Fifth Avenue vents the real truth, unpleasant as it may be to some. He himself and his fellow Israeli shop assistants are trampling silently but eloquently on the myths of the old Zionist dotards.

The young Israeli shop assistants and waiters in the restaurants and bars of Forty-Second Street's pick-up area, where the "playhouses" are decked with yellow flags and the windows of the sex shops dealing overtly in pornography and covertly in prostitution lurk demurely, are efficient and obliging. These dead souls consider themselves lucky in that they can embark, without fear of the police or the immigration authorities, on a career in their new home, legally and with first-class, authentic documents.

But what about those who have entered the United States illegally and without a work permit? I have met some of them too.

On the far side of the Hudson in New Jersey, looking for a certain Sabra whom a mama in Jerusalem had asked me to greet, I stumbled upon a whole nest of Israelis, skulking illegally in America. In an old two-story house, deep in a neglected garden hidden from the street and the eyes of the police, were living twelve young fellows from Israel whose papers were not quite in order.

The house belonged to a morose man of middle years who chatted passably in English but whose accent made it clear he had been born in Tel Aviv. It was a long time since he had left Israel. He had acquired full American citizenship and his own trucking business. He afforded his fellow countrymen protection, providing them with a roof and thereby running the risk of getting into difficulties with the police. But this he did not for sentimental reasons. He cruelly exploited these lads, who, being outside the law, would agree to anything just to get a foothold in the land of Columbus.

The boys were all drivers, and day and night they sat at the wheels of their boss's trucks in return for half the wage earned by their fellow drivers—black Americans.

These were real white slaves. And there are any number of such hideaways from the Atlantic to the Pacific. Successful Israelis conceal their illegal-immigrant fellow countrymen and fleece them, exploiting their fleeting hope that they too may be able to establish themselves in America.

The bitter irony, the historical twist, is that the Sabras, instead of opening up the Negev Desert in their own country, as the fathers of Zionism foresaw and dreamed, are energetically opening up the American continent, which was habitable long before they arrived. According to one official of the Israeli Consulate in New York, if one scrupulously totaled up all the demobilized soldiers who have fled to America, one would discover a whole contingent of the Israeli wartime army living there.

Not only Sabras and credulous repatriates from Western countries, however, flee from Israel. Brand new citizens, who have only just received their menorah passports, run away too. The national heroes of not so long ago, those who fought for the right to go from the USSR to their historical homeland, the Russian emigrants, are on the run. For such people the road back to the USSR is completely sealed off. They flee, they know not where, without money and without hope, trying to find somewhere to hide and get their breath back, to recover after the final collapse of all their illusions.

When a Jew who has come from America or from France returns whence he came, no one in Israeli official circles is embarrassed. After all, such a person exchanged a high standard of living for a lower one. Is Israel to blame if his idealism did not last long? The fact of the matter is that more than 30 percent of the Americans who come to Israel leave within a year. They do the country no harm thereby.

Quite the contrary! From Israel's point of view, this is a highly profitable kind of tourism. A family lives there for a year, spending dollars left and right, more than any other group of foreign tourists, who are not all that easy to lure, and quits the country with an empty purse, leaving a substantial legacy of hard currency behind in Israeli banks.

But when the Russian Jews start to flee—anywhere at all, even to the back of beyond—things are getting too hot for comfort. What will the world's Jews say—the genuine Zionists, who are brimming over with pride in their courageous Russian brothers? What will the people say who give all the money that goes toward settling and installing the Russian Jews in their ancient homeland?

Israel will go to any lengths to obscure and hide from prying eyes this phenomenon, which is a great danger to the future of the state and which is spreading like a cancerous growth. After all, if the Russian Jews who have sacrificed so much to get here flee at once without a backward glance, is this not an indictment?

Their flight often begins long before the Israeli frontier is reached—in Vienna, where the only staging post for immigrants is situated. The Russian Jews arrive here by air and by rail in order to board the El Al Boeings and be borne away on wings emblazoned with the Star of David, home to their native land, to the land of their ancestors.

Despite the Israeli visa they received in Moscow, by no means all the Jews arriving in Vienna hasten toward the planes whose doors the staff of Sokhnut hold hospitably open. They recoil in hostility from the Israeli representatives who are meeting them and rush into the embrace of the HIAS [a Jewish communal organization] staff, who will take them to Rome and then get them a visa to some other country, even to one as remote as New Zealand.

The ones who flee when they get to Vienna more often than not began their difficult and dramatic shedding of their Soviet citizenship with a pure faith in, and an ardent impulse toward, Israel and Israel alone. While the months and years of torment spent in obtaining the precious visa went by, however, depressing and graphic letters were arriving from Israel from those who had managed to get there earlier. These letters, portraying, sometimes truthfully, sometimes exaggeratedly, the real nature of the country toward which these others were striving, cooled enthusiasm and sowed despair.

For these people there was no road back. To remain in the USSR after they had publicly proclaimed that they were Zionists amounted to suicide, and they somberly embarked on their journey in order to turn aside in Vienna, in search of illusory comfort in some remote spot on our unfriendly planet.

The remainder, also alarmed and already largely unenthusiastic, continued on their way to the Promised Land. They had no wish to renounce their dreams, and the hope was still warm within them that all was not so gloomy as it appeared from the letters of the preceding wave of immigrants, from hearsay, and from rumors.

They came to their senses three or four months later, after vain efforts to seek out something good, something cheering, something to set one's mind at ease, something to make all the rest worth enduring and to help shut out the bad things. A frenzied search began for ways of escape from this "paradise," to shake its dust from their feet before it was too late.

And here the erstwhile ardent Israeli patriots discovered with horror that in their beloved historical homeland they had fallen into a primitive trap. The snare was sprung as soon as they had set foot in the Holy Land at Lod airport. Even earlier in fact, at the Viennese castle of Schönau, when the Israeli officials had begun issuing them food and money and giving them the airplane tickets and baggage receipts, the clinging web of debts had begun to enmesh each of them, becoming ever more tenacious the longer they stayed in the country.

In order to leave Israel, this original ransom, which was of a size well beyond the means of a penniless fugitive from the USSR, had to be repaid to Sokhnut. It was a cunning stratagem, coolly conceived beforehand, to secure the immigrants, to pin them to the spot, to bind them hand and foot, to keep in the country against their will, broken, devastated people.

Yet it turned out to be by no means an easy matter to break the angry and wrathful Soviet Jews, who had still not cooled down from the heat of the battle with the Soviet authorities, and to make them love Israel in the repulsive form she assumed in their eyes—eyes which now opened to a reality incompatible with the rosy haze of Zionist hallucination. People sold the residue of their possessions, even their linen, and searched the whole world to find relatives and friends, whom they abjectly begged to ransom them. With relief they flew up into the air from those same grey concrete landing strips at Lod, which they had recently kissed, falling upon the concrete as the first piece of sacred earth they had longed to see. Now they cursed this earth and this country that had brought about their cruel disillusionment, broken their lives, and dissipated their last hopes.

These crushed and wretched people arrived in Rome, where the Jewish emigration services pointedly turned their backs on them. How so? Ah, they were now no longer heroic Jewish warriors from the USSR but traitors to the Zionist idea, deserters from Israel. The so-called *iordim*— the descenders.

It was now not the Jewish but the international charity institutions that took them under their stern and austere wings, and their miserable refuge became the crowded honeycomb of tiny rooms in the lodging houses on the Via Alexandria.

Here for six months and in some cases a year, they hung about in want and dispiriting inactivity until some government took pity on them and gave them a visa. Some of them went to seed. They became unrecognizable. Theft, crookedness, and prostitution became widespread. The Rome police arrested many. Neighbors began to regard with hostility the people from Via Alexandria, who had quite recently enjoyed the reputation of heroes and whose behavior had filled the whole Jewish world with pride.

This tragedy is stubbornly hushed up in Israel, and the precise number of fugitives from the Holy Land is suppressed. There are thousands of them, and their number is growing all the time. New measures are already being taken and new obstacles are being set up in the path of the runaways. The Italian authorities, not without pressure from Israel, have made it more difficult to get an Italian entry visa. These changes primarily concern former Soviet emigrants or others who have no permanent passport but simply a temporary passport. Since 1973 Italy has refused to give people with these temporary passports visas to enter Italy. Need it be said that all Russian Jews have such passports?

On occasions, the Israeli press expresses its attitude to this phenomenon. To its great shame, this more often than not takes the form of laying down the law. Here is a sample. A certain Eliazer Akabas domineeringly reads the riot act on the pages of *Nasha Strana*.

> The task of Sokhnut representatives in foreign countries is to facilitate the repatriation of Jews to Israel, not to serve as a channel of return or emigration to other countries....
> It is essential that we take all the necessary measures to stop repatriates and in particular repatriates from the Soviet Union leaving Israel. Israel must not be turned into a transit point. We can well manage without this "Jacob's ladder" on which Jews from the Soviet Union and other countries have taken the place of the ascending and descending angels.

Mr. Akabas's injunctions reached the ears of those for whom they were intended. Now not only HIAS—the Jewish emigration center in Rome—but even the non-Jewish organization on the Via Alexandria has slammed their doors in the faces of former Soviet Jews fleeing from Israel. The ultimate irony is that the only refuge left a Russian Jew in Rome is the Union of Russian (Orthodox) Churches.

The crowning stage of this drama, which has imparted to it a ring of tragedy, are those two hundred families that have gone back to Vienna and there hang around the Soviet Embassy, begging to be allowed to return to the Soviet Union.

Grigory Vertlieb, whose name not so long ago was frequently in the newspapers as one of the heroes of the Leningrad hijacking trial, reached Israel by a miracle. The trial led to two death sentences, which were commuted only when the whole world was up in arms. For their own propaganda purposes, Israeli loyalists wheeled this same Grigory Vertlieb all the way across Europe, and I myself shared the platform with him at a vast meeting in the Mutualité in Paris. This Vertlieb, no other, has been wearing his pants out in Vienna for over a year, calling Israel every name under the sun, giving interviews to Soviet journalists and endeavoring, hitherto unsuccessfully, to find some tiny crack through which he can creep back to his native Leningrad and forget all about his nightmare-like Zionist odyssey.

It is hard, sometimes almost unbearable, to stay in Israel, but to go back to the anti-Semites in the country where you were born would be even more dreadful. What bitterness one finds in these two sayings, current among Russian immigrants in the Holy Land:

"I'll die for Israel, but don't ask me to live there."

"What efforts it took to get out of Russia, but it takes even more to stay here."

Not long ago a Russian Jew died in Israel. Not a single newspaper mentioned his death. No friend was found to honor the deceased's memory with an obituary. I too might well not have noticed this case had the name Semyon Ladyzhensky not seemed familiar. Of course (I remembered) it's Senya the Crowing Cock! "Twice Jew" of the Soviet Union, that same Senya upon whom even *Izvestia* bestowed the necessary space for a lengthy anti-Semitic satire. What didn't they accuse him of in that article in order to work up anti-Semitic feelings in the Russian reader! He was a thief, a blackguard, a speculator, a rogue, anything you can think of, this man, whom the newspapers dubbed with the underworld nickname Senya the Crowing Cock, though at the time this *cock* was approaching sixty. In his passport, however, he was known by his real name, Semyon Ladyzhensky, and in paragraph 5 of that same Soviet passport, in black and white like a brand, it said: nationality—Jewish. As they say in the Soviet Union, old Semyon was an invalid of the fifth paragraph.

He had the good fortune to be one of the first Muscovites to reach the sacred land of Israel and discovered earlier than many others that he did not belong. He had left his family in Moscow, frightened to share his Zionist dreams. By dint of unbelievable efforts, he obtained a re-entry visa.

The Moscow authorities did not give him time to find his feet before they presented him with the bill. He had to go into print with some anti-Israeli disclosures. He had no alternative, and in those same pages where he previously had been stigmatized, a newly respectable Semyon Ladyzhensky now branded the Zionists. After this, both Jews and Russians began to treat him with unconcealed disdain, and the authorities, having squeezed him dry, also turned fastidiously away. His acquaintances avoided him, suspecting with some foundation that he was connected with the KGB. He feared that, having made use of him, they would try to get rid of him and exile him to Siberia.

Things were bad for the old man. An outsider to everyone, with no friends and no relatives, he wandered around Moscow like a hunted animal, looking at the enormously long lines outside the shops and recalling the shop windows in Israel bursting with goods. So once again he applied to go to the land of his ancestors. The Soviet authorities did not endeavor to detain him and escorted him to Chop Station with all dispatch. From there he traveled to Vienna and from Vienna to Lod—by the now familiar route. Here he was cheerfully saddled with debts, had his feelings dragged in the mud, and was sent to Haifa to look for a place to live. In Haifa his tribulations came to an end. He hanged himself, thus solving the problem of his debts and also the most acute problem of all: where on this earth does a Jew belong?

He was buried free of charge. Sokhnut footed the bill from those monies that American Jews give generously to Israel so that their Russian brethren can gain a foothold in the Promised Land.

Almost every day airliners with a heavy load of repatriates from the USSR land at Lod airport. Their occupants know nothing and are therefore full of hope. Every day other planes bear away from Israel those who, coming to from the initial shock, desperately break out of their bonds and, robbed of all they possess and with only their children in their arms, escape from the trap that is called their historic homeland. People will go to any, sometimes the most unseemly, lengths just to get out. They are prepared to change their skin, to have plastic surgery done on their face, to excoriate from their body like warts any hint of their Jewish origin. They want to be like all the rest, to disappear into the crowd, to answer just for their own sins and not for those of a whole nation—a nation with which they have long had no links save its common misfortunes. Thus Israel becomes the climax of their assimilation and that final drop which causes the cup to brim over, shattering their remaining illusions, thrusting them toward an irreversible break.

Before they leave Israel, while they are still stagnating in overcrowded Ulpans, vainly searching for the chance of getting hold of some money in order to buy their freedom from Sokhnut, some families, Jewish families, proud of their history and their forebears, who had long resisted enforced assimilation and brought their children here in order to have them reared, rush into the arms of the Christian church and there seek sanctuary at the feet of Russian Orthodox priests.

The increasingly frequent cases of Soviet Jews accepting the Christian faith here in the land of Abraham and Rachel have led to disconcerted murmurings in the Israeli press. Christian priests have been accused of missionary activity and of improperly inveigling wavering spirits. There have even been attempts to burn down Christian missions in Jerusalem.

This is just another lie. I know well several families who took this step and who left Israel with the assistance of the Orthodox church. I have no wish to evaluate what they did. Although I myself am an atheist, I believe that religion, whatever its tendency or persuasion, is not a toy that can be adapted to changing circumstances or tried on like a shirt as need demands.

I got to know Igor B., a Muscovite and formerly a teacher of English language and literature at the university, after I had arrived here in Jerusalem. He was recently married to a young Russian woman, and they were excitedly awaiting the birth of their child, who would be born in the Holy Land, a true Israeli, a Sabra. Both Igor and his wife Ira had been atheists all their lives and had not the slightest notion that Ira's Russian origins would cause them so much bother.

They were surprised and dumbfounded to discover that if Ira did not accept Judaism with all the concomitant religious rites their as yet unborn child had in store for him the unenviable fate of being a social misfit in his own country, a second-class citizen.

Igor and Ira made up their minds to flee without a backward glance. But where was the money to come from? In complete despair they went to the Russian Orthodox Mission. The holy fathers took them in and promised them assistance. Then, as a sign of gratitude for the sympathy they had been shown and to break the final threads, which even before that had bound them only tenuously to the Jewish faith, the young parents christened the newborn child and themselves accepted Orthodoxy. The holy river Jordan served as a baptismal font. Today the family lives in New York, where they traveled at the expense of the holy Fathers, who also helped them to get a visa.

My very old friend Heinrich G. had his children baptized
into the Orthodox faith in Jerusalem. I played the fatal role
of tempter in his destiny, and to this day I suffer pangs of
conscience. Heinrich is a somewhat unlucky but extremely
talented film director, who was my colleague and neighbor
in Moscow. Our families were friends for many years, attending each others birthday celebrations and, of course,
the premieres of each other's films.

I felt a strong bond with this subtle, extremely perceptive
artist. I knew his past, which was very little different from
the lot of most Soviet young men of our generation. During
the Second World War he had been a gunner and radio
operator in the air force, had been shot down, lost an eye
and wore thereafter a velvet eye patch, which made him
look a little like Moshe Dayan.

The only Jewish thing about G. was his name. Like most
of us, he was fully assimilated. He was educated in Russian
culture, made films in Russian, and Russian was his native
and only language.

He greeted the turbulent awakening of national consciousness in me with amusement, considering it just
another enthusiasm. For a long time he could not take seriously my heated, impassioned arguments about the destiny of our nation, about the culture whose renaissance we
could and should achieve, about Israel, the only place in the
world where all this could be freely undertaken. Only when
he saw the risk I was prepared to take to accomplish my
purpose, when the visa to Israel I had fought for was in his
hands, did he give in and asked me to send him a summons
to Israel. He arrived in Israel a year after I did, leaving behind him in Moscow a life that had been running smoothly
and a secure reputation as a talented artist. That is to say, he
sacrificed everything to join the nation from which he had
always been so remote and, even at this late stage, to offer it
his gifts.

He found me unemployed, morose, and dismayed. Other
acquaintances were no better off. He soon realized that like

the rest of us he was no use to anyone here, and his sacrifice had been meaningless.

At over forty his life was broken. He had twin daughters growing up, to whom the country and its language were alien. He was down-and-out and, swallowing his pride, subsisted on degrading hand-outs from Sokhnut. There were not even the vaguest prospects of getting work or having a movie camera in his hands.

In the Ulpan at Qatamon, full of sound like an Eastern bazaar, he sat alone, completely torpid, surrounded by posters of the films he had made in Russia; his aspect made me apprehensive about his mental state.

Salvation came from the Russian Orthodox Mission. One of the very priests who had helped Igor B. discovered G. and invited him to make a documentary film about the parts of Jerusalem linked with the name of Jesus Christ.

My friend had always been an atheist. He agreed to make this film because he saw in it interesting artistic possibilities. Moreover, it was work, for which he had waited so long. Thereafter, he would live not on charity but on what he had earned with his own hands.

Heinrich G. made the film. I have not seen it, but it is said to be a film of talent, which fits into the pattern of the rest of this subtle artist's work. Suddenly like a bolt from the blue the news reached the Russian immigrants: Heinrich's children had been baptized. They had been converted to Orthodoxy and were going to America.

I saw no more of G. He kept out of my way, avoided meeting me, and left Israel without saying goodbye. But when I reflect on what happened, and I think a great deal about my old friend's act, I neither judge nor accuse him. He was always honest and meticulous. He could not have taken this step for personal advantage in order, through the good offices of the Orthodox Mission, to obtain a free ticket to America. What he did must have been a statement—his protest against the snare for immigrants that the Jewish state had become. His soul had been so seared by the cold indifference of his fellow countrymen that he finally and irreversibly turned his back on the Jews he had joined so uncircumspectly.

The Jews flee from Israel. They dismiss the commandments of their forefathers, which once evoked holy awe, or turn from them to Christianity. For two thousand years Jews scattered across the face of the earth, daily, in every prayer addressed their God in hope: "Next year in Jerusalem!"

And now particularly since the Yom Kippur War a fresh hope illumines the Israeli countenance, now lacking its former assurance: "Next year in... New York, London, Paris, Munich, Frankfurt... anywhere but Jerusalem."

According to a report in the newspaper *Maariv*, the number of Israelis applying for Canadian entry visas in January 1974 was twice that of the same month in the preceding year.

According to statistics of the Israeli electric company, there are thirty-eight thousand apartments in which no electricity has been consumed for many years. These apartments are locked up and empty. Their owners have long since left Israel, not selling their dwellings simply because they do not trust the stability of the Israeli pound. Furthermore, a significantly large number of apartments, approaching one hundred thousand, have been sold or are rented by people who preferred to live in foreign parts.

A sinister symptom of the bankruptcy of the Zionist idea of the ingathering of the nation from the diaspora has been the way in which people who are loyal and dedicated to the regime and whose blood and sweat went into the bond that secured the state's foundations have begun gradually to leave the country.

I would like to quote the story of one family, which I heard in Herzliya from a man who asked me not to mention his name. He is an Iraqi Jew. Twenty years ago as a young boy, he was repatriated to Israel together with the rest of his large family, all of whom were deeply imbued with Zionist fervor. Only his eldest brother was indifferent to Zionism, preferring to seek his fortune in Latin America. This family gave its all and hoisted onto its shoulders the heavy burden of its newly acquired country. After the appropriate train-ing, one brother became a professional intelligence agent and has been working in the field for around ten years in one of the Arab countries. Another brother is an officer in the commandos. Both of them are constantly risking their lives. Both serve not out of obligation but from conviction.

The narrator himself is not a soldier, although he took part in three Arab-Israeli wars, was injured several times, and is sufficiently disabled to have been discharged from the reserve. He has five children. He lives frugally, hardly able to make ends meet, even with the assistance of his brother in Latin America. He is deeply disturbed about what awaits his sons who are growing up. The same portion is in store for them—endless fighting until they are either killed or maimed like their father.

The mother, as head of the family, has now decided, with the agreement of all the brothers, to say farewell to Israel and go to join the eldest brother in Latin America. The mother's decision is final, and the sons, who by now have had most of the Zionism knocked out of them, were not inclined to demur. Even the one who had been working as a secret agent abroad came home and joined his family.

In the newspaper *Haaretz,* another such Israeli, one Eliezer Livna, asks with unconcealed nostalgia:

Are we really in a vicious circle?
Society's initiative has been sapped. The standard of living is falling, and there is increasing lack of discipline and indifference. Laxity and evil hold sway in our society. Crime once again con-quers the law, and the state is robbed within the framework of the law itself. Hordes of officials go on gobbling up the taxes levied from the people and throwing fresh bureaucratic monkey

wrenches into the nation's works. The country does not respect its leaders' words, for it sees their deeds.

And Jews leap out of the vicious circle and forsake the unfriendly shores of Palestine.

In international forums the Israeli representatives impress the world with their lists of dead souls, asserting shamelessly that the country's Jewish population is increasing rapidly and more and more new land is needed to settle them. In point of fact a lot of the old lands are still empty, and where building works are going on it is not Jewish but Arab hands that are putting up the houses.

Opposite my house, for two years a new building has been rising, built of golden Jerusalem stone. It still lacks its roof. Every morning Arabs are brought here to work—they are Palestine refugees living in a camp somewhere in Samaria. They work slowly and unhurriedly, doing almost everything by hand. They carry the sand in buckets, move the stone in wheelbarrows. Melancholy Arab music, thick as honey, flows from a tiny transistor on the sill of an empty, frameless window.

As I write these words, the Arabs are laying bricks at the same level as the floor where I live. Their faces are tanned deep bronze, and they wear kafiyahs. When I lift my eyes from the manuscript, I always encounter their glances—not malevolent but smiling, uningratiating, and without fear. They look at me almost mockingly, as might restrained and patient hosts at a chance guest who has overstayed his welcome.

This is their home is what their confident look asserts. These walls they are building will sooner or later be theirs. The house in which I live, but which was built by their hands, will also pass to them. Their children will come from the refugee camps and live in all the houses in these parts.

They look at me from the scaffolding of the house they are

building and smile at me a warm smile, without malice. But I have no time to smile. My mind is in a turmoil, and the walls of the room, with portraits of my children hanging on them, breathe down on me a sepulchral chill, although outside the southern sun is hot enough to drive men mad.

chapter nine

THE OPEN WOUND

The incandescent white gravestones reverberate the mercilessly fierce heat of the sun. A multitude, an endless multitude of gravestones with the biblical lettering of the ancient Hebrew alphabet inscribed upon the stone. It seems as though sarcophagi from time immemorial have floated up and emerged from legendary depths into the light of day, into the blazing sun, which has lost none of its intensity since the days when a young Jew from Nazareth went on his last journey. His name was Yeshua Ganotsri, for two thousand years remembered in reverence by the gentiles as Jesus Christ, the Son of God.

The imprint of history lies not upon these gravestones. The stone is fresh and un-yellowed. The graves too are fresh, and the women are still alive who mourn those dead. For here beneath these stones lie only men—young husbands and beardless sons, Jewish soldiers in the military cemeteries of Israel.

There are thousands of graves. Each settlement has two cemeteries, a civilian and a military. Frequently the gravestones of the military cemeteries are in greater profusion. This is the price the Jews have been paying for a quarter of a century. They just cannot settle the account for the right to have their own state, born in the restless brain of the Viennese journalist Theodor Herzl. The central military cemetery extends its ranks of gravestones like columns of soldiers in the very heart of Jerusalem, on Mount Herzl.

Jewish mothers weep. Hot and dry though it is in Palestine, young eyes aged by widowhood are never dry of tears, as death claims the men one after the other—first the husband, then the son, then the grandson.

I remember distinctly the first piercing of my heart in that land by the aching sensation of constant, endless losses. It was not at the numberless military cemeteries one sees as one travels through Israel that I sensed this pain. I did not feel it as I gazed at the columns of figures ranged impassively on the pages of a statistical handbook. I first felt that sinking bitter pang in the pit of my stomach when I visited the home of a couple of elderly Jerusalem school teachers. They lived in a simple stone house overhung by old pine trees in the part of the town called Moshav Germanit, named in honor of the German Jews who once built the clean little narrow streets of a German settler's village.

We were the guests of German Jews who had made a happy and timely escape from Hitler and dropped fresh roots here in the inhospitable, stony soil of Palestine. They have been living here for more than forty years. Their children were born here and know no other country.

I cannot remember now who took us to see them. We Russian Jews, the first of the present wave of immigrants, were at that time in fashion. Many people, both in Israel and elsewhere in the world, were in ecstasy over us and our stubbornness that had breached that blank wall behind which we had been locked away for decades. We were known as the *courageous Jews*. People were proud of us and loved us, and those kind, sincere idealists, who have not yet become extinct in Israel, invited us to their homes, one after

the other, and with a heartfelt thrill absorbed our impassioned speeches and gazed with maternal tenderness
and pride into our eyes, still blazing with the unquenched
flames of recent battles.

In this house also, they listened to us eagerly, hanging on
our every word. We had already grown used to being regarded as heroes by our spell-bound listeners and without
the least constraint ascended the pedestal erected for us.

For all that, I managed to detect that the faces of our hosts
seemed prematurely aged and that in their eyes there lurked
a profound, inescapable sorrow such as nothing could dis-
pel and which would dwell there forever. I also observed on
the walls a large number of paintings, some in oils and some
in water colors—amateur paintings, not the work of a master, but executed with sincere feeling and enthusiasm—and
all the work of the same hand. I made up my mind that they
were the artistic efforts either of our kind host or hostess,
and in order to give them pleasure I began to praise the
paintings, trying to persuade them on no account to give up
their hobby.

"They aren't our paintings," said the hostess, smiling
tenderly. "They were done by our son. He died. In Sinai."

And that was all she said, turning her attention again to
the stories of my comrades.

When we were about to go, the door opened and in came a
tall, thin young man about twenty with a black bandage
running across his forehead and cheek and covering his eye.
His right shirt sleeve was pinned up with a safety pin close
to the shoulder, where one could discern the short stump of
an arm. "And this is my younger son," the hostess said,
introducing him, and added, "now, my only son."

It was at that moment I sensed the price that this country,
unloved by the world, pays for each extra day of life and
how paltry our sufferings and anguish were in comparison
with theirs. Then, with each new encounter I became more
and more convinced that the whole of Israel is one vast open
wound, never healing and with blood always streaming

from it. The wound is two thousand years old, but it is freshly and painfully pierced here today in the land of Palestine.

I am weary, my feelings are numb from the sight of hosts of photographs from family albums, portraying young men who will never grow old.

There are the voices of their mothers and wives:

"He was killed on the Golan Heights."

"He was blown up by a mine."

"He was shot down by a rocket."

"He was burnt to death in his tank."

"He didn't survive. He died in a hospital."

In a kibbutz in the Valley of Jezreel, close to the mountain ridge of Ephraim, there lives a family who befriended us. The family has a daughter, widowed quite young when her husband was killed. It didn't happen in the Six Day War of 1967 or in the Yom Kippur War of 1973. It happened in between the wars, in the *peaceful* years, when, even so, almost every day someone died on the frontier. She was left with two young daughters and is unlikely to remarry: there are very few eligible young men around, and each year their number is less and less.

Once again the father and mother are alone. Their only son has grown up and is training in a school for military pilots. He is already flying a Skyhawk, and somewhere there lurks a Soviet rocket with his name on it. Every morning when they switch on the radio his parents hold their breath, then heave a sigh of relief to learn that, thank God, a day has passed without any hostilities in the air.

It is a miracle that the parents themselves are still alive. Just before the Second World War they managed to escape—she from Poland, and he from Belgium. The Nazis exterminated their families in the gas chambers, burnt them in the ovens of the crematoria, and scattered their ashes over the fields of Europe. My friends, to fill the places of all those who perished, put out a shoot here in the Middle East, and the torrid eroding wind threatens to destroy it too. They already have one grave in a military cemetery. Their only son, the final bearer of the family name, still unmarried and without issue, flies in a supersonic fighter across the stormy but ever cloudless sky of ancient Judea.

Of losses like these, irreplaceable and sapping the life-blood of a nation already living by virtue of a miracle, an Israeli woman, I. Har-Shafi, has written with deep poignancy in a short piece called "Five Basalt Headstones." I quote it almost in full, because it is a cry from the heart and editorial cuts would be inappropriate.

> Azkara for the dead of the Sturman family. That was what the announcement said. I was afraid to go. I tried to procrastinate, to deceive myself. How could I be late for what had already happened. But there might suddenly be a miracle and the wheel of time and the wheel of fortune might move onward.
>
> However I might try to delay, nothing could now be changed. The number of basalt stones could not become one less.
>
> The fate of the Sturman family is a fact more terrible than all the definitions people have tried to give it: the legend of the Sturman family ... the curse hanging over the Sturman household ...
>
> A curse. A blessing. These are just words ...
>
> The Sturmans are smiles which send you mad, they are hands rocking a baby. This is a household of women, who have escorted on their last journey to the cemetery at Ein-Harod a father, a husband, a son, a grandson, and a brother. All their menfolk committed to this earth for eternal safekeeping.
>
> The Sturmans are the scroll of flame of Israel's wars ...
>
> This story of life and death is the price we pay.
>
> The story of one family. The row of basalt headstones, like a recurring refrain.
>
> Chaim, son of Moshe Sturman, Moshe, son of Chaim and Atara Sturman, Chaim, son of Moshe and Reuma Sturman. Wall and tower. The War of Liberation. The operation on Green Island after the Six Day War.
>
> Comrades and friends came to be present at the ceremony where yet another basalt tablet was put up in memory of the Sturman family. The second grandson of Chaim and Atara Sturman, Amir, who fell at the Suez Canal, was buried in the military cemetery—the last grave on the right.

In Ein-Harod the dead are not forgotten. They are at home, surrounded by life's eternal stream. Tall trees cover them with their leaves. They are remembered every day. They are a living presence.

But this is a special day. The day when Chaim is remembered, the hero of Atara's youth. It almost coincides with the day when the settlement of Ein-Harod was founded.

Then follows an account of how Chaim Sturman, the founder of this dynasty where every man died a soldier's death, was killed by an Arab bullet, leaving behind him a son, who had in store for him the very same fate. This son was called Moshe. And the author continues:

Moshe was a young man with a great shock of hair and a gentle smile. Moshe gazes at me from a photograph which shows him holding his son Chaim in his arms.

Then Moshe went into the army. Each time he came home there was a celebration in the young family. Once grandmother went to see him off on the bus and young Chaim began to cry: "I want to go too." Grandmother tried to quiet him, to distract him, and didn't even have time to say "Shalom" to Moshe.

He never returned. And there was Moshe's fresh grave next to Chaim's grave.

Grandmother Atara raised her grandson Chaim, who was always full of laughter.

She accompanied him also on his last journey.

Now she looks at her menfolk, smiling from their photographs: Chaim, Moshe, Chaim, Amir.

The people who have come to the cemetery to honor their memory look at the plaque with the names of the dead. Names. A long row of names on the clean granite. And that is the most frightening thing of all. Oh God, let there be no more!

Reuma, Moshe's wife and Chaim's mother, says: "They fell in battle, but not one of them was a man of war."

Tamar, the daughter of Atara and Amir's mother, says: "He was just beginning to live. Just starting to make his way in life . . . and he was my son."

We dispersed quietly from the cemetery, taking a last look at the Sturman graves. The black basalt cries out mutely: "Let there be no more."

I would very much like to know how many ardent supporters of Israel who have taken this country up like a hobby, an intense, almost painful passion, like a game of cards, have read this piece. Those soft-hearted and sentimental diaspora Jews who have made Israel an idol which they worship at a respectful and safe distance. They are no less proud of it than of their own healthy bank account. Excitedly, like little boys playing at war, in the drawing rooms and cafes of New York, Paris, and London, they argue until they are hoarse, until they are in a frenzy, over the military map of the Middle East, recarving it in their mind's eye, extending frontiers, attacking head on and on the flanks, bringing off lightning victories, evoking the ecstasy and envy of the whole non-Jewish world.

I would very much like to know whether they visit the military cemeteries, those crowds of Jewish tourists from all over the world, who inundate Israel during the holiday season, consume the kosher food with relish, bask on the beaches beneath the same sun that once warmed their forebears, and, with patronizing tenderness, pat the harrassed locals on the back and say: "We are proud of you. Since you created our state we can hold our heads up."

You cannot see the military cemeteries from the gleaming windows of the luxury hotels, from the pale blue waters of the swimming pools where the tourists cool their bodies from the heat of the day. Behind the barrier of fresh tropical vegetation, the sighs of the widows and the tap of the young invalid's crutches cannot be heard.

I would very much like to know whether those smug and sated people ever give a thought to the fact that the Israel that has become the object of their enthusiasm is made up of living men and women, Jews just like themselves, but whom fate has placed not in Brooklyn or Whitechapel, but here in the melting pot, in the dragon's maw, of endless war and blood-letting. Do they realize that enough is enough and that there is not so much Jewish blood left that it can be spilled so liberally?

I, who live in Israel and who have staked not only my own

life but the lives of my children, see all this in a far from rosy light. In hopeless anguish I see my people in the guise of an old, old man, who having for centuries tramped alien streets has finally wandered home to the place of his birth. He wearily picks his way on his bruised and naked feet over the sharp hot stones. The dry thorny branches pluck at his clothes and tear at his flesh. He walks through his ancient homeland and blood drips down from his wounds. Each drop sinks into the sand and brings forth not a flower but a white gravestone. Behind the old man stretches a multitude of gravestones. And still he goes on, his lifeblood ebbing away.

How much blood is there left in him?

Can he keep going much longer?

chapter ten

CHIPS IN A DIRTY GAME

The battle of the Russian Jews with the Soviet regime and their isolated victories in it at first appeared as a miracle not only to the astounded world, but to us too, active participants in these events. In the whole history of Soviet power nothing comparable had ever happened. Any manifestation, not only of opposition but of even the slightest dissatisfaction, had been suppressed in the most cruel manner, without a whisper of protest either from the rest of the country or from a much vaunted world opinion.

What had happened? Was it possible that the omnipotent regime before which the whole globe quails was frightened by a sorry little band of recalcitrant Jews? Nothing would have been simpler than for the Soviet government to have polished them off as it might a fly, without even raising an eyebrow in response to the half-hearted protests of Western intellectuals and the short-lived indignation of the world's Jews.

With wariness and surprise, we discovered that the regime was making concessions. It snapped its jaws, sometimes showing its claws and fetching blood, but nevertheless a narrow crack had opened in the Iron Curtain, and Jews, speechless with unexpected happiness, crowded and pushed toward it, making for Israel. First there were scores, then hundreds, then thousands.

Like everyone else, I tended initially to ascribe this miracle to the force of the explosion of Jewish national feeling plus a hitherto unknown degree of support for us by the world's Jews, demonstrating that we were one nation and that under pressure from us even a monster like Soviet power was forced to beat a retreat. I was amazed and exceedingly proud. Then, observing other facets of this process, I began to have my first doubts.

The man in Moscow who held in his hands the fate of Jews wishing to go to Israel was a most fascinating person, General Giorgy Minin. He was one of the heads of the anti-Zionist section of the Committee of State Security of the USSR, the KGB. Although he had the rank of general, when we saw him he was always in civilian clothes. He was comparatively young and charming, polite and quite cultured, which made him something of an odd man out in his place of work. Not without a certain degree of irony, he demonstrated to the flabbergasted Jewish intellectuals whom he invited to come and talk to him fairly fluent conversational Hebrew and read aloud to them, with a slight accent, extracts from *Maariv*.

General Minin, like a well-fed cat playing with a mouse, loved these face-to-face, man-to-man encounters with Jewish intellectuals, which took place in an office especially allocated to him on the first floor of the Moscow visa department in Kolpachny Lane. Down below in the reception hall and in the street there was a buzz of conversation from the crowds of Jews. They were unceremoniously brought to order and dealt with by hefty militiamen and the general's mettlesome assistants like Major Zolotukhin or Captain Akulova. Unlike this general, these assistants were invariably in full KGB uniform.

The general's office, however, was filled with the murmur of calm and friendly conversation. Smiles were exchanged, and there were even handshakes on saying goodbye. The general endeavored to drive a wedge into the Jewish movement by splitting off the intelligentsia from the rest. Consequently, he strung us along, making a show of respect and at times indulging in the kind of frank revelations that one rarely hears from the lips of officials.

These were his words to me, and time has confirmed the total accuracy of what he said.

Surely you don't think that we are frightened by your pressure and that you have achieved anything which wasn't a part of our own plans? You see yourselves as heroes, don't you? In fact you're mere cogs, puppets in a vast and complex game in which we pull the strings and you dance to our tune. And you aren't the only ones.

Not a single person would have left Soviet territory had his desire not coincided with our interests. Yes, yes, there's no need to be surprised. A strong Israel accords with Soviet interests. In that case the Arabs will always be needing our help and hanging on to our coattails. This is why, although we pillory Israel in the press and curse her in every quarter, we still send Jews there from Russia. For form's sake we dig in our heels, imprison someone now and then, but we still keep letting them go. And a great many of them are very young and have done their military service in the Soviet army.

This permits us to adopt a different one with the Arabs. If you don't behave yourselves, we say, we'll allow more Jews to go to Israel. If you decide to be obedient, we shall cut off the flood. And we might even put a stop to it altogether. You must admit it's an admirable arrangement.

As he said this he winked at me and laughed.

Oh, what terrifying truth there was in the general's words. Let us just cast our minds back.

In the spring of 1971, when the whole world was watching the first large groups of emigrants leaving the USSR for Israel (my own family was swept out in that flood), a series of events were unfolding in the Sudan. There was an anti-Communist uprising, the expulsion of Soviet diplomats from Khartoum, and very nearly a break in diplomatic relations with the Soviet Union. Around the same time, almost every day for several months in succession, there were planes landing at Lod Airport in Israel, disgorging hundreds of Soviet Jews. The Arab embassies in Moscow became anxious and sent a rain of protests. Talks began. The Sudan tempered its anticommunism, relations became somewhat more normal, and the planes of Soviet Jews arrived at Lod less frequently and half empty. As for the Soviet Jews themselves, those who had not managed to slip out at the appropriate moment and went on trying to obtain a visa began to find themselves in prison or dismissed from their jobs, subjected to humiliations and mockery, while world public opinion was mystified that its protests caused not the slightest embarrassment or reaction.

After a time the Soviet authorities once again began to hand out visas left and right, and thousands of families from Moscow, Leningrad, Riga and Vilna, Minsk and Kiev flooded into Israel. The Israeli immigration authorities were knocked off their feet and kept working day and night to absorb the unexpected deluge of new citizens.

A routine check made it clear that there was nothing unexpected at all about this torrent. Everything was completely natural. It was precisely at that moment that the Egyptian president Anwar Sadat took it into his head to have a little of his own way, show his independent character, and expel from the country the Soviet military specialists. In Moscow Giorgy Minin responded by opening the valve of Jewish emigration a little wider. One lot of airplanes transported the Soviet military specialists whom Sadat had expelled from Cairo Airport to Moscow, while others took Jews from the USSR to Israel, thereby increasing the might of the Arabs' enemy. Sadat could not take it. He relented and even asked for forgiveness. General Minin was not long in showing corresponding flexibility. The valve began to close, and the Israeli immigration authorities had time to get their breath back.

Soviet gendarmes are very expert at catching fish in muddy water. Close scrutiny of the last few years' events lifts the veil from some highly curious phenomena.

For years now, throughout Russia, or to be more precise among the most enlightened and intellectual sections of the population, a democratic movement has been developing—illegal opposition to the regime involving the unique phenomenon of *samizdat,* typewritten, duplicated, uncensored protest literature, frequently antigovernment, circulating in thousands of copies. *Samizdat* included a journal called *A Chronicle of Current Events,* which appeared regularly, also of course unofficially, in which were recorded with pedaritic meticulousness and strict documentary accuracy based on the testimony of eyewitnesses all the crimes of Soviet power, all the infringements of human rights in the USSR. The journal left the country by clandestine routes. Its contents appeared in the Western press, giving rise to one scandal after another. The Soviet Union was no longer hermetically sealed off from the outside world. For all who wished to see the truth, the brutal inner workings of the system were on view like fish in an aquarium.

The KGB wore themselves out looking for the culprits. They imprisoned the "democrats" and herded them into psychiatric hospitals, but the movement did not expire and the journal continued to appear with the same clockwork regularity as before. Sometimes there were changes of style when new authors came forward to replace those who had been seized.

More than half the "democrats" were Jews. The Jewish emigration to Israel was of more assistance than anything else in helping to rid Russia of its creative opposition. Among the first floods of emigrants were a disproportionately large number of "democrats." Sometimes they included non-Jews or half-Jews or quarter-Jews. The KGB made no difficulties about supplying them with visas, allowing them to jump the waiting list and even speeding up their departure as if they were apprehensive that by some mischance the emigrants might change their minds and remain in Russia to "sow discord among the native Russians."

I shall never forget one curious episode that took place at Sheremetievo Airport. We were seeing off Boris Tsukerman, an eminent figure in the Russian democratic movement. This gifted physicist enjoyed the reputation among the "democrats" of being a walking reference book on Soviet jurisprudence, both criminal and civil, and employed his extensive knowledge to fight openly and legally with Soviet power, which was constantly breaking its own laws and infringing the citizens' already curtailed rights. Boris Tsukerman acted as unpaid council for those being wronged, and his scrupulously argued protests exposed the regime's most reactionary types, pinning them down or forcing them to backtrack. Most of the legal documents aimed at the defense of human rights that the "democrats" produced were formulated and compiled by Tsukerman.

Now he was leaving, having received his visa with exceptional speed. Representatives of the authorities, both in and out of uniform, hung about in abundance among the crowd of well-wishers, waiting impatiently for this disturber of the peace to be taken up into the air and never more to set foot on Russian soil.

When Tsukerman and his wife and children had made their way to the plane and were no longer visible to us in the terminal, a crowd of breathless Russian peasant women charged noisily into the building. They were simple country women in men's boots and padded jackets, with warm shawls on their heads. When they discovered that they were late for the send-off, they began to wail with one voice, as at a village wake, lamenting the Jew Tsukerman's departure, as if he were one of their nearest and dearest. They were peasant women from Naro-Fominsk, not far from Moscow, where at one time the authorities had closed the Orthodox church. Boris Tsukerman, however, had won it back through the courts, and it had once again been opened for services. As a result of this, in Naro-Fominsk he had acquired something approaching the reputation of a saint.

The blood of the Russian democratic movement was ebbing away. The KGB was killing two birds with one stone. On the one hand they had flung a tasty morsel to the Western liberals: "Have a taste of that! You wanted these people to be allowed to emigrate. There you are! We're not the tyrants you took us for."

The liberals gobbled down the morsel, their stomachs rumbling with pleasure, not of course missing the opportunity of first thrusting it in the face of the anti-Communists: "And you said they were animals! See how wrong you were! A dialogue with these people is possible."

The other side of the coin was that it had been possible to expel from Russia quietly and without any bloodshed an unacceptable social stratum representing a danger to the authorities—the initiators of resistance to the regime. The result was not slow to emerge: the democratic movement in Russia is at its last gasp. The unofficial journal *A Chronicle of Current Events* has ceased to exist, and *samizdat* has withered and dried. The lonely figures of the Russian "democrats" do not frighten the KGB. Before long, they too, unless they drink themselves silly, will find a Jewish fiancée for an arranged marriage and forsake the USSR to the accompaniment of sighs of relief from the secret police.

For its own ends, the KGB cunningly exploited the attraction for the Jews of emigrating to Israel, and herein lies one of the reasons why the authorities put up with Jewish emigration and why they are not thinking of putting an end to it. It would be unwise to lose such a high trump card in a dirty game, at which others apart from the Soviet Union are playing.

Soviet power has used the right to emigrate, wrested from it by the Jews, for a further unsavory end. In every case, the individual leaving the USSR is subjected to a moral execution. At the factory or plant where he worked or at the insti-

tute where he studied, a general meeting of all his colleagues, at which he himself would be present, was bound
to be held. At these meetings, anti-Semites great and small
are, as it were, let loose and, to the accompaniment of
whoops of encouragement from the bosses, they publicly heap
abuse on the unfortunate, scoff at him with impunity, all of
which he must endure or else risk losing his exit visa. These
moral pogroms are a superb safety valve through which the
dissatisfaction and wrath of the Russian population can be
released, and the "Jesuits" of the KGB make unlimited use
of it for letting off superheated steam. People leave this kind
of meeting with the feeling that it is not the ruthless, totalitarian regime that is responsible for all their misfortunes
but these Jews, who are betraying Russia by going to live in
hostile Israel.

In short, the Soviet authorities have turned the concessions they were forced to make the Jews to considerable
advantage. And they derive direct material advantage as
well. It is well known that most Jewish families belong to
the comparatively well off part of the population. When
they leave, they are obliged to pay a thousand dollars per
head for a visa. They are forbidden to take money and valu-
ables with them, which is to say in plain language, they are
robbed of all they have earned. The elderly are deprived of
the pensions earned during a long working life and faced
with the horrendous prospect of penury in their declining
years. To a certain degree, the apartments vacated by the
Jews when they leave afford the authorities an opportunity
to alleviate the country's perennial housing crisis.

The USSR has turned Jewish emigration to Israel into
quite a profitable commercial enterprise. Developing a taste
for the whole business, the authorities introduced the celebrated education tax. As if they were in a slave market, they
sold Jews to Israel according to a scale of prices based on the
individual's educational standard. This was selection with
a vengeance. It stank to heaven—so much so that the flabbergasted West squeamishly held its nose. The authorities

eventually had to retreat beneath a hail of taunts and gob-
bets of spittle. The ransom was rescinded and the world
calmed down, but robbery without the ransom continues to
this day, and no one minds as long as things do not get any
worse.

These are the ways in which the USSR uses Soviet Jewry
in its manipulations at the present time, while the whole
world's inquiring attention is focused on their uneasy lot.

And what about those in other countries, in Israel and the
United States of America, who keep this problem constantly
on the boil? How much do they make out of their righteous
works in defense of Russian Jews? Do they make anything at
all? Perhaps their efforts are altruistic?

Let us take a look. Let us first agree that we will have
everything out in the open, keep nothing back, even if it
emerges that there is not much to choose between the lot of
them, everybody who fancies it having his pound of the
wretched immigrants' flesh, their hands so filthy that even
raw lye would not get them clean.

When we were still in Russia, cut off from the rest of the
world, when the only snippets of news to reach us came
over the air, through the marauding whoops and whistles of
the Soviet jamming stations that muffled what seemed to us
to be the one remaining channel of accurate information,
our intuition rather than our reason alerted us to a sort of
strange, inert coolness seeping through the Israeli Russian-
language radio broadcasts. We felt an incomprehensible
and frightening neutrality. Jewish sit-ins were being staged
in various Russian cities. Signatures were being collected
for petitions to the authorities. Foreign journalists and diplomats of various embassies risked their positions to meet
us secretly. They carefully concealed and took away with
them for transmission to the West our written appeals for
help. There these appeals soon appeared in the newspapers
and were broadcast on the radio in various languages,

alarming the world, causing it to lie awake at night and cast suspicious glances in the direction of Moscow, where serious events were beginning to unfold and where once again there was a distinct whiff of Jewish blood in the air.

Yet Israel reacted to events in the USSR with greater coolness and restraint than anyone else. The appeals we transmitted to Israel, sent by all manner of routes—by correspondents, diplomats, and tourists—disappeared without a trace, as if they had evaporated somewhere on the way, while what was sent to other countries was broadcast very rapidly indeed over the air or found its way into the newspapers. Kol Israel [the voice of Israel radio broadcast], however, would read out our letters—by no means all of them—after all the others, when its silence was becoming awkward, and it would do so somehow unwillingly, through gritted teeth, always citing as a source a foreign press agency or newspaper, as if justifying its involvement in such an obscene matter as Zionism.

When those of the first group of the movement's activists reached Israel, they were received by the head of the government, Mrs. Golda Meir. They rushed up to her with puzzled questions: "Why does Israel say nothing? Why doesn't it help the Jewish movement in Russia? You should be raising the roof!"

They were dumbfounded by her cold response: "Put padlocks on your mouths."

Not only we, but some Israelis whose consciences troubled them, were asking puzzled questions. This is what Dr. C. Rosenblum, editor of the newspaper *Yediot Achoronot*, wrote in an article called "It's neither Ethical nor Reasonable."

Many immigrants from the USSR here in Israel are filled with deep displeasure. They assert that it has been caused by Jerusalem's inactivity in the matter of liberating Jews from Russia.

And this is the absolute truth! There exists a tacit but strong and stubborn resistance on the part of the government to anything that remotely resembles an active struggle for the rights of emigration from the USSR. Anyone who has had direct experience of the government's attitude in this crucial question is aware of this. The government's reaction to proposals containing an element of un-compromising struggle remind one of an Italian strike: no resistance, not even an argument, but plain inactivity.

Those who publish our newspapers are in no doubt about this. About two years ago, in those days when only a tiny trickle of immigrants was emerging from Russia, Golda Meir asked them to "lower the pitch a little" in articles about repatriation. She said: "It will only harm those Jews still in Russia who also hope to come back to us. They might be blinded by the floodlights we direct at them. If we make a fuss about repatriation, the Soviets will stop all repatriation, even the present infinitesimal numbers, so we must be circumspect." And she added: "Our silence earns the gratitude of those Russian repatriates who still have relatives in the USSR wishing to come to Israel."

However, quite soon afterwards it became apparent that the newly arrived repatriates of the Soviet Union were of the opposite opinion. They demand (their own experience in the USSR has convinced them) that Israel should "raise the pitch" in struggling for the return of their brethren....

There were some editors who rose in revolt against these efforts to gag them. They showed resistance, not for sensational reasons, but on account of the harm which they believed was caused by keeping silent, and they stated: "We do not share your opinion and we will print everything that in our view is important." In response to this Golda Meir said: "In that case my friends, I shall have no alternative but to subject your articles to censorship." And censorship was imposed upon us, thus putting an end to the argument. Censorship is, after all, the most powerful of arguments. It affects everybody, both the pro's and the con's....

Once again there was calm in the country. The repatriates from the Soviet Union were amazed and, having no other outlet, began an "individual struggle" for the liberation of their brethren in the USSR. Their meetings and hunger strikes by the Wailing Wall are still fresh in the memory.

Not all Russian immigrants, however, confined themselves to singing psalms by the Wailing Wall. Many extended their activities to the United Nations and Washington, and this alarmed the Jerusalem government, since the campaign began to flare up in various parts of the world without its participation. In the light of such a development, governmental inactivity became "dangerous" for the government itself.

Consequently, the ambassador and other of our government's emissaries in the United States embarked upon a vigorous war— not against the Soviet Union but against those repatriates who were attacking the Soviets in the U.S.A., and a scandal resulted. . . .

Many former Soviet Jews began to shower our government with requests that lists of Jews demanding permission to leave Russia should be published. The government rejected this suggestion in horror and to this day pays no heed to the request of our brothers and sisters. . . .

The most depressing expression of this phenomenon was the case of the United States Senator Jackson, a person who has fought persistently for the free repatriation of Soviet Jews.

We simply threw him to the wolves and turned out backs on him. He applied the brakes on the whole American administrative machine in order to force it to make the extension of economic ties with the Soviet Union a condition of the abolition of the education tax. And what did we do?

We stood idly by on the sidelines, as if it had nothing to do with us. Nor was that all. We are without doubt partly to blame for the fact that many American Jews turned away from Senator Jackson.

You may well ask: "What is the explanation of Jerusalem's policy on this issue?" Here is a clear answer: "It wishes to draw a veil over the question of Jewish repatriation from the USSR so that it is easier to incline the Soviets toward the re-establishment of diplomatic relations with us." In our opinion, this course is not only unprincipled but also ill-advised.

I intentionally included this long quotation from an Israeli newspaper in order to show what awaited us on arrival in Israel.

The true picture became more apparent to us gradually and with terrifying clarity. Official Israel, i.e., the Socialist party that rules the country, grovels subserviently before the Soviet Union as behooves an ideological younger brother, forgiving it everything, even cultural and, latterly, physical genocide, too, directed against its Jewish population. We, on the other hand, had escaped from the USSR as fierce anti-Communists who had experienced at first hand all the delights of the socialist paradise. As such we were unacceptable to the Israeli ruling clique. We were a danger to it and should our numbers ever become sufficiently large, we would become its gravediggers.

Dr. Julius Margolin, a man who lived an amazing life, a gifted crusading publicist and one of the most interesting political figures in the Jewish state, did not live to see our arrival but died a few months before the first groups of repatriates, the vanguard of the Soviet Jews, fought their way through to Israel. He spent five terrifying years in Stalin's dungeons and, from 1946 onwards, strove untiringly to awaken the conscience of Israel, getting absolutely nowhere. This is what his comrade-in-arms Golda Yelin wrote in the preface to the dead man's articles (a collection entitled *Jews in the Soviet Union*), published in 1973.

These articles, which were written in the 1950s, are being published for the first time. The fact that articles on a subject such as this could not be published in Israel either in Russian or in Hebrew when they were written tells us a great deal. Anyone, however, who thinks that this kind of thing happened only in the past is making a mistake. Even today, in spite of all the changes that have taken place with regard to the fate of Jews in Soviet Russia, these articles can only be published in a primitive edition of this nature. Moreover, the vast amount of material possessed by the new repatriates from Soviet Russia has scarcely any access to the press, particularly in the Hebrew press....

That same censorship that once stifled Margolin's voice is still at work, and the voice of the latest repatriates is unable to reach the people of Israel. We must not permit precious materials about the history of Jewish sufferings in Communist Russia to share the fate of Margolin's articles and, as were his, be circulated in typescript twenty years after they are written.

We were far from being the first of Israel's unloved and unwanted sons.

It was the most awful betrayal, at which the mind boggles. When we came into contact with the Israel of which we had dreamed and which we had sought for so long, we ran our heads into a brick wall and were paralyzed with shock.

Of course, these people who ran the show could not slam the country's doors in our faces. Their continued silence was already becoming a disgrace. They started adding their voice to the general chorus, but it was an insincere and hypocritical voice. In order to put us firmly in our places, impose limits on our ambitions, and sap our desire to take any kind of active steps, the bureaucratic apparatus was hurled into the fray—the most callous and uncouth apparatus of its kind I have encountered in my life. Yes, in some ways the bureaucracy was worse than the Soviet variety. After all, the Soviet bureaucracy works; in Israel they sit on their hands—a real oriental bureaucracy, it combines xenophobia with laziness. We were given a cruel working-over. In a spirit combined indifference and hostility, our bureaucratic overlords had us running the gauntlet and on the rack, which by no means all of us could endure. Many were broken and almost all sank into apathy.

One need only say that the Israeli Ministry of Immigrant Absorption—and I am ready to swear that this has been done purposely—was given to the most Marxist of all the socialist parties in the ruling block, Mapam. The party myrmidons in this ministry relieve their pro-Communist feelings on the anti-Communists who arrive from Russia. The immigrant is subjected to refined humiliations, an assault is made on his sanity with the same relish as was extant in those Soviet institutions where Jews seek exist visas.

Initially cooling down and then crushing and paralyzing the mass of immigrants who so unexpectedly came tumbling down upon its head, Israel has managed to transform the Russian Jews into something striking in its cynicism, an unbeatable card.

You will recall that before the authorities let any of us out of the Soviet Union they arranged pogrom meetings, at which we Jews figured as the cause of all the Russian people's tribulations. Having finally escaped to what we thought was our home, we Russian Jews once again become scapegoats for all disasters and misfortunes, but this time those of the Israelis. A justification was found for the resounding failures of the state's economic policies, the awful destitution of the impoverished areas, the highest taxes in the world, the heavy stench of the housing crisis—for all these things. But of course! The Russian Jews were to blame for all these things. They were swallowing up all the money. That was why the taxes were high. That was why there was nowhere to live. If your children could not get into university, it was because preference was being given to theirs.

A tiny parochial country—where in very truth if you sneeze in the north at Rosh Pina, then in Eilat, the southernmost point, they will say "Bless you!"—was enveloped in a poisonous cloud of unfriendly rumors, and we began to sense hostility toward us in every quarter. Occasionally, the government would mutter something indistinctly intended to convey the impression that it was defending the immigrants, but it did not manage to find time to spell out distinctly, with all the means at the disposal of its propaganda apparatus, and make it clear to the confused population that *not a single Israeli pound was being spent on the immigrants at the expense of the indigenous Israeli population and that all this money was being given by diaspora Jews.* The very fact therefore of the appearance of this Russian wave of immigrants was a blessing for the country. Precisely because of these people, hundreds of millions of dollars (dollars, not worthless Israeli pounds) were cascading into the Israeli treasury like golden rain, rescuing the rickety economy from the brink of crisis and creating full employment for the country's able-bodied population.

This was not done. On the contrary, the newspapers and television, even the variety stage, excelled each other in describing the fairy tale "privileges" of the Russian immigrants, evoking thereby the annoyance and covetous spite of the natives. Their just anger over the social and economic bedlam prevailing in the country, over their very hard lives with nothing better in prospect, was adroitly diverted into a safe channel. The Russian immigrants became the scapegoats, and the noxious wave of hostility flooded over them instead of over the government.

Here is one example of many. If an immigrant has somehow managed to scrape together, more often than not on credit and at a high rate of interest, the money to buy a car, the police attach to it, like a stigma, a number surrounded by a white band, informing everyone that this is an immigrant's car. Hooligans from the poor areas go looking for these white bands in places where the cars are parked at night and scratch their bodywork, slash their tires, and break their windows.

The country is simply not aware that the immigrants get nothing for nothing. Their every step in their "native" land is expressed in a special document, the Teudat Ole, in round sums of money which have to be repaid with interest. People are enmeshed in debts like a fly in a spider's web, and in this situation their feelings are no different from those of that fly upon which the spider casts a greedy eye.

In Beersheba, the center of the Negev Desert region in the south of Israel, the Selyutin family from Minsk lived for a year. Both he and his wife are doctors. They have two children, and in addition both grandmothers live with them. In order to pay a thousand dollars for each living soul in the family and leave the USSR, they sold everything they could and brought with them only the most essential things: their clothing, linen, and their books—their personal library, which every educated family in Russia possesses.

One year was enough for them to realize that their coming to Israel had been a very serious error. The road back to Minsk was sealed off, and in desperation they applied to go to Germany. Someone had told them that there was a shortage of doctors there.

Alas, however, when you leave Israel, as when you leave the USSR, you have to pay a ransom. On the basis of their Teudat Ole, they were rendered an account, which they were unable to pay. After all, in Russia they had had their own apartment and possessions, which they had acquired over the years. By selling it all they had been able to scrape together the money for the ransom. Furthermore, there were relatives and friends to whom they could rush for help if worse came to the worst. Here in Israel, they were on their own and without possessions, but the bill had to be paid. There were the tickets for themselves and their luggage from Vienna to Tel Aviv, their board and lodging in the Ulpan where they had been taught the essentials of Hebrew, and many, many other things. For a second time they had to pay a price for freedom. This time it was in Israel, their so-called historical homeland.

They paid. I saw them do it. Every last agorot. They almost had to sell the clothes they stood up in. Everything went that had survived Soviet plunder. They sold their bed linen for next to nothing, and their whole library of Russian books—the family's one remaining treasured possession, its last link with its roots and former life—went for a song.

Svetlana and Yefim Selyutin were not alone in their fate; they shared it with hundreds of families who emigrated from Russia and who had the will and the energy to decide to continue their flight, this time out of Israel. Dramas like these the Israeli government conceals from its own people and even more carefully from Jews in the diaspora.

So the unexpected and unwanted arrival of the Russian Jews was used within the country as a lightning conductor by the insolvent Israeli politicians. They did not derive their advantage from the wretched crowds of bemused immigrants inside Israeli frontiers. The main dividend was squeezed out of foreign countries. For all they were worth, laying on the pathos and the sobbing, they began to exploit the responsive sensitivities of the world's Jews to the sufferings of their fellows. Hundreds of Russian Jews with even the most rudimentary knowledge of a European language (I myself was one of them) were sent across the world to speak, under the watchful eye of Israeli officials, at meetings in Jewish communities in the United States, Canada, Argentina, Australia, England, and France, asking their fellow-Jews for material help, melting hearts, and loosening purse strings. People's sufferings were ruthlessly exploited, crudely and tactlessly paraded for all to see. Personal grief was put on show as if it were part of an exhibition. I recall how after a series of public appearances in New York, the sister of David Chernoglaz, who in Russia had served a prison sentence on account of her desire to emigrate to Israel, was reduced to a state of nervous collapse requiring medical attention. Several other people, whose spiritual traumas were thrown open to the well-fed public for guided tours, returned from their travels almost out of their minds.

On the other hand, the money came rolling in. Tens, hundreds of millions of dollars tumbled into the bottomless pit of the Israeli treasury, and all under the same ruse: "Help the Russian heroes." A slogan was coined—"Settling each Russian immigrant family in Israel costs $35,000" (in 1976 this was changed to $60,000), and on the basis of this inflated figure millions of dollars were raised from distraught and deeply moved ordinary Jewish men and women. They were and still are being shamelessly skinned. They were dishonestly told and are still being told that this money was a gift to a Russian immigrant, but a careful watch was kept to ensure that donors did not discover the true situation.

The unsavory truth is that most of this money never had been destined for the immigrants. It was used for quite different purposes: to plug the holes in the Israeli state budget. Those miserable crumbs that reached the Russian Jew were given to him in the form of a *loan*, on which he had to pay interest. He did not, however, pay the money back to his American benefactor but to the Israeli treasury, which had turned even the gift into a source of income.

Something of a grain of truth emerged on one occasion at a meeting in Chicago. A Russian emigrant, the former Moscow lawyer Boris Kogan, who had been sent to America to extort money, could stand no more of it, and while addressing his audience drew the curtain very slightly aside and hinted at the real situation of the Russian Jews in Israel.

What a fuss he caused! Kogan was quite literally silenced and removed from the platform. He was there and then thrown out of his hotel and left without means of support, subsequently spending a long time on the streets of New York, sheltering under the roofs of kind folk he happened to encounter and managing with very little food. He never did return to Israel, not even to collect the few wretched belongings he had brought from Russia. He feared the consequences.

Once while I was in New York he wandered into my hotel, the luxurious Drake Hotel right in the heart of fashionable Manhattan, where he himself had once had a magnificent suite when he was in the management's good graces. When I offered him some supper, for a long time he was unwilling to accept, but he then overcame his embarrassment and agreed, gobbling the food greedily down without taking time to chew it. He was drawn and emaciated, and his eyes were frozen in despair.

Until then I had only known him very slightly. I tried to recall what I knew of him. He was a bachelor. He had come to Israel alone, sacrificing the most precious thing in his life—his parents. They were feeble, ailing, old folk, both of whom were bed-ridden, in need of constant attention, and thus were unable to undertake the journey. He was obsessed with the idea of serving his nation and assumed the burdensome sin of leaving them to the mercy of fate to die within unfriendly walls without a single loved one beside them.

In Israel he quickly realized that his sacrifice had been in vain and that he was one of many who had been cruelly deceived. His profession was a rare and unusual one. He was one of the few specialists in the world in the field of international maritime law and had a fluent knowledge of four languages: Russian, French, English, and Italian. The only place in Israel, however, where he could find application for his talents was the port of Haifa, where he worked as an ordinary porter, humping crates and sacks about on his back. Although his health was not particularly good and he was unable to see adequately without eyeglasses, he accepted this unaccustomed physical work without complaint, blaming no one for his fate and considering that perhaps the most useful thing he could do for the country he loved to the point of pain was dragging heavy loads about.

His knowledge of languages finally won him a trip to the United States to collect money. The rest of the story you know. Where he is now and what has become of him I have no idea.

The shameless charity fraud continues to this day. Hundreds of new green unfortunates who have just escaped from Russia take their bleeding wounds on tour across the continents of the world and like puppets, whose strings are pulled by those who accompany them, parade their grief and probe their sores, evoking in response waves of sympathy and showers of clinking coins. Million after million comes cascading down past the palms of the performers into the deftly placed hands of the organizers of these circuses, the cold and calculating Israeli political hacks.

When we began our Moscow fight for the right to emigrate freely to Israel, in our wildest flights of fancy we could not have anticipated the kind of unrestrained speculation, political intrigues, and buying and selling that this movement of ours would become. For several years now Russian Jews have been a fashionable topic all over the world and scarcely any eminent politician, particularly one who strives to achieve fame, can ignore this issue. Their interest is completely selfish, based on long-term considerations and having nothing whatsoever to do with the fate of the Russian Jews. Anyone who has a mind can warm his carefully manicured, grasping hands at the conflagration of our sufferings.

In America and England, in France and Australia, in almost every country, all kinds of committees and commis-

sions have sprung up like mushrooms. They all have impos-
ing budgets with staffs of paid officials and honorary members from senates and congresses, parliaments and governments. The campaign for Russian Jews has become a
profitable and lucrative profession, and if, heaven forbid,
our movement in the USSR should cease or dry up,
thousands of people who shout the odds at meetings and in
commissions for a high remuneration would be left without
a crust of bread.

And what about the statesmen? Good God, what honeyed
smiles they flashed in my direction when I was brought to
the United States and taken from city to city, from meeting
to meeting, from banquet to banquet like an exhibit, an ar-
chetypal symbol of the Russian Jew. They treated me with
informality, almost like an equal, slapping me on the back
in front of the cameras and television cameras. They called
me their friend and sometimes even their brother, never
forgetting to address the microphone. Yet they did not even
remember my name. When on one occasion, I phoned one
congressman at the number on his visiting card, which he
had solemnly thrust into my hand on a platform in front of
thousands of people, inviting me simply and unceremoniously to visit his home ("my wife and children will be thril-
led!"), for a long time he could not remember me and then
somewhat drily observed that he was rather busy and asked
me to phone later, though he did not suggest when. His tone
exuded amazement and annoyance. He clearly regarded me
as a fool. Nor was he very wide of the mark. I was still
inexperienced in the ways of Western democracy and took a
great many things at face value.

We Russian Jews were just the chips in a vast and dirty
game, which the Soviet Union and Israel were playing.
People from the United States were also involved, playing
for the same stakes, but with a good deal less skill.

The presidential election was close at hand. Russian Jews
had become a salable commodity in America. The two com-
peting parties in the election were fighting over them,

shedding television tears about their fate and radiating syn-
thetic toothpaste-advertisement smiles in their direction,
for both the Republicans and the Democrats were endeavoring to collect the votes of their Jewish supporters.

The lengths that these men of consequence were prepared
to go to, vying with one another in advertising the high
quality of their love for us! I was in Pittsburgh, busy with
my dreary run-of-the-mill business. One meeting followed
another in synagogues, restaurants, private houses. The
same old speeches with slight variations, depending on
whether there were more women than men in the audience.
The same entourage with their capacious briefcases for
money and checks.

My voice was hoarse and overworked, my nerves were
tense, for however many times you say the same old things,
each time you become tense and strung-up because for you
the subject of the meeting is still your own wound and the
sufferings of individuals close to you. I was brought back
late to the hotel by my camp-followers, solicitously fed in
the restaurant, money being no object, for I would be
needed the next day and the day after, needed in good working order like a well-oiled machine.

Very late on one such evening in my Pittsburgh hotel, I
received a telephone call from Washington—Washington,
where I had neither acquaintances nor friends. Someone
was ringing at the behest of Senator H. and inquired politely
when I could see the senator, who would very much like to
talk to me about an important matter. I had not the slightest
idea who Senator H. was, but my attendants explained to
me with reverently rolling eyes that he was an important
figure on the staff of McGovern, the Democratic party presidential candidate, and on no account should I allow a
chance like that slip through my fingers. I honestly could
not manage to grasp what this chance was that had come my
way, but I was too self-conscious to ask, not wishing to
demonstrate once again, for the umpteenth time, my verita-
bly staggering Russian slowness to catch on.

It was agreed that on the following day precisely at noon I would be waiting for the senator in a room he would order in the restaurant at the Pittsburgh airport, where he would fly in for one hour simply to meet me, before returning to Washington. American efficiency! The very thought of it still fills me with a feeling of ecstasy.

At a few minutes before twelve the plane from Washington landed, and at precisely midday the senator appeared in the airport restaurant, where I, in keeping with my Russian habit of arriving very early for a rendezvous, had already been hanging about for a full hour. He was young, a bundle of American energy, with the obligatory American smile spreading right across thirty-two top-quality teeth, and he got straight down to business.

The senator was aware that I had been a film director in Russia and, according to his information, had made some quite successful films. He knew too that dozens of other film people from the USSR had arrived in Israel and found themselves in a difficult situation. The film industry in the Jewish state was very small and the new immigrants could not find work. He, Senator H., who was a great friend of Israel and in particular of the heroic and courageous emigrants from Russia, proposed the following: to found in Israel a new film company with a large amount of capital raised in the United States and to provide work for the new arrivals. This would be a vast project involving millions of dollars. There would be work for everybody. Hundreds more of my colleagues would come flooding from Russia when they heard about the opportunities. I could not believe my ears.

Right there at the table on one of the restaurant napkins the senator drew up a contract in his own handwriting, and we both put our signatures to it. I then hurriedly (the senator was looking at his watch, as there were just a few minutes left before the return flight) compiled a list of all the film people who had come to Israel from the USSR, and with that list Senator H. dashed on to the runway, where the

Washington plane was already revving up its engines. I was left in the restaurant by myself at the table, and the waiter, who had been paid in advance for the lunch, kept taking suspicious sidelong glances at my excited glowing countenance—I must have seemed slightly unhinged.

Later Senator H. sought me out in New York, and I signed a pile of official papers drawn up by the lawyers—with each fresh signature a huge film company was being born before my very eyes, and I could not wait to get back to Israel in order to cheer up my friends, roll up my sleeves, and finally get down to the work I loved.

I was happy. The senator had become a guardian angel and benefactor for all those of us who had already lost hope of ever using their skills again. In the eyes of American Jews, this man was adorned with the halo of an ardent admirer of their Russian brethren—a man who with deeds and not just words was helping them to establish themselves in their historic homeland.

More than five years have passed since all this happened, and neither I nor my friends have made any films. Many of them have already left Israel and fled to various parts of the world.

In the United States, the election was over and with it ended the hunt for votes and the need for the trump card that we represented. Promises and obligations went on to the rubbish heap along with the election posters. We were used, our hopes were aroused, and as soon as the need for us had passed they forgot all about us.

Now I am just a shade wiser. I bear no grudge against Senator H. Such is the style and the law of the life he leads. Since then I have had a host of such "friends," all tarred with the same brush.

It was not only private individuals—singly or in herds, under the flags of committees and commissions, or without even a fig leaf—who derived benefit from the song and dance that surrounded us but even such serious institutions as the U.S. State Department and the CIA.

In a hollow among the Bavarian Alps lies the city of Munich, of sad and inglorious memory, where to this day the *Bierkeller* that gave its name to Hitler's first putsch is reverently preserved as a memorial and shown to visitors and tourists. It was here that the harbinger of a new order emerged in Europe and with it the final solution of the Jewish Question, heralding the first puffs of smoke from the chimneys of Auschwitz and Treblinka. In this same Munich, its wartime ruins now rebuilt and the faces of its plump burghers gleaming more rosily than ever, at Arabella Strasse 18 (now Englische Garten 1) there stands a multi-story building occupying a whole block. It is built of dull grey concrete and looks like a barracks.

As distinct from neighboring hotels, the Arabellahaus and the Sheraton, it has no glowing neon sign on its roof and no yard-high letters across its facade. Only by the main entrance, if you look carefully, will you find a small plate with the name of the institution etched demurely upon it. The well-built figures of guards in civilian clothes loom behind the thick glass doors, which only open when a button is pressed inside the building.

The monotonous, endless corridors within are like those of a prison. Grey shadowy figures flit along them, disappearing through countless doors. The turnings in the corridors are closed off by iron partitions with inset iron doors just like the watertight doors in submarines, heightening still further the building's similarity to a prison.

It is Radio Liberty—its Munich section. The other section is at 30 Forty-second Street in New York.

Radio Liberty transmits broadcasts in Russian and in a dozen other national languages to the Soviet Union twenty-four hours a day, fighting a fairly energetic ethereal duel as part of the ideological encounter between Communist East and the capitalist West.

The Soviets have long had Liberty stuck in their craw.

There are special jamming stations in various parts of the USSR to stifle its broadcasts. It is lambasted in the pages of the Soviet press as the regime's most baleful enemy. Just the mention of the word *Liberty* causes a gnashing of teeth in the Kremlin. The state security services conduct an unceasing secret war against this radio station.

A huge staff of officials services this gigantic enterprise. Previously it was financed by the CIA, but when this occasioned a public scandal, its funding was transferred to the U.S. Department of State.

Of course it was not easy to gather together the highly qualified, polyglot personnel to service the station. Initially emigrants who left Russia during the Revolution were drawn into the work; later came those who fled with the Nazis after the Second World War. Among others, former policemen and burgomasters, direct participants in Hitler's plan for the final solution of the Jewish Question, entrenched themselves.

Quite a colorful company, isn't it? It does not always smell too good. The main thing is the low level of qualifications. The odd "nonreturnee"—Soviet tourists or seamen who found political asylum in the West—occasionally supplemented the station's staff, but attaining its professional level was clearly beyond them.

And suddenly, what a stroke of luck, as if from heaven! The Jews! The Russian Jews at the cost of considerable sacrifices had broken through the Iron Curtain, at first in a tiny stream and then in an ever-increasing flood—on average 3,000 souls per month. They poured into Israel, letting all the world know that their aim, their dream was to live in the historic homeland of which they had dreamed for centuries, to build their own Jewish state. In their requests to the visa department, in letters to Brezhnev and Kurt Waldheim (and to U Thant before him), Soviet Jews trying to obtain permission to emigrate did not fail to stress their loyalty to the land of their birth and gave assurances that once they had left its frontiers they would indulge in no activities hostile to the USSR.

It was simply impossible to find better personnel to swell the sparse ranks of Liberty, which ranks had become decidedly thinner in recent years as old-stagers reached pensionable age. Those in charge of the radio station lowered their hands into the torrent of immigrants in order to catch the nice little fish they needed.

One could not ask for more. The array is dazzling. First-class experts in the Russian language, who received their higher education in Moscow and Leningrad, radio and TV announcers, editors, actors, directors. Here is a Jew from Kazan—he will be fine for the Tatar section. And for the Byelorussian and Ukrainian departments, there are Jews from Minsk and Kiev who speak the languages without an accent. You might think you were in the Kreshchatik (the main street of Kiev) or the Komarovka (the main square of Minsk). And what a find for the Caucasian section the Georgian Jews are! The Bokhara Jews from Dushanbe and Tashkent make splendid reinforcements for the Tadzhik and Uzbek sections.

So the hunt began to recruit Jews into the ranks of anti-Soviet mercenaries, fighting for the liberty of the Russian, the Byelorussian, the Ukrainian, the Tatar, the Uzbek, the Georgian, the Tadzhik, and many, many other nations among whom these Jews had lived and from whom they had been only too pleased to skedaddle as soon as the opportunity presented itself.

And what about their historic homeland? Who is going to build the Jewish state, about which they fantasized so loudly and untiringly in their statements and open letters to the whole world?

In justification of most of these people it should be observed that they did not find themselves in Munich instead of Tel Aviv of their own free will, exchanging the long-cherished bread of life in their own state for a joyless crust

262   *Farewell, Israel!*

in another foreign country. Israel greeted its Soviet sons inhospitably, and the diploma of a Soviet university or an academic degree in Russian language and literature became a passport to unemployment and, consequently, to beggary.

Many of these people I knew both in Moscow and in Israel, and I can testify that they had not the least desire to become involved in politics and that the career of a professional anti-Soviet mercenary had no charms for them whatsoever. They had, after all, grown up and lived in the USSR, and their friends and relatives still living there might easily become hostages. No, many of them were not tempted by this prospect, and if they had known that this was where their impulse to live in Israel would end they would perhaps not have moved from where they were and would not have smashed up their own lives and those of their families.

Roaming back and forth in Israel looking unsuccessfully for work, depressed by the unfriendliness of those who surrounded them, despairing of the apparent impasse in which they found themselves, these people sooner or later fell into the clutches of the Radio Liberty talent scouts. These wily old hands with Jewish faces, fairly correct Russian and quite a few years of CIA service under their belts, exhorted and lured their prey with high salaries, rent-free apartments, and life in Europe, the center of culture.

They scoured the Ulpans like thieves in the night. These specially commissioned huntsmen, e.g., Max Ralis, David Anin, and Jean Lecache, had a good nose for profit. They would usually appear at twilight, not drawing unnecessary attention to themselves, even somewhat embarrassed by their mission, but guessing unerringly where the candidate they needed was living. They were usually accompanied by a man whose tracking was faultless, one Itzhak Almagor, who for a long time held down a job as a secretary of the society Irgun Akademaim, an association for persons with higher education originating from the USSR. Not long before, Itzhak Almagor had been promoted and become president of the society. In his hands was concentrated all the information about persons with higher education arriving from the USSR, and he offered a very wide range of goods to potential purchasers. So far as I am aware, he received a specific reward for each head he was able to offer.

Looking for the right people, catching specialists speaking various languages among the mass of immigrants from the USSR, goes on not only with the assistance of talent scouts scouring the Ulpans under cover of night. For some time, mysterious advertisements have been appearing in the Israeli Russian-language newspapers *Nasha Strana* and *Tribuna,* directed toward immigrants from the USSR who have experience of journalism and a good command of Bashkir, Tatar, Uzbek, and Tadzhik. They are mysteriously invited to dial a particular number and to ask for a certain Mr. Sergeev.

Anyone who is even faintly knowledgeable can see the ears of Radio Liberty sticking through this innocuous advertisement. It is just a different form of recruiting. Its purpose remains the same—gathering qualified mercenaries and lowering them into the mire of the cold war, a war far removed from the genuine interests of Soviet Jews. Obviously, all this ferment of activity on the part of the talent scouts in Israel, although slightly camouflaged and not completely out in the open, could not be a secret to the authorities. According to my information, this work is carried on with their knowledge and with no small assistance from them. No less a person than Nehemiah Levanon, the head of a mysterious department of the Israeli Ministry for Foreign Affairs, is in contact with those who run Liberty, making recommendations and rejecting candidates who appear dubious. Israel does what favors it can for the U.S. In the absence of suitable goods for export it trades in people, hapless immigrants from the USSR.

The result of this energetic activity is that a lot of Jewish faces have begun to appear in the studios of Radio Liberty, in Munich and in New York. Jews unable to find a niche in

Israel are making broadcasts in the various national languages of the USSR. The Soviet secret services are well aware of what is happening at Radio Liberty. Their agents are active there. I remember being in Munich at the radio station, walking along an interminable, prison-like corridor and talking to one of the heads of Radio Liberty, Mr. Francis Ronalds. In a Russian not without flaws, he cut me short and suggested that we seek a more suitable place for our chat. "The walls here have ears," he observed without a shadow of irony, as if he were uttering a commonplace. "It may well be that one in ten of my staff works for the KGB."

What about that! The recent scandalous case of the Soviet agent Marin, returning to the USSR after having spent nine years wearing the mask of a political refugee working at Radio Liberty simply bears out Mr. Ronalds's suspicions.

Moscow is consequently fully informed of the number of Soviet Jews who have been recruited by Radio Liberty. I will not go into the matter of how the KGB can take cruel revenge on their relatives and friends in the Soviet Union. Recruiting such large numbers of Jews to work for its most deadly enemies gives the Kremlin a pretext to fan the flames of official anti-Semitism even more energetically and a convenient excuse to halt emigration to Israel altogether and seal the crack in the Iron Curtain forced open by Jewish tenacity.

I wonder whether the State Department, which is responsible for Radio Liberty, has foreseen this possible eventuality? Those very same people who day and night selflessly agonize over the fate of the wretched Soviet Jews are, in pursuance of rather squalid departmental interests, quite cold-bloodedly digging those self-same Jews' graves. Here sentiment and fine words are set aside; they do what is expedient. We, all unaware, were from the very beginning toys in the hands of political operators, chips stacked on the table for the use of the players—the USSR, Israel, and the United States of America.

chapter eleven

THE FUNERAL KNELL

$\mathbf{M}$eyer Weisgal, veteran of the Zionist movement and for many years close collaborator of the first president of Israel, Chaim Weizmann, writes in his memoirs:

There is the inevitable (and tiresome) question, before as well as after the establishment of the state: "Why Palestine?" Why could not the Jews, a people of such enormous creative energy, have taken over empty lands in Uganda or the Argentine and made them bloom? Why Palestine, why Jerusalem? Think of all the problems you would have saved yourselves with the Arabs if you had gone somewhere else? In March, 1968, I was asked all these questions again by J. B. Priestley, when he spent a few days in Rehovot. I began with a story. Following the Six Day War, after the city of Jerusalem had been reunited, there appeared a cartoon in one of the Israeli papers. It showed "Yisrolik," the little fellow with the fatigue cap whom the cartoonist Dosh has made into a symbol of the young state, offering King Hussein advice as to how to get back the city. "Do what we did. Say over and over again for two thousand years, 'Next year in Jerusalem.'"

His witty advice to a certain extent contains the answer to the question why the Jewish state was proclaimed in Palestine and

265

not anywhere else and why the Jews are so preoccupied with Jerusalem.

"Next year in Jerusalem!" This sacramental phrase has been, as it were, the umbilical cord tying the Jews of the world to the land of Israel for two thousand years. On feast days and for that matter on every other day of the year, Jews say these words and moreover not just once a day but more often. All of Jewish expression, religious, liturgical, folkloristic is permeated with a longing for Zion.

And what is more, in whatever far-flung latitude the Jews might live, everywhere they identify with their remote forebears growing the "fruits of the earth" in the Middle East, in the Holy Land. In Eastern Europe when sometimes the earth is still covered with snow and the frost at times still severe, children from the Jewish shtetels plant young saplings, because in the far off land of Israel it is the day of "Tu B'Shevat," also called the "New Year of the Trees," the time of the first blossoming of the almond trees in the land of their ancestors. . . .

In New York it is perhaps an overcast autumn day of drenching rain, yet the Jews pray for rain, for in the far-off land of Israel the earth yearns for the reviving moisture from heaven.

And it is no accident that the land of our forefathers is usually called simply "Eretz"—country, earth, land. There is no need for further explanation and amplification—for the Jew it is the only land which is his. [M. Weisgel, *So Far* (London: Weidenfeld & Nicholson, 1971), pp. 251–52.]

On November 29, 1947, this two-thousand-year-old Jewish dream came true. With 33 votes in favor, 13 against, and 10 abstentions, the United Nations passed the *historic* resolution to establish a Jewish state in part of the territory of Palestine. I purposely stress the word *historic*, for only now, when oil diplomacy has plunged us into an energy crises sending a shudder through all Europe, when the world's whole attention is concentrated on the Middle East and the subsequent fate of Jerusalem may become the spark to precipitate a third world war involving the use of weapons of mass destruction, only now has astonished humanity begun to grasp that this *historic* resolution was the dynamite detonator attached to the world's oil supplies.

That same ill-fated resolution, greeted with such ecstasy

by Jews in every part of the world, signed the Jewish nation's death warrant, against which there was no right of appeal, the death sentence of a nation which had for so many centuries astonished the world with its fantastic capacity to survive and its apparent immortality.

The state of Israel was born in unbelievable torment. The vote of each United Nations delegate was fought over by both sides: the Jews and the Arabs. Political passions, still not cooled after the Second World War, relegated the Palestine question to the periphery, muted its poignancy and danger, and made it an object of customary behind-the-scenes trading. The world did not treat this problem seriously and linked it simply with secondary interests.

For the Jews, after millennia of wandering in alien lands, the foundation of their own state was a question of the first importance and one involving the most intense emotion. This clouded their reason to such an extent that they did not in their joy perceive that they had entered a minefield where it seemed impossible for them to survive.

The same Meyer Weisgal, who was a witness and direct participant in those memorable events, recreates in his memoirs an authentic picture of how it all happened:

A two-thirds majority was required for ratification, and every single vote counted. Weizmann was again called to action. One week before the vote he went to President Truman and convinced him that the Negev must be part of the Jewish state. American objections were dropped. Weizmann then telephoned Léon Blum [leader of the French socialists and at that time a member of the French government] and got the French—who had been expected to abstain—to vote for Partition. And Weizmann rocked the United Nations with his speech....

That night there was a Labor Zionist rally called at the St. Nicholas Arena. When it had been planned, the outcome of the vote was unknown; it was not even certain that there would be any outcome. Expectation was tense, and when the car, escorted by police, finally reached the door of the Arena and Weizmann appeared at the entrance the cheering engulfed the building. He was lifted out of my protective grasp on to the shoulders of the people and carried into the hall.

Such, in Meyer Weisgal's words, were the atmosphere and the enthusiasm when the Jewish state was born.

More than a quarter of a century has now elapsed since those historic days. A quarter of a century of ceaseless, exhausting, bloody fighting to preserve what was artificially created in the all of the General Assembly of the United Nations. All that time the conflagration of an endless, viciously cruel war has been blazing in the Middle East, now flaring up ominously, now dying down a little and smoldering, time and again jerking the rest of the world into a response and sometimes placing it on the verge of total catastrophe.

And what are the fruits that the Jewish people have harvested, a people who have in their long history undergone the incredible sufferings of dispersion? Fresh numberless sacrifices, the galling weariness of world public opinion, the never-ending sequence of anti-Semitic outbursts—not on the trivial day-to-day level but on a national scale sanctioned by the authorities and embracing whole countries—this has been the legacy.

Despite the prophecies of the Zionist leaders, Israel has not become a magnet for the world's Jews. In a quarter of a century Israel has somehow managed to gather together in the territory that was formerly Palestine just one-fifth of the Jewish population of the diaspora. In New York City alone there live to this day more Jews than in the whole of Israel. There are more in Paris than in Tel Aviv and more in London than in Jerusalem.

It has turned out to be difficult, in fact simply impossible, to imbue all Jews with the idea of Zionism, to arouse them and make them foresake the cozy corners they have lived in for generations. These places were not always safe, but on the other hand they were familiar and capable of supplying their needs, whereas they were asked to exchange them for an even less secure existence in a hot and unfamiliar climate, far removed from both physical and material well-being and enveloped in a fog of medieval religious fanaticism.

For two thousand years the Jews dreamt of returning to Zion, and these dreams, this hope, preserved a nation, saved it from disintegration, from vanishing into dust, as was the fate of other nations. The realization of this dream, the return of the Star of David to the holy ruins of Jerusalem, should have been a mighty impetus toward the blossoming of an ancient nation, toward its renaissance. Alas! The trumpet sound of the shofar at the Wailing Wall, proclaiming to the world that a miracle had occurred and that on the ruins of the ancient kingdoms of Judah and Israel the Jewish state had been reborn like a phoenix rising from its own ashes—this clarion call resounded across the continents of the world where for centuries exiles from the Holy Land had sought shelter. Despite all expectations, the creation of the state did not infuse new blood into the ancient veins but, on the contrary, laid the Jewish nation low and catastrophically accelerated the previously slow process of assimilation and disintegration. One after another, Jewish communities began to collapse, and their ranks became sparse and thin. This did not happen, however, because their members were draining away to Israel, but because of mixed marriages, because of conversions to different faiths—because of precipitate flight from the Jewish faith into the saving depths of assimilation.

However paradoxical this may sound, it is a fact—tragic and unanticipated. Even the most superficial analysis of events in the Jewish world since 1947 confirm it eloquently and inescapably. The renaissance has not come.

In a preceding chapter I have already examined in some detail the way in which the very large Jewish community in the USSR began to break up and decline from the time of their birth of Israel. The clumsy efforts of certain over-zealous Zionist authors, who in most cases have never lived in Russia and who superficially and subjectively analyze the fate of Soviet Jews from a safe distance, cannot be taken seriously. Their stubborn assertions that it was not the creation of the state of Israel that brought to life official anti-Semitism in the USSR and that the whole thing began considerably earlier sound far from convincing.

For example, the eminent American expert on Soviet Jewish problems, William Korey, in his *The Soviet Cage: Anti-Semitism in Russia*, exonerates the state of Israel from blame for the national catastrophe of Jews in the Soviet Union, asserting without a shred of evidence that the persecution of Jews in the USSR began much earlier, in the first half of the 1930s. He substantiates his thesis by pointing to the notorious Great Purge trials, in which many of the accused were Jewish.

It is true that during the Stalinist purges many Jews were liquidated, but so too were an even greater number of Russians, Georgians, Kazaks, and Ukrainians. Stalin annihilated hundreds of thousands of people—not however on an ethnic basis but simply because he suspected that they might be members of a political opposition.

Not a single Jew suffered at that time simply because he was a Jew. Korey's assertion is untrue. I affirm on the basis of my own first-hand experience and my committed knowledge of this subject that right up to the creation of the state of Israel there was no trace of official anti-Semitism in the USSR and that Jews were not subjected to any kind of repressions specifically on the basis of their origins.

The persecution of Jews in the USSR, the cruel suppression of any form of national self-awareness among them and, as a consequence of this, the accelerated disintegration of a once mighty community, its dispersal, and destruction coincided with the troubled and tortured birth of the state of Israel.

Scarcely anyone then foresaw what a disaster for the whole Jewish community this event would turn out to be.

The funeral knell tolled not only for Soviet Jews. From the new-born state's first steps, the sinister tolling rang out for an equally distinct group of Jews, the Jewish communities of Moslem countries of the Middle East and North Africa.

From the Atlantic coast of Africa, from Casablanca in Morocco, where for centuries Jewish life has prospered, through Tangier and Rabat, Algiers and Oran, Tunis and Tripoli, Cairo and Alexandria, Baghdad, Beirut, and Damascus, right across to the Indian Ocean, like hundreds of oases, Jewish communities dotted the Moslem world. Ancient synagogues dwelt peacefully side by side with mosques, and the Mosaic law was confessed with the tacit blessing of the Koran.

At various periods and in particular during the Middle Ages, a period of aggressive expansion in the Arab Caliphate, which victoriously overwhelmed the whole of North Africa and surged via Spain into Europe, the Jews of the Moslem countries achieved great heights in the cultural, economic, and social life of their times and gave many famous names to the world.

At the moment when the state of Israel was created in Palestine, there were more than a million Jews living in the Arab world, in compact communities among their Arab neighbors, preserving from time immemorial their national structure, culture, religion, and the stable peace of the Jewish family—a tested protector of the fabric of their national life and an almost insuperable barrier to assimilation.

This life, ordered for centuries, collapsed after 1947 as if there had been an earthquake. The Jewish state was created in Palestine despite the desperate resistance of the Palestinian Arabs and the governments of neighboring Moslem countries. The Arabs rallied against the Jews beneath the green banner of Holy War. The armies of Egypt, Syria, Iraq, and Trans-Jordan joined in battle against the Jewish settlers, against the prisoners who had survived Hitler's death camps. Blood flowed in profusion, both Arab and Jewish, and two related nations, deriving from the same Semitic roots, conducted a relentless fratricidal war, whose end even today, more than a quarter of a century later, is not in sight.

The year 1947 made the Arabs and almost all orthodox Mohammedans, at a stroke, the irreconcilable foes of the Jews. Crowds of Palestinian refugees fleeing from the scourge of war to the neighboring Arab countries added yet more fuel to the fire of national and religious fanaticism.

The era of peace for the Jews in Moslem countries was over. A wall of hatred sprang up around dozens of Jewish communities from Casablanca to Baghdad. There were the first outbreaks of pogroms and the spilling of innocent blood, and the Jews, to save their children, abandoned their property and forsook the places that for centuries had been their homes, in whose Jewish cemeteries their ancestors rested, leaving behind them empty and often devastated synagogues. The death agony of the great and celebrated Sephardic Jewish community had begun.

The highest price Jews paid for the creation of their own state in Palestine was the almost complete liquidation in the space of a few years of all the Sephardic communities in places where they had existed for more than a thousand years. The Jews either went into exile or were expelled by force. The Jews of Algeria and Morocco—the two largest communities in the Islamic countries—moved in two directions. One stream, in which was concentrated the elite—doctors, engineers, lawyers, businessmen, highly skilled workers—without pausing long to think, made for France, which until the Second World War had been the colonial overlord of these countries and, therefore, did not dare to slam her doors in the faces of her erstwhile subjects. There are now more than three hundred thousand Arab Jews living in France.

The most desperate and adventurous Sephardic Jews made their way to the Latin American countries and the United

States. There, beyond the ocean, a pitiful minority amid foreign ways and customs, bereft of their main source of support—the traditionally strong Jewish family, which had broken up into a host of fragments during the flight—they began hastily and even readily to submit to assimilation in order to withstand the new conditions and at least survive physically.

In France too the Jewish refugees from Arab countries soon laid down their burden of former traditions under the influence of close and, as it transpired, deleterious contact with their co-religionists, the Ashkenazic Jews, who long before had been exposed to a hefty dose of "assimilation radiation" and were even somewhat ashamed of being Jews at all.

The French Jews, both Ashkenazim and Sephardim, are vying with one another like sprinters striving to breast the tape in their efforts to dissolve among the French. This is how the picture of the community's collapse looks to a very well-informed person, the director of the Gence Juive pour Israel, Menachem Giladi:

Only ten thousand Jewish-born French schoolchildren from an overall national Jewish population of 550,000 are receiving their education in Jewish educational institutions. This is taking into account the fact that most Jewish schools in France are housed in good, high-quality buildings, and three thousand of the pupils at these schools receive scholarships from the Fonds Social Juif Unifié from kindergarten to university entrance. Even in such enticing conditions, an increase in the number of those wishing to study at Jewish schools cannot be achieved. The overwhelming majority of young French Jews are quickly becoming assimilated and breaking their links with the Jewish community.

In the opinion of Menachem Giladi, this process is to a large extent facilitated by the fact that educated Jewish youth avidly absorbs liberal and left-wing ideological doctrines and regards Judaism as no more than an obstacle on the road to universal equality and fraternity.

Although Hebrew is included in the range of languages

studied in French elementary schools, Jewish pupils very rarely display any inclination to study the official language of the state of Israel and of the Jews as a whole. The children's parents usually encourage the study of English or any other modern foreign language.

A final result of the movement toward assimilation is the large number of mixed marriages, which in percentage terms are increasing at a catastrophic rate. All the signs indicate, Giladi concludes, that in a generation the French Jewish community will have lost its best members.

And so the creation of the state of Israel uprooted the Arab Jews from their age-old habitations, where they had previously made no attempt to conceal their consanguinity with an ancient biblical nation, flung them far and wide throughout the world, plunged them into the seething cauldron of assimilation, i.e., of national suicide. Seeking justification for the metamorphoses that has overtaken his fellow countrymen in exile, the Tunisian Jew Albert Memmi—today a famous French writer and professor of sociology at the Sorbonne—in an interview for the journal *Intellectual Digest* expressed doubt as to whether his own forebears in the Sahara had ever been Jews at all. Perhaps, he suggested, they were just Berbers converted to Judaism, since according to his information most North African Jews are simply Berber nomads who have accepted Judaism.

The same thing happened to the Jews in those Arab countries that were formerly British colonies. The best and most dynamic section of the Egyptian and Iraqi Jewish communities also found refuge not in Israel but either in the British Isles or in other English-speaking countries such as Canada, Australia, or New Zealand. They energetically made a 180° about-face and hurriedly discarded all that was Jewish in order to array themselves in more convenient and contemporary attire.

Such has been the fate of one torrent of Jewish refugees from the lands of Islam, scattered all over the planet by the hurricane provoked in the Arab world by the birth of the state of Israel. Another torrent, consisting mainly of the least educated Arab Jewish community, on or around the poverty line, did not dare take the risk of living among completely alien and unfamiliar neighbors and went to join its co-religionists in Palestine. These refugees formed the nucleus of the Sephardic community in Israel, rapidly forming a *lumpenproletariat*. Their impoverishment was further heightened by being juxtaposed to the comparatively thriving background of the extremely successful Ashkenazic Jews. They entered into a most intense social and even racial conflict with their fair-skinned brethren. I am deeply convinced that in the not too distant future they will become that uncontrollable explosive force that will lead to the fall of the Third Temple, i.e., the demise of the present-day state of Israel—the end, that is, of that same state to whose birth they owe their exile from their old haunts and the loss of their ancient traditions and mores that preserved them so long as a nation, the state whose genesis in 1947 rang out like a funeral knell above the heads of the Moslem world's Jewish communities.

Eastern Europe was another extremely sensitive area that reacted sharply and painfully to the creation of the state of Israel. Poland, Czechoslovakia, Hungary, and Romania were countries with extensive and quite conspicuous Jewish populations, over which the tumbrels of the Second World War rolled relentlessly, leaving just a sorry handful of survivors. When the Soviet Union drove the Nazi occupying forces from Eastern Europe, established its own rule, and implanted its Communist doctrine in the new soil, it needed loyal executors of its policies. The Czechs, Poles, Hungarians, and Romanians inspired no confidence. On the other hand, the local Jews could be relied upon completely. They were filled with a feeling of gratitude toward the Soviet Union for rescuing them from Hitler's yoke, and they were more inclined than others to believe in Communist ideology, which proclaimed in its tablets the most progressive slogans of universal equality and brotherhood—all of which the Jews had dreamt for centuries. They therefore placed themselves fully at the disposal of the new authorities and fairly rapidly achieved success in their chosen field. The tiny little groups of Jews that had not been wiped out, comprising less than a sorry 1 percent of the overall population of these countries, acquired in just a few years colossal and previously unthinkable influence and power, occupying the most important posts in the ruling party, in science, the economy, the army, culture, and in the repressive police apparatus.

Jews like Rudolf Slansky in Czechoslovakia and Matyas Rakosi in Hungary achieved the summits of power, becoming the general secretaries of the Communist parties of their respective countries. The people of Poland went in fear of the names of their new Jewish bosses, such as members of the Party Central Committee Minc and Berman. Romania was graced with a still more brightly ascending star, the Jewess Ana Pauker, who took up the reins of power. To a significant degree the Soviet Union established its dominion in Eastern Europe with a few skillful and dedicated pairs of Jewish hands. This was an old technique. In 1940, when, under an agreement with Hitler the Soviets had occupied the Baltic countries of Lithuania, Latvia, and Estonia and forcibly joined them to their empire, they had for the first time used this "fifth column," in the form of the local Jewish communities, to consolidate their presence and subdue the subjugated nations. The Jews were accorded outward signs of favor and initially even entrusted with the reins of power. This naturally evoked a whirlwind of anti-Semitism among the subject nations, at first concealed and festering under the pressure of the Soviet jackboot, then bursting out into the open when the Nazis came. It is, after all, well known that the mass destruction of the Jewish population of Vilna, Kaunas, Riga, and Tallinn was perpetrated largely not by Germans but by Lithuanian, Latvian, and Estonian volunteers, members of punitive detachments who wreaked cruel vengenace on their erstwhile friends and neighbors for the latter's short-sighted and unseemly role as "Russificators" and zealous instruments of the policies of the Soviet occupation forces.

Soviet power eventually renounced the services of the Jews, finding trained national cadres to replace them. All this was in accordance with the well-known principle: the job is finished, the workmen can go.

The same thing happened in Eastern Europe. The people of those countries grew to hate their Jews even more intensely, and things reached the state of open pogroms, like those in the town of Kalisz (in Poland), with dozens of dead and injured. It is true that the Communist authorities initially suppressed harshly any manifestations of anti-Semitism, seeing in it a threat to the new order, which was dependent on the Jews to a considerable degree. True servants and instruments were soon recruited, however, trained from among the indigenous population. Jews in important posts began to be an obvious nuisance, and ways were sought to get rid of them.

A pretext was not long in presenting itself: the proclamation of the Jewish state in Palestine. Beneath the banner of anti-Zionism, a relentless attack from above was launched against the vestiges of the Jewish population in the Eastern European countries, the so-called peoples democracies.

Following the Soviet Union's infectious example, its loyal satellites masked garden-variety anti-Semitism with anti-Zionism and pitilessly began to finish off the insignificant number of Jews who had only recently survived the Nazi ax. The main charge was Zionism and espionage on Israel's behalf.

The Jews found themselves between the hammer and the anvil, between the blind hatred of the enslaved population and the merciless bayonets of the political police implementing the anti-Semitic behest of the Communist authority. A rash of widely publicized trials broke out from the

Baltic to the Black Sea. They were crudely staged and as alike as peas in a pod regardless of the host country, for there was but one director and one prototype—the Soviet Union.

Rudolf Slansky, general secretary of the Communist party of Czechoslovakia, Laszlo Rajk, and many, many other Jews were shot as Israeli agents. The prisons were filled with thousands of Jews. The sparse and fragmentary Jewish community of Eastern Europe, of which only a few hundred thousand out of four million had survived Hitler's gas chambers, was delivered an ultimate and conclusive blow, after which it sank into a final state of coma. And as soon as a first opportunity presented itself, as for example during the Hungarian uprising of 1956 or the months of Dubcek's "Prague Spring" in 1968, the final vestiges of the Jewish community in those countries made a run for it and dispersed all over the world.

There was no need to flee from Poland. In 1968 Gomulka accused the country's whole Jewish population of being sympathetic to Israel and expelled the last remaining Jews, rendering the home of Maidanek and Auschwitz finally clean of Jews, *Judenfrei,* a goal that had eluded even the SS executioners. There remain but four thousand Jews of the millions and millions.

The last few tens of thousands of Polish Jews, plundered by the authorities and humiliated, found refuge not in Israel, the source of all their misfortunes, but in the neighboring countries of Scandinavia, where they fervidly turned their back on Judaism and entered the Christian faith and strove for all they were worth to be known to the natives as Polish immigrants.

Thus came to an end the existence of one of the most colorful and picturesque sections of the world's Jewish community, the Jews of Eastern Europe. They were stamped out largely by the Germans in the Nazi death camps, and after the creation of the state of Israel, they were finished off by local Communists.

For some time, the ancient Jewish cemeteries, the unusual architecture of the old Jewish quarters, and the exotic buildings of the synagogues will remain like museum exhibits, as a reminder of the Jews who once inhabited these places. But they will soon fall into disrepair and decay, and new contemporary buildings will erase these last traces.

New York Times correspondent Henry Camm visited the Polish city of Wroclaw, which until 1945 was the center of the German province of Silesia and was then called Breslau. In former times this city had a reputation as a center of the Jewish culture and religion. There are just a few hundred Jews left in Wroclaw today, writes Camm, many of whom do not want any one to know they are Jews. All the younger ones have left. Only the elderly remain—those who survived the Nazi camps or the "safety" of exile in the Siberian regions of the Soviet Union. They live in a state of apathy, drawing miserable pensions and waiting to die.

Perhaps they had not really noticed that on the doors of the main synagogue, which has long been boarded up, someone had drawn a Nazi swastika and written with lucid brevity *Kike*. A foreign tourist rubbed out the swastika, not noticing that he was being watched by two young fellows holding dogs on leads. They came up to the tourist, and one of them sneered in German: *Jude!* The other spat with feeling, and then they both disappeared around the corner, their dogs at their heels.

What Henry Camm saw in Wroclaw, I have observed in Warsaw, in Krakow, Prague, and Bratislava. And everywhere former Jewish quarters are deserted, as they might be after a pogrom, and terribly lonely and inhospitable. You leave them with an aftertaste of bitterness in your heart, leaving behind death, decay, finality.

We have examined the unfolding destiny of the Jewish community, or more precisely its tragic culmination, in the Moslem Middle East and North Africa and in Communist

Eastern Europe after the creation of the state of Israel. The communities in these places were literally destroyed. The Jews of the world suffered an irreplaceable loss.

But how did the reality of the re-creation of Jewish statehood make itself felt on the way of life of Jews in the rest of the world—in the wealthy countries of Western Europe, in Latin America, in the Republic of South Africa, in Australia, or on the Asian continent?

The news of the creation of the Jewish state did not descend upon the Jews in these portions of the world like a devastating hurricane but was simply the catalyst speeding up a chemical reaction, bringing to life forces which had until then been slumbering deep down within the Jewish community, forces in part constructive and in part destructive. In certain quarters nationalist, Zionist, and extremist factions became active, taking Israel as their banner and the object of their devotion. In other sections of the Jewish population, tendencies to assimilate became accentuated.

India, where until 1947 fifteen thousand Jews lived, a tiny group that was not absorbed into the ocean of half a billion souls. Today the number of Jews in India has declined to eight thousand. Seven thousand of them live in Bombay alone. The Israeli catalyst stirred up and threw into utter confusion the rhythm of the life of this community. Some Indian Jews were carried away by Zionist enthusiasm and rushed to Israel; others, fearful of remaining in districts denuded of their Jewish population, also began to emigrate but in differing directions—to the United States, England, Australia, where they submitted to the power of assimilation. Many tiny Jewish communities in India have disappeared entirely, including several villages whose populations were entirely Jewish. The present rate of emigration of Jews from India is about thirty-five persons per week. Soon, not a single Jew will remain.

Something similar is happening to the Jews of Iran, who have lived there since the time of Artaxerxes, Esther, and Mordecai. Since the creation of the state of Israel, a great many Jews have left Iran altogether, and many have moved into Tehran from small towns, weakening local communities and bringing them into decline. There are at present forty-five thousand Jews in Tehran and a further twenty thousand in other Iranian cities. Life in the capital has rapidly made its mark on the attitudes of its Jewish citizens and caused a sharp increase in the tendency to assimilate. An ever-increasing number of Jews have begun to forsake their national traditions, and their children spurn a Jewish education.

The emergence of Israel has polarized Jewish circles in the diaspora and led, as for example in France, to a schism in the community, where Jews are divided into left and right, supporters and opponents of Israel, and wage with one another a mutually weakening war. This delights the anti-Semites and confirms the zeal of those who desire to assimilate.

A further crisis, also closely linked with Israel, threatens the Jewish population in this part of the world. The attitude to Israel of the governments of countries where Jews live sometimes confronts the Jews themselves with intractable problems. If the state shows preference to the Arabs, then Jews are obliged to oppose their own government, with all the unpleasant consequences flowing therefrom, or to make a conclusive break with the Jewish community and move into the camp of Israel's enemies.

In most countries where relations with Israel are somewhat strained, Jewish inhabitants are suspected of having dual loyalties, and they are persecuted for this, in particular in those places where national feelings run high. France, which has placed an embargo on the supply of arms to Israel and persistently woos the Arabs, has, according to newspaper reports, given evidence of the first notable signs of this. In order to avoid espionage on Israel's behalf and also to allay fears of sabotage, the French have begun to cut down the number of Jews working in the aircraft industry.

The situation of the Jews on the Latin American continent, whose governments are of volcanic instability, is yet more complicated. One military junta succeeds another in power, first the extreme right then the extreme left.

There are about sixty thousand Arabs living in *Chile*. They were bitter opponents of the now defunct Allende regime and are supporters of the right-wingers who have now seized power. The affection of the powers that be has, therefore, undergone a corresponding shift from the Jews to the Arabs. In a review of the situation of Chilean Jews, the British member of Parliament, S. C. Davis, records a sharp deterioration in the relations between Chile and Israel because the Israeli Embassy in Santiago offered political asylum to a number of Allende's supporters. Naturally, for this reason, fear and uncertainty are rife among Chilean Jews.

The rapprochement between Latin America and the oil-rich Arab world which is proceeding at a rapid pace, heightens the tensions in the Jewish community and increases the flood of emigrants from the South American continent.

Where do they go? To Israel? Only the most paltry number do so, and even they do not linger long in the Jewish state. Most of them flee to the United States and Canada, hoping that there perhaps they will manage to weather the storms they believe to be imminent.

Recently there has been a perceptible increase in Arab propaganda in *Australia*. Twenty thousand Australian Arabs, supported by Arab embassies in Canberra, are taking an active part in political life and in student movements. This has intensified the anti-Semitic epidemic on the fifth continent. It is precisely in Australia that one of the few legal Nazi parties in the world is active. The Nazis publish a magazine called *Stormtrooper*, and in 1970, in elections to the Senate, they received twenty-five thousand votes. A further extreme right-wing party is active in Australia, the League for the Defense of Australians' Rights, which distributes extremely anti-Semitic literature, including the *Protocols of the Elders of Zion.*

Not long ago Australian Jews discovered a danger to themselves from the opposite quarter: all kinds of left-wing extremists show ever-increasing solidarity with the Arabs and are conducting an extensive campaign directed ostensibly against Zionism, but under cover of which it is not hard to discern primitive anti-Semitism.

The situation of the powerful *South African* Jewish community, which until recently seemed to be confidently embarked on a course toward enviable economic prosperity, is even more complicated and involved. The second and third generations of Jewish families who emigrated at the beginning of the century, mainly from Lithuania, have become an inalienable part of the white minority and its policy of apartheid.

Israel has introduced further complications into the lives of South African Jews. Pumping each year increasingly large sums of money from the pockets of prosperous Johannesburg and Cape Town Jews, it provokes displeasure in certain circles at the constant and irreversible flow of capital abroad.

Israel's policy on the black continent has always been aimed at winning the sympathy of the young states that have emerged from the former colonial territories. Israel helped them with credits, instructors, and weapons, wooing the blacks in every possible way. This purchased affection cost Israel dear, and one of the forms of payment she had to make for it was being forced to support on all international platforms the uncompromising struggle by the African countries against their white racist neighbor. This naturally gave rise to indignation in the Republic of South Africa.

It would, of course, be naïve to think that purchased affection can be sincere. It only needed some large and enticing financial handouts from the oil-rich Arab countries to entice the governments to turn their backs on Israel, break off diplomatic relations, and drive out like sworn enemies Israeli instructors. They now present a united front of hostility to the Jewish state across the whole black continent. Anti-Semitism, which was previously unknown in Africa, has now begun to befuddle black brains. The President of *Uganda*, Idi Amin, has stated officially that the six million Jews annihilated by Hitler received their just deserts and has foretold yet more terrible blows against the Jews in the not too distant future.

We see from the foregoing that the creation of the state of Israel, instead of strengthening the Jewish nation, became the destructive factor that for more than a quarter of a century now has been laying low one Jewish community after another, thrusting them toward self-destruction, dissipating with unforseen speed that which had been stubbornly and agonizingly preserved for thousands of years.

chapter twelve

THE VISIT OF THE OLD LADY

To the little remote town of Güllen after many years of absence comes a fabulously wealthy old lady, a multimillionairess born in those parts. The inhabitants of the town are choking in the grip of poverty, plagued by unemployment and ruin, and only the old lady's arrival and her philanthropy can save them. The lady actually is prepared to save the little town, but she imposes one condition. The citizens of Güllen must take vengeance upon a man who once, in his youth, insulted the old lady and is now living out his allotted span respected and honored among them. Yet they must kill him if they expect to receive the old lady's restoring charity, kill a man to whom they feel no enmity, alongside whom they have lived all their lives. To fulfill the whim of the philanthropist and save themselves from poverty, they must be transformed from good-hearted, ordinary men and women into calculating murderers. Initially they are plunged into distraction, then gloom. But rather quickly they find dozens of justifications for their act. The human being is sacrificed, and the murderers who but

285

recently were respectable citizens stretch out their hands for their reward without a shadow of repentance.

This is the plot of a Friedrich Dürrenmatt tragicomedy, *The Visit.* Its situation, however, down almost to the last detail is being enacted today. Not on the stage but in real life and with this one difference; it is not the life and death of an individual human being that is at stake but that of a whole country with a population of three million.

In the struggle with Israel, the Arab world is now using its most effective weapon—the threat of oil starvation and economic crisis for all countries that do not support its strivings to destroy the Jewish state. The effect has turned out to be rather striking; just like the men and women of the town of Güllen, the countries of our planet with scarcely a single exception have accepted this dictate without complaint. And this is so regardless of their social system—from the traditional democracies to unashamedly totalitarian regimes, from the pinkish left to the brown of the right. In deference to Dürrenmatt's characters, one must say that they did not at once yield to the old lady's blackmail. The nations of the world, however, have begun to break off relations with Israel and adopt a hostile attitude toward her, dooming her to perish, and they have done this without the flicker of an eyelid. To the six million victims of the Nazi terror the world has scarcely had time to forget they will add a further three million Jewish victims. No one, after all, is in any doubt that the collapse of the state of Israel will involve the death of almost every last member of the population.

It is now clear to all—both to those who love Israel, to those who hate her, and to those who are indifferent—the whole world, exuding respectability but afraid of being starved of oil and unwilling to give up its comfort, is ready to sacrifice the Jews, this nation whose tenacity for life verges on the indecent and that somehow still inhabits our crowded planet.

How many times has this already happened?

In Jerusalem, close to Mount Herzl there stands in a valley of the Judean Hills a museum called Yad ve-Shem. It is a memorial dedicated to the victims of the European catastrophe, the six million Jews tortured by the Nazis, a third of my nation. A mountain of books and scientific treatises has been dedicated to the study and cataloguing of their incredible holocaust. Here the uneasy conscience of humanity exposes the murderers, the Nazis, comparing them with the beasts and denying them the right to be called men.

By exposing and stigmatizing specific murderers, humanity, as it were, purges its soul of the sin and washes its hands. The planned destruction of the Jewish nation by nazism, however, was carried out with the silent complicity and frequently even with the participation of the European nations among whom the Jews lived. On the huge, horrific photographs at Yad ve-Shem, which make the visitor's blood run cold, both the victims and the executioners are marked out. We see not only Germans firing at naked men and women on the edge of an antitank ditch but also Lithuanian policemen using truncheons to smash in the skulls of rows of Jews laid out in the courtyard at the Ninth Fort in Kaunas; Poles obligingly and readily hanging their own Jews under German supervision; Ukrainian SS men from the "Galicia" division, who in cruelty and monstrous behavior excelled their German mentors.

Six million Jews were annihilated before the eyes of hundreds of millions of people. Six million ordinary human beings. And who resisted this? Who cried out in anguish? Who risked his personal peace and quiet to stretch out a hand to the unfortunates?

I shall be told that there were such people, and several examples will be quoted of the fearlessness and spiritual beauty of individuals who staked their lives to save a Jewish family or a Jewish child.

At the Yad ve-Shem museum names of the righteous Gentiles, those who were unafraid to give succour to the unfortunates, have been scrupulously collected. In honor of each of these heroes, the grateful Jewish community has planted a tree on the mountain slope, and the leafy avenue leading to the memorial is actually called the Avenue of the Righteous. Beside each fondly tended tree stands a stone plaque bearing the name of the righteous one and the country in which each saved the life of a Jew.

> Aczinsky, Mark (Poland)
> Caliguri, Coelia (Italy)
> Christiansen, Anna (Denmark)
> Fédy, Giles and Marie (France)
> Gabis, Antonina (USSR)
> Jansen, Andres and Ida (Holland)
> Richter, Emma (Germany)

Like all visitors to this ghastly museum, I bow my head in the shade of the young trees before each name on the plaques, paying my tribute of admiration and gratitude to these men and women. As I do so, my heart grows cold from yearning and despair. There are in all three-hundred-and-thirty trees, and the museum records contain a further several hundred names, in whose honor fresh trees will be planted. That is all. These were all the righteous of the occupied world, the only ones to risk their lives. The unconcern and indifference of hundreds of millions of people led to this tragedy; but these men and women are living out their days on earth with an untroubled conscience. With what excruciating reproach to humanity this sorry little grove cries out from the slope of Mount Herzl in Jerusalem! How terrible and unambiguous the warning it issues to the Jews who survived and to those who were born after the catastrophe—that they have no future while the world is as it is and their fate continues to hang on a single thread that might break at any moment. Today the world gazes calmly and unemotionally at the preparations for Israel's extinction, and the prospect of a further three million Jewish victims does not disturb its serenity.

For when in the 1930s the Nazis invited the Western democracies to accept the Jewish refugees who were being

expelled from the Third Reich under pain of death, the vaunted Western democracies averted their gaze and, shroud-
ing themselves in immigration quotas, declined to offer refuge to the poor wretches, thereby dooming them to annihi-
lation. Even such an out-and-out scoundrel as Hitler's hench-
man Joseph Goebbels wrote in his diary that by refusing
to accept the Jews, Roosevelt and Chamberlain had given
their blessing to the vile act of the Nazi executioners.

France and Switzerland, abounding in humaneness and
the democratic spirit, closed their frontiers in the face of the
flood of Jews fleeing from Germany, and those who managed to break through illegally were extradited and handed
back to the Gestapo.

The Soviet Union, where in 1939 there was still no mention of anti-Semitism, also greeted Jewish refugees from Poland with bayonets and drove them back in considerable
numbers to certain death.

A sad symbol of international cynicism was the tragic
odyssey of the shipload of Jewish children that sailed from a
German port, seeking a country that would agree to provide
shelter for the children. For weeks, as if striken with the
plague the ship sailed back and forth from one port to
another, from one country to another, and everywhere, off
the coast of Africa, by the shores of Latin America, in the
roadsteads of U.S. ports, they encountered the same wall of
indifference and hostility. Any excuse was used to deny the
ship permission to moor, and the doomed vessel sailed on
across the Atlantic waves until it was sunk by a submarine
and the cold ocean depths gave shelter to the Jewish children, on whom the whole world had turned its back.

Sad and tragic though it be, it remains a fact that there is
no place on our vast planet where the Jew can peacefully
live out his days. If they are tolerated in one country today,
then no one can vouch for their fate tomorrow. There is no
state on earth, no nation on earth, excepting those among
whom the Jews have never lived, which can boast that its
hands are clean of Jewish blood. Everywhere, in differing

epochs, under the most varied social systems, even after a long period of peaceful coexistence with the Jews, sooner or later, with fatal inevitability, the venom would burst forth and the blood of innocent men and women would be shed in profusion, intoxicating the vicious perpetrators of pogroms.

According to the calculations of the experts, if the Jewish population of the world had developed in normal circumstances, it would now have reached 150 million. After all, two thousand years ago ancient Judah could, in a moment of strategic danger, summon to her banners up to a million men. The Jews have always been known for their prolific families. Ten or more children in a family was from generation to generation on ordinary, run-of-the-mill occurrence. Why then are there only about 14 million of us on the earth at the present time? Our blood has been let, and we have been destroyed systematically and with diabolical regularity throughout our whole history. Our path on earth, as that of no other nation, is strewn with corpses beyond number. No other nation can boast such a terrible record of the number of its members violently done to death. And no one's death provoked such indifference and sometimes even unconcealed satisfaction among the bystanders as did the death of a Jew. So it was in barbaric medieval times and so it is in our present enlightened era. Much has changed under the sun but not the attitude to the Jew. We are like lepers on the earth, and in those places where our blood is still warm in our veins we are endured with the greatest difficulty.

You will recall how soon after the Second World War, when the conscience of humanity for a brief moment was stung with shame for what it had done, Soviet Communism began to prepare a retribution against its Jews, against the vestiges of a nation, against those who had survived Hitler's gas chambers. Who in the USSR took a stand against this? Who raised an angry voice in protest? The country was silent; the Russian people were silent. And not just silent.

The whole mob—the mindless masses and the Party and state bosses—whooped in pursuit, anxious to get a blow in.

And what about Poland, the country of Auschwitz, Maidanek, Treblinka, whose fields, as no others, are heavily fertilized with the ashes of millions of Jews? That same Poland, where only a few sorry thousands of Jews were left alive, initiated against them the ultimate pogrom in 1968 and, having first robbed them, expelled them from the country. Nor did the Polish people contradict their leaders; on the contrary they expressed delight, both overtly and covertly.

This is why there are so few of us left on the earth, and very, very soon the winds of history will finally obliterate our tracks altogether. We are being violently done to death in every generation, and those who survive seek physical salvation in assimilation, in joining other nations, in mingling with them completely and without a trace. Today this epidemic has assumed such disastrous proportions that it would be no exaggeration to postulate the complete disappearance of the Jewish nation in two generations, that is to say, in the beginning of the next century.

In the United States, the most mighty citadel of the Jewish community, mixed marriages among the young have reached 40 percent, and according to the information of Rabbi Solomon Sason, in certain Jewish communities in France the percentage is as high as 90 percent.

The Soviet Union is hardly worth mentioning. There a whirlwind of assimilation, zealously assisted by the authorities, is already sweeping through its third generation. According to Soviet figures, while all the other nationalities of the USSR show a definite annual growth in numbers, only the number of Jews continually declines.

As the saying goes, there's no need to look far for an example. I have among my papers an interesting photograph of myself and some friends of my youth. Ten or so young Jewish fellows, all of whom had graduated from university, had a photograph taken as a souvenir in the central square of the city of Vilna, I think, in 1950. We were all then just over twenty. All were bachelors. Yura, Grisha, Danya, Yasha, Ilya, David. Some of us had been born there in Lithuania in tiny shtetels and had managed to absorb a charge of Jewish culture. Others had come from remote Russian regions of the USSR, to a large extent assimilated by our environment, but even so making no effort to hide our Jewishness or finding it in any way a burden. Jewish mamas, and in those days there were still a high concentration of Jews living in Vilna, viewed us hopefully as suitable fiancés for their daughters.

We, however, had tasted the delights of bachelor life and were in no hurry to get married. We had one friend, Leonid, who was already married and encumbered with two young daughters. His portion hardly made us feel ecstatic. Furthermore, in our hearts we rather scorned him. He was married to a Russian girl and had in a cowardly fashion agreed under pressure from his wife to register their daughters under her Russian name and not under his Jewish name. Naturally, the girls acquired their nationality not from their father but from their mother. Leonid's act, his concession to his wife, seemed to us to be an insult to his manly dignity, something rather distasteful and capitulatory. At that time we never thought of such concepts as assimilation. We reasoned like men and fathers-to-be and censured Leonid not because he had turned his back on his Jewishness but because wishing to provide a more comfortable future for his daughters he had foregone his paternal rights.

All this was at the time of the first outbursts of officially inspired anti-Semitism in the USSR, now more than thirty years ago. All the young men on the photograph are thriving today, long married, and fathers of families. And what else?

I won't mention Leonid, the object of our scorn. His daughters are Russian according to their passports and, protected by their mother's Russian surname, successfully contracted marriages with young Russians, whose surnames they took, making Leonid's grandchildren second-generation Russians. When their grandfather, this same Leonid, dies, the last shred of evidence capable of arousing suspicion that Leonid's posterity has even a drop of Jewish blood in its veins will disappear.

My remaining friends also paid their tribute to assimilation. The tribute was a great one. Out of the seven of them, only two married Jewish girls. Yura's wife is a Byelorussian, Yasha's a Ukrainian, Ilya's a Lithuanian, and Grisha's and David's wives are Russian. Consequently their children are not registered in their documents as Jews. Only Danya and I married Jewish girls, and only we two left the USSR and settled in Israel. Only we have Jewish children. The issue of all the other members of this former bachelor fraternity has forever left the bosom of the Jewish community.

This example reflects better than statistics the course of rapid assimilation of the present generation of Jews, assimilation leading to the complete disappearance of the nation. The young men on the photograph are not exceptions. Their progress is absolutely typical of my contemporaries. The way that Danya and I chose is the way of the minority and, as I now realize, far from being the best way.

Having sought refuge in Israel, this last asylum of the Jewish community, we have perhaps saved ourselves from assimilation but, on the other hand, have condemned our children and ourselves to physical extinction.

Israel is doomed and is unlikely to survive a decade. I think with bitterness and a yearning, sinking heart that in 1985 this state will no longer be on the map of the world. She will be pitilessly and relentlessly swallowed up by her Arab neighbors, who with force and hatred will descend upon her, and in the place of the Jewish settlements with their biblical names resurrected from oblivion, the desert winds will sweep the sands across mass graves, like those overgrown with grass all over Europe in 1945.

It is quite impossible for Israel to withstand the colossal oil riches and the military potential that her neighbors are buying up all over the world. And no one will come to her aid. She even sticks in the craw of her handful of well-wishers, an irritant; her very existence prevents them from having a quiet life and receiving as others do the munificent handouts of the oil sheiks and kings.

Israel will put up a desperate fight. Her citizens have learned how to do this, but it will not save them. Internally torn apart by an incurable social affliction, her lifeblood squeezed from her by growing pressure from without, she will fall inevitably and very soon, taking all of us down with her.

The old lady's visit has already begun and the residents of Güllen having made peace with their consciences are ready for the sake of their own well-being to offer the exacted sacrifice.

From ancient times, in popular superstition death has been portrayed as a blind old woman with a scythe. It is her visit to my door that I sense.

She stands, her scythe poised to end the tragic and glorious journey of a most ancient nation, a nation whose tenacious hold on life has surpassed that of all others. Her eyeless skull broods over the last convulsions of an undying tribe.

I know that having written this book I shall be accused of all the deadly sins and, at the very best, of pessimism. I do not conceal that I am a pessimist. My life's experience and what I have seen around me have made me such. And can a Jew be any other? I only once met an optimist of Jewish origin . . . in a lunatic asylum. A psychiatrist friend of mine invited me especially to see the miracle.

As a nation we stand at the edge of the abyss, being engulfed at breakneck speed. This century will pass and in the new one there will be no Jewish nation. It will remain in the pages of the history books as an example of amazing longev-

ity, deep wisdom, and incomparable patience and endur-
ance. And down upon the men and women of the earth, if
they themselves survive and contrive not to destroy all
things living, will gaze with sad, Jewish eyes from the walls
of the churches, our last kinsman, the Son of God, Who
came forth from the belly of a nation loved by none.